BUSINESS ORGANISATIONS AND CORPORATE LAW

A Comparative, Comprehensive and Functional Approach

BUSINESS ORGANISATIONS AND CORPORATE LAW

A Comparative, Comprehensive and Functional Approach

Shashank Moda

GLOBAL INDIA PUBLICATIONS PVT LTD
NEW DELHI
www.globalindiapublications.com

Published by :

Global India Publications Pvt Ltd
11, Darya Ganj, New Delhi - 110 002
Phone : +91-11-45355555
E-mail : info@globalindiapublications.com
Website: www.globalindiapublications.com

ISBN: 978-93-80228-91-4

Published and Printed by Mr. Pranav Gupta on behalf of **Global India Publications Pvt Ltd** at Times Press, New Delhi.

PREFACE

Business Laws is the field of law concerning companies and other business organizations. This includes corporations, partnerships and other associations which usually carry on some form of economic or charitable activity. The most prominent kind of company, usually referred to as a "corporation", is a "juristic person", i.e. it has separate legal personality, and those who invest money into the business have limited liability for any losses the company makes, governed by corporate law. The largest companies are usually publicly listed on stock exchanges around the world. Even single individuals, also known as sole traders may incorporate themselves and limit their liability in order to carry on a business. All different forms of companies depend on the particular law of the particular country in which they reside.

The law of business organizations originally derived from the common law of England, but has evolved significantly in the Twentieth century.

Other types of business organisations, such as cooperatives, credit unions and publicly owned enterprises, can be established with purposes that parallel, supersede, or even replace the profit maximization mandate of business corporations.

"A corporation is described to be a person in a political capacity created by the law, to endure in perpetual succession." Americans in the 1790s knew of a variety of corporations established for various purposes, including those of commerce, education, and religion. As the law of corporations was articulated by the Supreme Court under Chief Justice Marshall, over the first several decades of the new American state, emphasis fell, in a way which seems natural to us today, upon commercial corporations. Nonetheless, Wilson believed that, in all cases, corporations "should be erected with caution, and inspected with care." The actions of corporations were clearly circumscribed: "To every corporation a name must be assigned; and by that name alone it can perform legal acts." For non-binding external actions or transactions, corporations enjoyed the same latitude as private individuals; but it was with an eye to internal affairs that many saw principal advantage in incorporation. The power of making by-laws was "tacitly annexed to corporations by the very act of their establishment." While they must not directly contradict the overarching laws of the land, the central or local government cannot be expected to regulate toward the peculiar circumstances of a given body, and so "they are invested with authority to make regulations for the management of their own interests and affairs."

As theorists such as Ronald Coase have pointed out, all business organizations represent an attempt to avoid certain costs associated with doing business. Each is meant to facilitate the contribution of specific resources investment capital, knowledge, relationships, and so forth - towards a venture which will prove profitable to all contributors. Except for the partnership, all business forms are designed to provide limited liability to both members of the organization and external investors. Business organizations originated with agency law, which permits an agent to act on behalf of a principal, in exchange for the principal assuming equal liability for the wrongful acts committed by the agent. For this reason, all partners in a typical general partnership may be held liable for the wrongs committed by one partner. Those forms that provide limited liability are able to do so because the state provides a mechanism by which businesses that follow certain guidelines will be able to escape the full liability imposed under agency law. The state provides these forms because it has an interest in the strength of the companies that provide jobs and services therein, but also has an interest in monitoring and regulating their behaviour.

Business Law is the law of the most dominant kind of business enterprise in the modern world. Business law is the study of how shareholders, directors, employees, creditors, and other stakeholders such as consumers, the community and the environment interact with one another under the internal rules of the firm. In the preparation of this book I am thankful to my family, friends and colleagues who supported me in writing of this book.

I am very much thankful to Mr. Pranav Gupta, Director, Global India Publications Pvt Ltd, for his kind cooperation and support for this book.

Shashank Moda

CONTENTS

1

Company and Corporate Law

Introduction

An association of a number of individuals for the purpose of carrying on some legitimate business. This term is not synonymous with partnership, though every such unincorporated company is a partnership. Usage has reserved this term to associations whose members are in greater number, their capital more considerable, and their enterprises greater, either on account of their risk or importance. When these companies are authorized by the government they are known by the name of corporations. Sometimes the word is used to represent those members of a partnership whose names do not appear in the name of the firm; as A. B. & Company.

Companies law is the field of law concerning companies and other business organizations. It is an establishment formed to carry on commercial enterprises. This includes corporations, partnerships and other associations which usually carry on some form of economic or charitable activity. The most prominent kind of company, usually referred to as a "corporation", is a "juristic person", i.e. it has separate legal personality, and those who invest money into the business have limited liability for any losses the company makes, governed by corporate law. The largest companies are usually publicly listed on stock exchanges around the world. Even single individuals, also known as sole traders may incorporate themselves and limit their liability in order to carry on a business. All different forms of companies depend on the particular law of the particular country in which they reside.

The law of business organizations originally derived from the common law of England, but has evolved significantly in the Twentieth century. In common law countries today, the most commonly addressed forms are:

- Corporation
- Limited company
- Unlimited company
- Limited liability partnership
- Limited partnership
- Not-for-profit corporation
- Partnership
- Sole proprietorship

Many countries have forms of business entity unique to that country, although there are equivalents elsewhere. Examples are the Limited-liability company (LLC) and the limited liability limited partnership (LLLP) in the United States.

Other types of business organisations, such as cooperatives, credit unions and publicly owned enterprises, can be established with purposes that parallel, supersede, or even replace the profit maximization mandate of business corporations.

For a country-by-country listing of officially recognized forms of business organization, see Types of business entity.

There are various types of company that can be formed in different jurisdictions, but the most common forms of company are:

- *a company limited by guarantee.* Commonly used where companies are formed for non-commercial purposes, such as clubs or charities. The members guarantee the payment of certain (usually nominal) amounts if the company goes into insolvent liquidation, but otherwise they have no economic rights in relation to the company.
- *a company limited by guarantee with a share capital.* A hybrid entity, usually used where the company is formed for non-commercial purposes, but the activities of the company are partly funded by investors who expect a return.
- *a company limited by shares.* The most common form of company used for business ventures.
- *an unlimited company* either with or without a share capital. This is a hybrid company, a company similar to its limited company (Ltd.) counterpart but where the members or shareholders do not benefit from limited liability should the company ever go into formal liquidation.

There are, however, many specific categories of corporations and other business organizations which may be formed in various countries and jurisdictions throughout the world.

US Companies Law

In the United States, corporations are generally incorporated, or organized, under the laws of a particular state. The corporate law of a corporation's state of incorporation generally governs that corporation's internal governance (even if the corporation's operations take place outside of that state). The corporate laws of the various states differ in some cases significantly - from state to state. Because of these differences, corporate lawyers are often consulted in an effort to determine the most appropriate or advantageous state in which to incorporate, and a majority of public companies in the U.S. are Delaware corporations. The federal laws of the United States and local law may also be applicable sources of corporate law.

Companies Law Theory

"A corporation is described to be a person in a political capacity created by the law, to endure in perpetual succession." Americans in the 1790s knew of a variety of corporations established for various purposes, including those of commerce, education, and religion. As the law of corporations was articulated by the Supreme Court under Chief Justice Marshall, over the first several decades of the new American state, emphasis fell, in a way which seems natural to us today, upon commercial corporations. Nonetheless, Wilson believed that, in all cases, corporations "should be erected with caution, and inspected with care." The actions of corporations were clearly circumscribed: "To every corporation a name must be assigned; and by that name alone it can perform legal acts." For non-binding external actions or transactions, corporations enjoyed the same latitude as private individuals; but it was with an eye to internal affairs that many saw principal advantage in incorporation. The power of making by-laws was "tacitly annexed to corporations by the very act of their establishment." While they must not directly contradict the overarching laws of the land, the central or local government cannot be expected to regulate toward the peculiar circumstances of a given body, and so "they are invested with authority to make regulations for the management of their own interests and affairs."

The question then arises: if corporations are to be inspected with care, what - if not the commercial or social conduct, or the by-laws is to be inspected and by whom? Do corporations have duties? Yes: "The general duties of every corporation may be collected from the nature and design of its institution: it should act agreeably to its nature, and fulfill the purposes for which it was formed." Who sees that corporations are living up to those duties? "The law has provided proper persons with proper powers to visit those institutions, and to correct every irregularity, which may arise within them." The Common Law provided for inspection by the court of king's bench. In 1790, at least, "the powers of the court of king's bench [were] vested in the supreme court of Pennsylvania." As for the dissolution of corporations, there seems not to have been much question that a corporation might "surrender its legal existence into the hands of that power, from which it was received. From such a surrender, the dissolution of the body corporate ensues." Nor does there seem to have been much question that by "a judgment of forfeiture against a corporation itself, it may be dissolved." However, Supreme Court Justice Wilson, lecturing in his unofficial capacity, at least, suggests his displeasure with the doctrine that corporate dissolution cannot be predicated "by a judgment of ouster against individuals. God forbid such is the sentiment of Mr. Justice Wilmot that the rights of the body should be lost or destroyed by the offences of the members."

As theorists such as Ronald Coase have pointed out, all business organizations represent an attempt to avoid certain costs associated with doing business. Each is meant to facilitate the contribution of specific resources investment capital, knowledge, relationships, and so forth towards a venture which will prove profitable to all contributors. Except for the partnership, all business forms are designed to provide limited liability to both members of the organization and external investors. Business organizations originated with agency law, which permits an agent to act on behalf of a principal, in exchange for the principal assuming equal liability for the wrongful acts committed by the agent. For this reason, all partners in a typical general partnership may be held liable for the wrongs committed by one partner. Those forms that provide limited liability are able to do so because the state provides a mechanism by which businesses that follow certain guidelines will be able to escape the full liability imposed under agency law. The state provides these forms because it has an interest in the strength of the companies that provide jobs and services therein, but also has an interest in monitoring and regulating their behaviour.

Companies Law

Law schools typically offer either a single upper level course on business organizations, or offer several courses covering different aspects of this area of law. The area of study examines issues such as how each major form of business entity may be formed, operated, and dissolved; the degree to which limited liability protects investors; the extent to which a business can be held liable for the acts of an agent of the business; the relative advantages and disadvantages of different types of business organizations, and the structures established by governments to monitor the buying and selling of ownership interests in large corporations.

The basic theory behind all business organizations is that, by combining certain functions within a single entity, a business (usually called a firm by economists) can operate more efficiently, and thereby realize a greater profit. Governments seek to facilitate investment in profitable operations by creating rules that protect investors in a business from being held personally liable for debts incurred by that business, either through mismanagement, or because of wrongful acts committed by the business.

Corporate law

Corporate law is the law of the most dominant kind of business enterprise in the modern world. Corporate law is the study of how shareholders, directors, employees, creditors, and other stakeholders such as consumers, the community and the environment interact with one another under the internal rules of the firm.

Corporate law is a part of a broader companies law (or law of business associations). Other types of business associations can include partnerships (like most law firms), or trusts (like a pension fund) or companies limited by guarantee (like some universities or charities). Corporate law is about big business, which has separate legal personality, with limited liability or unlimited liability for its members or shareholders, who buy and sell their stocks depending on the performance of the board of directors. It deals with the firms that are incorporated or registered under the corporate or company law of a sovereign state or their subnational states. The four defining characteristics of the modern corporation are:

- Separate Legal Personality of the corporation (the right to sue and be sued in its own name i.e. the law treats the company as a human being),
- Limited Liability of the shareholders (so that when the company is insolvent, they only owe the money that they subscribed for in shares),
- Transferable Shares (usually on a listed exchange, such as the London Stock Exchange, New York Stock Exchange or Euronext in Paris),
- Delegated Management, in other words, control of the company placed in the hands of a board of directors.

In most developed countries excluding the English speaking world, company boards are appointed as representatives of both shareholders and employees to "codetermine" company strategy. Corporate law is often divided into corporate governance (which concerns the various power relations within a corporation) and corporate finance (which concerns the rules on how capital is used).

Corporate Law in Context

Definition: The word "corporation" is generally synonymous with large publicly owned companies. In the United States, a company may or may not be a separate legal entity, and is often used synonymously with "firm" or "business." A corporation may accurately be called a company; however, a company should not necessarily be called a corporation, which has distinct characteristics. According to Black's Law Dictionary, in the U.S. a company means "a corporation or, less commonly, an association, partnership or union that carries on industrial enterprise."

The defining feature of a corporation is its legal independence from the people who create it. If a corporation fails, its shareholders will lose their money, and employees will lose their jobs, though disproportionately affecting its workers as opposed to its upper executives. Shareholders, however owning a part piece of the company, are not liable for debts that remain owing to the corporation's creditors. This rule is called limited liability, and it is why corporations end with "Ltd." (or some variant like "Inc." and "plc"). In the words of British judge, Walton J, a company is...

> *"...only a juristic figment of the imagination, lacking both a body to be kicked and a soul to be damned."*

But despite this, corporations are recognized by the law to have rights and responsibilities like actual people. Corporations can exercise human rights against real individuals and the state, and they may be responsible for human rights violations. Just as they are "born" into existence through its members obtaining a certificate of incorporation, they can "die" when they lose money into insolvency. Corporations can even be convicted of criminal offences, such as fraud and manslaughter.

History

Although some forms of companies are thought to have existed during Ancient Rome and Ancient Greece, the closest recognizable ancestors of the modern company did not appear until the second millennium. The first recognizable commercial associations were medieval guilds, where guild members agreed to abide by guild rules, but did not participate in ventures for common profit. The earliest forms of joint commercial enterprise under the *lex mercatoria* were in fact partnerships.

But with the expansion of international trade, Royal charters were increasingly granted in Europe to merchant adventurers. The Royal charters usually conferred special privileges on the trading company (including, usually, some form of monopoly). Originally, traders in these entities traded stock on their own account, but later the members came to operate on joint account and with joint stock, and the new Joint stock company was born.

Early companies were purely economic ventures; it was only belatedly realized that an incidental benefit of holding joint stock was that the company's stock could not be seized for the debts of any individual member. The development of company law in Europe was hampered by two notorious "bubbles" (the South Sea Bubble in England and the Tulip Bulb Bubble in Holland) in the 17th century, which set the development of companies in the two leading jurisdictions back by over a century in popular estimation.

But companies, almost inevitably, returned to the forefront of commerce, although in England to circumvent the Bubble Act 1720 investors had reverted to trading the stock of unincorporated associations, until it was repealed in 1825. However, the cumbersome process of obtaining Royal charters was simply insufficient to keep up with demand. In England there was a lively trade in the charters of defunct companies. However, prevarication amongst the legislation meant that in England it was not until the Joint Stock Companies Act 1844 that the first equivalent of modern companies, formed by registration, appeared. Soon after came the Limited Liability Act 1855, which in the event of a company's bankruptcy limited the liability of all shareholders to the amount of capital they had invested. The beginning of modern company law came when the two pieces of legislation were codified under the Joint Stock Companies Act 1856 at the behest of the then Vice President of the Board of Trade, Mr Robert Lowe. That legislation shortly gave way to the railway boom, and from there the numbers of companies formed soared. In the later nineteenth century depression took hold, and just as company numbers had boomed, many began to implode and fall into insolvency. Much strong academic, legislative and judicial opinion was opposed to the notion that businessmen could escape accountability for their role in the failing businesses. The last significant development in the history of companies was the decision of the House of Lords in *Salomon v. Salomon & Co.* where the House of Lords confirmed the separate legal personality of the company, and that the liabilities of the company were separate and distinct from those of its owners.

In a December 2006 article, *The Economist* identified the development of the joint stock company as one of the key reasons why Western commerce moved ahead of its rivals in the Middle East in post-renaissance era. Of course one should not underestimate the effects of early industrialisation either.

Corporate Personality

One of the key legal features of corporations are their separate legal personality, also known as "personhood" or being "artificial persons". However, the separate legal personality was not confirmed under English law until 1895 by the House of Lords in *Salomon v. Salomon & Co.* Separate legal personality often has unintended consequences, particularly in relation to smaller, family companies. In *B v. B* Fam 181 it was held that a discovery order obtained by a wife against her husband was not effective against the husband's company as it was not named in the order and was separate and distinct from him. And in *Macaura v. Northern Assurance Co Ltd* a claim under an insurance policy failed where the insured had transferred timber from his name into the name of a company wholly owned by him, and it was subsequently destroyed in a fire; as the property now belonged to the company and not to him, he no longer had an "insurable interest" in it and his claim failed.

However, separate legal personality does allow corporate groups a great deal of flexibility in relation to tax planning, and also enables multinational companies to manage the liability of their overseas operations. For instance in *Adams v. Cape Industries plc* it was held that victims of asbestos poisoning at the hands of an American subsidiary could not sue the English parent in tort. There are certain specific situations where courts are generally prepared to "pierce the corporate veil", to look directly at, and impose liability directly on the individuals behind the company. The most commonly cited examples are:

- where the company is a mere façade,
- where the company is effectively just the agent of its members or controllers,
- where a representative of the company has taken some personal responsibility for a statement or action,
- where the company is engaged in fraud or other criminal wrongdoing,
- where the natural interpretation of a contract or statute is as a reference to the corporate group and not the individual company,
- where permitted by statute (for example, many jurisdictions provide for shareholder liability where a company breaches environmental protection laws),
- in many jurisdictions, where a company continues to trade despite inevitable bankruptcy, the directors can be forced to account for trading losses personally.

Capacity and Powers

Historically, because companies are artificial persons created by operation of law, the law prescribed what the company could and could not do. Usually this was an expression of the commercial purpose which the company was formed for, and came to be referred to as the company's *objects*, and the extent of the objects are referred to as the company's capacity. If an activity fell outside of the company's capacity it was said to be *ultra vires* and void.

By way of distinction, the organs of the company were expressed to have various *corporate powers*. If the objects were the things that the company was able to do, then the powers were the means by which it could do them. Usually expressions of powers were limited to methods of raising capital, although from earlier times distinctions between objects and powers have caused lawyers difficulty. Most jurisdictions have now modified the position by statute, and companies generally have capacity to do all the things that a natural person could do, and power to do it in any way that a natural person could do it.

However, references to corporate capacity and powers have not quite been consigned to the dustbin of legal history. In many jurisdictions, directors can still be liable to their shareholders if they cause the company to engage in businesses outside of its objects, even if the transactions are still valid as between the company and the third party. And many jurisdictions also still permit transactions to be challenged for lack of "corporate benefit", where the relevant transaction has no prospect of being for the commercial benefit of the company or its shareholders.

As artificial persons, companies can only act through human agents. The main agent who deals with the company's management and business is the board of directors, but in many jurisdictions other officers can be appointed too. The board of directors is normally elected by the members, and the other officers are normally appointed by the board. These agents enter into contracts on behalf of the company with third parties.

Although the company's agents owe duties to the company (and, indirectly, to the shareholders) to exercise those powers for a proper purpose, generally speaking third parties' rights are not impugned if it transpires that the officers were acting improperly. Third parties are entitled to rely on the ostensible authority of agents held out by the company to act on its behalf. A line of common law cases reaching back to *Royal British Bank v Turquand* established in common law that third parties were entitled to assume that the internal management of the company was being conducted properly, and the rule has now been codified into statute in most countries.

Accordingly, companies will normally be liable for all the act and omissions of their officers and agents. This will include almost all torts, but the law relating to crimes committed by companies is complex, and varies significantly between countries.

Corporate Governance

Corporate governance is primarily the study of the power relations between the board of directors and those who elect them (shareholders in the "general meeting" and employees). It also concerns other stakeholders, such as creditors, consumers, the environment and the community at large. One of the main differences between different countries in the internal form of companies is between a two-tier and a one tier board. The United Kingdom, the United States, and most Commonwealth countries have single unified boards of directors. In Germany, companies have two tiers, so that shareholders (and employees) elect a "supervisory board", and then the supervisory board chooses the "management board". There is the option to use two tiers in France, and in the new European Companies (Societas Europea).

Recent literature, especially from the United States, has begun to discuss corporate governance in the terms of management science. While post-war discourse centred on how to achieve effective "corporate democracy" for shareholders or other stakeholders, many scholars have shifted to discussing the law in terms of principal-agent problems. On this view, the basic issue of corporate law is that when a "principal" party delegates his property (usually the shareholder's capital, but also the employee's labour) into the control of an "agent" (i.e. the director of the company) there is the possibility that the agent will act in his own interests, be "opportunistic", rather than fulfill the wishes of the principal. Reducing the risks of this opportunism, or the "agency cost", is said to be central to the goal of corporate law.

Corporate Constitution

The rules for corporations derive from two sources. These are the country's statutes (in the US, usually the Delaware General Corporation Law (DGCL); in the UK, the Companies Act 2006 (CA 2006); in Germany, the Aktiengesetz (AktG) and the Gesetz betreffend die Gesellschaften mit beschränkter Haftung (GmbH-Gesetz, GmbHG). The law will set out which rules are mandatory, and which rules can be derogated from. Examples of important rules which cannot be derogated from would usually include how to fire the board of directors, what duties directors owe to the company or when a company must be dissolved as it approaches bankruptcy. Examples of rules that members of a company would be allowed to change and choose could include, what kind of procedure general meetings should follow, when dividends get paid out, or how many members (beyond a minimum set out in the law) can amend the constitution. Usually, the statute will set out model articles, which the corporation's constitution will be assumed to have if it is silent on a bit of particular procedure.

The United States, and a few other common law countries, split the corporate constitution into two separate documents (the UK got rid of this in 2006). The memorandum of Association is the primary document, and will generally regulate the company's activities with the outside world. It states which objects the company is meant to follow (e.g. "this company makes automobiles") and specifies the authorised share capital of the company. The articles of association (or by-laws) is the secondary document, and will generally regulate the company's internal affairs and management, such as procedures for board meetings, dividend entitlements etc. In the event of any inconsistency, the memorandum prevails and in the United States only the memorandum is publicised. In civil law jurisdictions, the company's constitution is normally consolidated into a single document, often called the charter.

It is quite common for members of a company to supplement the corporate constitution with additional arrangements, such as *shareholders' agreements*, whereby they agree to exercise their membership rights in a certain way. Conceptually a shareholders' agreement fulfills many of the same functions as the corporate constitution, but because it is a contract, it will not normally bind new members of the company unless they accede to it somehow. One benefit of shareholders' agreement is that they will usually be confidential, as most jurisdictions do not require shareholders' agreements to be publicly filed. Another common method of supplementing the corporate constitution is by means of *voting trusts*, although these are relatively uncommon outside of the United States and certain offshore jurisdictions. Some jurisdictions consider the company seal to be a party of the "constitution" (in the loose sense of the word) of the company, but the requirement for a seal has been abrogated by legislation in most countries.

Balance of Power

The most important rules for corporate governance are those concerning the balance of power between the board of directors and the members of the company. Authority is given or "delegated" to the board to manage the company for the success of the investors. Certain specific decision rights are often reserved for shareholders, where their interests could be fundamentally affected. There are necessarily rules on when directors can be removed from office and replaced. To do that, meetings need to be called in order to vote on the issues. How easily the constitution can be amended and by who necessarily affects the relations of power.

It is a principle of corporate law that the directors of a company have the right to manage. This is expressed in statute in the DGCL, where §141(a) states, (a) The business and affairs of every corporation organized under this chapter shall be managed by or under the direction of a board of directors, except as may be otherwise provided in this chapter or in its certificate of incorporation.

In Germany, §76 AktG says the same for the management board, while under §111 AktG the supervisory board's role is stated to be to "oversee" (*überwachen*). In the United Kingdom, the right to manage is not laid down in law, but is found in Art.2 of the Model Articles. This means it is a default rule, which companies can opt out of (s.20 CA 2006) by reserving powers to members, although companies rarely do. UK law specifically reserves shareholders right and duty to approve "substantial non cash asset transactions" (s.190 CA 2006), which means those over 10% of company value, with a minimum of £5,000 and a maximum of £100,000. Similar rules, though much less stringent, exist in §271 DGCL and through case law in Germany under the so called *Holzmüller-Doktrin.*

Probably the must fundamental guarantee that directors will act in the members' interests is that they can easily be sacked. During the Great Depression, two Harvard scholars, Adolf Berle and Gardiner Means wrote *The Modern Corporation and Private Property*, an attack on American law which failed to hold directors to account, and linked the growing power and autonomy of directors to the economic crisis. In the UK, the right of members to remove directors by a simple majority is assured under s.168 CA 2006 Moreover, Art.20 of the Model Articles requires a third of the board to put themselves up for re-election every year (in effect creating maximum three year terms). 10% of shareholders can demand a meeting any time, and 5% can if it has been a year since the last one (s.303 CA 2006). In Germany, where employee participation creates the need for greater boardroom stability, §84(3) AktG states that management board directors can only be removed by the supervisory board for an important reason (*ein wichtiger Grund*) though this can include a vote of no-confidence by the shareholders. Terms last for five years, unless 75% of shareholders vote otherwise. §122 AktG lets 10% of shareholders demand a meeting. In the US, Delaware lets directors enjoy considerable autonomy. §141(k) DGCL states that directors can be removed without any cause, unless the board is "classified", meaning that directors only come up for re-appointment on different years. If the board is classified, then directors cannot be removed unless there is gross misconduct. Director's autonomy from shareholders is seen further in §216 DGCL, which allows for plurality voting and §211(d) which states shareholder meetings can only be called if the constitution allows for it. The problem is that in America, directors usually choose where a company is incorporated and §242(b)(1) DGCL says any constitutional amendment requires a resolution by the directors. By contrast, constitutional amendments can be made at any time by 75% of shareholders in Germany (§179 AktG) and the UK.

Director's Duties

The standard of skill and care that a director owes is usually described as acquiring and maintaining sufficient knowledge and understanding of the company's business to enable him to properly discharge his duties.

Directors are also strictly charged to exercise their powers only for a proper purpose. For instance were a director to issue a large number of new shares, not for the purposes of raising capital but in order to defeat a potential takeover bid, that would be an improper purpose.

Directors have a duty to exercise reasonable skill care and diligence - This right enables the company to seek compensation from its director if it can be proved that he hasn't shown reasonable skill or care which in turn has caused the company to incur a loss.

Directors also owe strict duties not to permit any conflict of interest or conflict with their duty to act in the best interests of the company. This rule is so strictly enforced that, even where the conflict of interest or conflict of duty is purely hypothetical, the directors can be forced to disgorge all personal gains arising from it. In *Aberdeen Ry v. Blaikie* (1854) 1 Macq HL 461 Lord Cranworth stated in his judgment that,

"A corporate body can only act by agents, and it is, of course, the duty of those agents so to act as best to promote the interests of the corporation whose affairs they are conducting. Such agents have duties to discharge of a fiduciary nature towards their principal. And it is a rule of universal application that no one, having such duties to discharge, shall be allowed to enter into engagements in which he has, *or can have*, a personal interest conflicting *or which possibly may conflict*, with the interests of those whom he is bound to protect... So strictly is this principle adhered to that no question is allowed to be raised as to the fairness or unfairness of the contract entered into..."

However, in many jurisdictions the members of the company are permitted to ratify transactions which would otherwise fall foul of this principle. It is also largely accepted in most jurisdictions that this principle should be capable of being abrogated in the company's constitution.

Corporate Litigation

Members of a company generally have rights against each other and against the company, as framed under the company's constitution. In relation to the exercise of their rights, minority shareholders usually have to accept that, because of the limits of their voting rights, they cannot direct the overall control of the company and must accept the will of the majority (often expressed as *majority rule*). However, majority rule can be iniquitous, particularly where there is one controlling shareholder.

Accordingly, a number of exceptions have developed in law in relation to the general principle of majority rule.

- Where the majority shareholder(s) are exercising their votes to perpetrate a fraud on the minority, the courts may permit the minority to sue.
- Members always retain the right to sue if the majority acts to invade their personal rights, e.g. where the company's affairs are not conducted in accordance with the company's constitution (this position has been debated because the extent of a personal right is not set in law). *Macdougall v Gardiner* and *Pender v Lushington* present irreconcilable differences in this area.
- in many jurisdictions it is possible for minority shareholders to take a *representative* or *derivative action* in the name of the company, where the company is controlled by the alleged wrongdoers.

Corporate Finance

Shares and Share Capital

Companies generally raise capital for their business ventures either by debt or equity. Capital raised by way of equity is usually raised by issued shares (sometimes called "stock" (not to be confused with stock-in-trade)) or warrants.

A share is an item of property, and can be sold or transferred. Holding a share makes the holder a member of the company, and entitles them to enforce the provisions of the company's constitution against the company and against other members. Shares also normally have a nominal or par value, which is the limit of the shareholder's liability to contribute to the debts of the company on an insolvent liquidation.

Shares usually confer a number of rights on the holder. These will normally include:

- voting rights
- rights to dividends declared by the company
- rights to any return of capital either upon redemption of the share, or upon the liquidation of the company
- in some countries, shareholders have preemption rights, whereby they have a preferential right to participate in future share issues by the company

Many companies have different classes of shares, offering different rights to the shareholders. For example, a company might issue both ordinary shares and preference shares, with the two types having different voting and/or economic rights. For example, a company might provide that preference shareholders shall each receive a cumulative preferred dividend of a certain amount per annum, but the ordinary shareholders shall receive everything else.

The total number of issued shares in a company is said to represent its *capital.* Many jurisdictions regulate the minimum amount of capital which a company may have, although some countries only prescribe minimum amounts of capital for companies engaging in certain types of business (e.g. banking, insurance etc.).

Similarly, most jurisdictions regulate the maintenance of capital, and prevent companies returning funds to shareholders by way of distribution when this might leave the company financially exposed. In some jurisdictions this extends to prohibiting a company from providing financial assistance for the purchase of its own shares.

Liquidations

Liquidation is the normal means by which a company's existence is brought to an end. It is also referred to (either alternatively or concurrently) in some jurisdictions as *winding up* and/or *dissolution*.

Liquidations generally come in two forms, either *compulsory liquidations* (sometimes called *creditors' liquidations*) and *voluntary liquidations* (sometimes called *members' liquidations*, although a voluntary liquidation where the company is insolvent will also be controlled by the creditors, and is properly referred to as a *creditors' voluntary liquidation*).

As its names imply, applications for compulsory liquidation are normally made by creditors of the company when the company is unable to pay its debts. However, in some jurisdictions, regulators have the power to apply for the liquidation of the company on the grounds of public good, i.e. where the company is believed to have engaged in unlawful conduct, or conduct which is otherwise harmful to the public at large.

Voluntary liquidations occur when the company's members decide voluntarily to wind up the affairs of the company. This may be because they believe that the company will soon become insolvent, or it may be on economic grounds if they believe that the purpose for which the company was formed is now at an end, or that the company is not providing an adequate return on assets and should be broken up and sold off.

Some jurisdictions also permit companies to be wound up on "just and equitable" grounds. Generally, applications for just and equitable winding-up are brought by a member of the company who alleges that the affairs of the company are being conducted in a prejudicial manner, and asking the court to bring an end to the company's existence. For obvious reasons, in most countries, the courts have been reluctant to wind up a company solely on the basis of the disappointment of one member, regardless of how well-founded that member's complaints are. Accordingly, most jurisdictions which permit just and equitable winding up also permit the court to impose other remedies, such as requiring the majority shareholder(s) to buy out the disappointed minority shareholder at a fair value.

Where a company goes into liquidation, normally a liquidator is appointed to gather in all the company's assets and settle all claims against the company. If there is any surplus after paying off all the creditors of the company, this surplus is then distributed to the members.

Mergers and Acquisitions

The phrase mergers and acquisitions (abbreviated M&A) refers to the aspect of corporate strategy, corporate finance and management dealing with the buying, selling and combining of different companies that can aid, finance, or help a growing company in a given industry grow rapidly without having to create another business entity.

Acquisition

An acquisition, also known as a takeover or a buyout, is the buying of one company (the 'target') by another. Consolidation is when two companies combine together to form a new company all together. An acquisition may be private or public, depending on whether the acquire or merging company is or isn't listed in public markets. An acquisition may be friendly or hostile. Whether a purchase is perceived as a friendly or hostile depends on how it is communicated to and received by the target company's board of directors, employees and shareholders. It is quite normal though for M&A deal communications to take place in a so called 'confidentiality bubble' whereby information flows are restricted due to confidentiality agreements. In the case of a friendly transaction, the companies cooperate in negotiations; in the case of a hostile deal, the takeover target is unwilling to be bought or the target's board has no prior knowledge of the offer. Hostile acquisitions can, and often do, turn friendly at the end, as the acquirer secures the endorsement of the transaction from the board of the acquire company. This usually requires an improvement in the terms of the offer. Acquisition usually refers to a purchase of a smaller firm by a larger one. Sometimes, however, a smaller firm will acquire management control of a larger or longer established company and keep its name for the combined entity. This is known as a reverse takeover. Another type of acquisition is reverse merger, a deal that enables a private company to get publicly listed in a short time period. A reverse merger occurs when a private company that has strong prospects and is eager to raise financing buys a publicly listed shell company, usually one with no business and limited assets. Achieving acquisition success has proven to be very difficult, while various studies have shown that 50% of acquisitions were unsuccessful. The acquisition process is very complex, with many dimensions influencing its outcome. There is also a variety of structures used in securing control over the assets of a company, which have different tax and regulatory implications:

- The buyer buys the shares, and therefore control, of the target company being purchased. Ownership control of the company in turn conveys effective control over the assets of the company, but since the company is acquired intact as a going concern, this form of transaction carries with it all of the liabilities accrued by that business over its past and all of the risks that company faces in its commercial environment.
- The buyer buys the assets of the target company. The cash the target receives from the sell-off is paid back to its shareholders by dividend or through liquidation. This type of transaction leaves the target company as an empty shell, if the buyer buys out the entire assets. A buyer often structures the transaction as an asset purchase to "cherry-pick" the assets that it wants and leave out the assets and liabilities that it does not. This can be particularly important where foreseeable liabilities may include

future, unquantified damage awards such as those that could arise from litigation over defective products, employee benefits or terminations, or environmental damage. A disadvantage of this structure is the tax that many jurisdictions, particularly outside the United States, impose on transfers of the individual assets, whereas stock transactions can frequently be structured as like-kind exchanges or other arrangements that are tax-free or tax-neutral, both to the buyer and to the seller's shareholders.

The terms "demerger", "spin-off" and "spin-out" are sometimes used to indicate a situation where one company splits into two, generating a second company separately listed on a stock exchange.

Distinction between Mergers and Acquisitions

Although often used synonymously, the terms merger and acquisition mean slightly different things.

When one company takes over another and clearly establishes itself as the new owner, the purchase is called an acquisition. From a legal point of view, the target company ceases to exist, the buyer "swallows" the business and the buyer's stock continues to be traded.

In the pure sense of the term, a merger happens when two firms agree to go forward as a single new company rather than remain separately owned and operated. This kind of action is more precisely referred to as a "merger of equals". The firms are often of about the same size. Both companies' stocks are surrendered and new company stock is issued in its place. For example, in the 1999 merger of Glaxo Wellcome and SmithKline Beecham, both firms ceased to exist when they merged, and a new company, GlaxoSmithKline, was created.

In practice, however, actual mergers of equals don't happen very often. Usually, one company will buy another and, as part of the deal's terms, simply allow the acquired firm to proclaim that the action is a merger of equals, even if it is technically an acquisition. Being bought out often carries negative connotations, therefore, by describing the deal euphemistically as a merger, deal makers and top managers try to make the takeover more palatable. An example of this would be the takeover of Chrysler by Daimler-Benz in 1999 which was widely referred to in the time.

A purchase deal will also be called a merger when both CEOs agree that joining together is in the best interest of both of their companies. But when the deal is unfriendly that is, when the target company does not want to be purchased it is always regarded as an acquisition.

Business Valuation

The five most common ways to valuate a business are

- asset valuation,
- historical earnings valuation,
- future maintainable earnings valuation,
- relative valuation (comparable company & comparable transactions),
- discounted cash flow (DCF) valuation

Professionals who valuate businesses generally do not use just one of these methods but a *combination* of some of them, as well as possibly others that are not mentioned above, in order to obtain a more accurate value. The information in the balance sheet or income statement is obtained by one of three accounting measures: a Notice to Reader, a Review Engagement or an Audit.

Accurate business valuation is one of the most important aspects of M&A as valuations like these will have a major impact on the price that a business will be sold for. Most often this information is expressed in a Letter of Opinion of Value (LOV) when the business is being valuated for interest's sake. There are other, more detailed ways of expressing the value of a business. While these reports generally get more detailed and expensive as the size of a company increases, this is not always the case as there are many complicated industries which require more attention to detail, regardless of size.

Financing M&A

Mergers are generally differentiated from acquisitions partly by the way in which they are financed and partly by the relative size of the companies. Various methods of financing an M&A deal exist:

Cash

Payment by cash. Such transactions are usually termed acquisitions rather than mergers because the shareholders of the target company are removed from the picture and the target comes under the (indirect) control of the bidder's shareholders.

Stock

Payment in the acquiring company's stock, issued to the shareholders of the acquired company at a given ratio proportional to the valuation of the latter.

Specialist M&A Advisory Firms

Although at present the majority of M&A advice is provided by full-service investment banks, recent years have seen a rise in the prominence of specialist M&A advisers, who only provide M&A advice (and not financing). These companies are sometimes referred to as Transition companies, assisting businesses often referred to as "companies in transition." To perform these services in the US, an advisor must be a licensed broker dealer, and subject to SEC (FINRA) regulation. More information on M&A advisory firms is provided at corporate advisory.

Motives Behind M&A

The dominant rationale used to explain M&A activity is that acquiring firms seek improved financial performance. The following motives are considered to improve financial performance:

- **Economy of scale:** This refers to the fact that the combined company can often reduce its fixed costs by removing duplicate departments or operations, lowering the costs of the company relative to the same revenue stream, thus increasing profit margins.
- **Economy of scope:** This refers to the efficiencies primarily associated with demand-side changes, such as increasing or decreasing the scope of marketing and distribution, of different types of products.
- **Increased revenue or market share:** This assumes that the buyer will be absorbing a major competitor and thus increase its market power (by capturing increased market share) to set prices.
- **Cross-selling:** For example, a bank buying a stock broker could then sell its banking products to the stock broker's customers, while the broker can sign up the bank's customers for brokerage accounts. Or, a manufacturer can acquire and sell complementary products.
- **Synergy:** For example, managerial economies such as the increased opportunity of managerial specialization. Another example are purchasing economies due to increased order size and associated bulk-buying discounts.
- **Taxation:** A profitable company can buy a loss maker to use the target's loss as their advantage by reducing their tax liability. In the United States and many other countries, rules are in place to limit the ability of profitable companies to "shop" for loss making

companies, limiting the tax motive of an acquiring company. Tax minimization strategies include purchasing assets of a non-performing company and reducing current tax liability under the Tanner-White PLLC Troubled Asset Recovery Plan.

- **Geographical or other diversification:** This is designed to smooth the earnings results of a company, which over the long term smoothens the stock price of a company, giving conservative investors more confidence in investing in the company. However, this does not always deliver value to shareholders (see below).
- **Resource transfer:** Resources are unevenly distributed across firms (Barney, 1991) and the interaction of target and acquiring firm resources can create value through either overcoming information asymmetry or by combining scarce resources.
- **Vertical integration:** Vertical integration occurs when an upstream and downstream firm merge (or one acquires the other). There are several reasons for this to occur. One reason is to internalise an externality problem. A common example is of such an externality is double marginalization. Double marginalization occurs when both the upstream and downstream firms have monopoly power, each firm reduces output from the competitive level to the monopoly level, creating two deadweight losses. By merging the vertically integrated firm can collect one deadweight loss by setting the downstream firm's output to the competitive level. This increases profits and consumer surplus. A merger that creates a vertically integrated firm can be profitable.
- **Absorption of Similar Businesses under Single Management:** Similar portfolio invested by two different Mutual funds namely United Money Market Fund and United Growth & Income Fund, caused the management to absorb United Money Market Fund into United Growth & Income Fund.

However, on average and across the most commonly studied variables, acquiring firms' financial performance does not positively change as a function of their acquisition activity. Therefore, additional motives for merger and acquisition that may not add shareholder value include:

- **Diversification:** While this may hedge a company against a downturn in an individual industry it fails to deliver value, since it is possible for individual shareholders to achieve the same hedge by diversifying their portfolios at a much lower cost than those associated with a merger.
- **Manager's hubris:** Manager's overconfidence about expected synergies from M&A which results in overpayment for the target company.
- **Empire-building:** Managers have larger companies to manage and hence more power.
- **Manager's compensation:** In the past, certain executive management teams had their payout based on the total amount of profit of the company, instead of the profit per share, which would give the team a perverse incentive to buy companies to increase the total profit while decreasing the profit per share (which hurts the owners of the company, the shareholders); although some empirical studies show that compensation is linked to profitability rather than mere profits of the company.

Effects on Management

A study published in the July/August 2008 issue of the Journal of Business Strategy suggests that mergers and acquisitions destroy leadership continuity in target companies' top management teams for at least a decade following a deal. The study found that target companies lose 21 percent of their executives each year for at least 10 years following an acquisition more than double the turnover experienced in non-merged firms. If the businesses of the acquired and acquiring companies overlap, then such turnover is to be expected; in other words, there can only be one CEO, CFO, etcetera at a time.

The Great Merger Movement

The Great Merger Movement was a predominantly U.S. business phenomenon that happened from 1895 to 1905. During this time, small firms with little market share consolidated with similar firms to form large, powerful institutions that dominated their markets. It is estimated that more than 1,800 of these firms disappeared into consolidations, many of which acquired substantial shares of the markets in which they operated. The vehicle used were so-called trusts. In 1900 the value of firms acquired in mergers was 20% of GDP. In 1990 the value was only 3% and from 1998–2000 it was around 10–11% of GDP. Organizations that commanded the greatest share of the market in 1905 saw that command disintegrate by 1929 as smaller competitors joined forces with each other. However, there were companies that merged during this time such as DuPont, US Steel, and General Electric that have been able to keep their dominance in their respective sectors today due to growing technological advances of their products, patents, and brand recognition by their customers. The companies that merged were mass producers of homogeneous goods that could exploit the efficiencies of large volume production. These "quick mergers" involved mergers of companies with unrelated technology and different management. As a result, the efficiency gains associated with mergers were not present. The new and bigger company would actually face higher costs than competitors because of these technological and managerial differences. Thus, the mergers were not done to see large efficiency gains, they were in fact done because that was the trend at the time. Companies which had specific fine products, like fine writing paper, earned their profits on high margin rather than volume and took no part in Great Merger Movement.

Short-run Factors

One of the major short run factors that sparked in The Great Merger Movement was the desire to keep prices high. That is, with many firms in a market, supply of the product remains high. During the panic of 1893, the demand declined. When demand for the good falls, as illustrated by the classic supply and demand model, prices are driven down. To avoid this decline in prices, firms found it profitable to collude and manipulate supply to counter any changes in demand for the good. This type of cooperation led to widespread horizontal integration amongst firms of the era. Focusing on mass production allowed firms to reduce unit costs to a much lower rate. These firms usually were capital-intensive and had high fixed costs. Because new machines were mostly financed through bonds, interest payments on bonds were high followed by the panic of 1893, yet no firm was willing to accept quantity reduction during that period.

Long-run Factors

In the long run, due to the desire to keep costs low, it was advantageous for firms to merge and reduce their transportation costs thus producing and transporting from one location rather than various sites of different companies as in the past. This resulted in shipment directly to market from this one location. In addition, technological changes prior to the merger movement within companies increased the efficient size of plants with capital intensive assembly lines allowing for economies of scale. Thus improved technology and transportation were forerunners to the Great Merger Movement. In part due to competitors as mentioned above, and in part due to the government, however, many of these initially successful mergers were eventually dismantled. The U.S. government passed the Sherman Act in 1890, setting rules against price fixing and monopolies. Starting in the 1890s with such cases as *U.S. versus Addyston Pipe and Steel Co.*, the courts attacked large companies for strategizing with others or within their own companies to maximize profits. Price fixing with competitors created a greater incentive for companies to unite and merge under one name so that they were not competitors anymore and technically not price fixing.

Failure of M&A

A book by Prof. Dr. Thomas Straub (2007) "Reasons for frequent failure in Mergers and Acquisitions" develops a comprehensive research framework that bridges rival perspectives and promotes a modern understanding of factors underlying M&A performance. The first important step towards this objective is the development of a common frame of reference that spans conflicting theoretical assumptions from different perspectives. On this basis, a comprehensive framework is proposed with which to understand the origins of M&A performance better and address the problem of fragmentation by integrating the most important competing perspectives in respect of studies on M&A Furthermore according to the existing literature relevant determinants of firm performance are derived from each dimension of the model. For the dimension strategic management, the six strategic variables: market similarity, market complementarity, production operation similarity, production operation complementarity, market power, and purchasing power were identified having an important impact on M&A performance. For the dimension organizational behavior, the variables acquisition experience, relative size, and cultural differences were found to be important. Finally, relevant determinants of M&A performance from the financial field were acquisition premium, bidding process, and due diligence. Three different ways in order to best measure post M&A performance are recognized: Synergy realization, absolute performance and finally relative performance.

Merger Waves

The economic history has been divided into *Merger Waves* based on the merger activities in the business world as:

Period	Name	Facet
1889 - 1904	First Wave	Horizontal mergers
1916 - 1929	Second Wave	Vertical mergers
1965 - 1989	Third Wave	Diversified conglomerate mergers
1992 - 1998	Fourth Wave	Congeneric mergers; Hostile takeovers; Corporate Raiding
2000 -	Fifth Wave	Cross-border mergers

Cross-border M&A

In a study conducted in 2000 by Lehman Brothers, it was found that, on average, large M&A deals cause the domestic currency of the target corporation to appreciate by 1% relative to the acquirers.

The rise of globalization has exponentially increased the necessity for MAIC Trust accounts and securities clearing services for Like-Kind Exchanges for cross-border M&A. In 1997 alone, there were over 2333 cross-border transactions, worth a total of approximately $298 billion. Due to the complicated nature of cross-border M&A, the vast majority of cross-border actions have unsuccessful anies seek to expand their global footprint and become more agile at creating high-performing businesses and cultures across national boundaries.

Even mergers of companies with headquarters in the same country are very much of this type and require MAIC custodial services (cross-border Mergers). After all, when Boeing acquires McDonnell Douglas, the two American companies must integrate operations in dozens of countries around the world. This is just as true for other supposedly "single country" mergers, such as the $29 billion dollar merger of Swiss drug makers Sandoz and Ciba-Geigy.

Corporate Insolvency

Insolvency means the inability to pay one's debts as they fall due. Usually used to refer to a business, insolvency refers to the inability of a company to pay off its debts.

Business insolvency is defined in two different ways:

- Cash flow insolvency
- Unable to pay debts as they fall due.
- Balance sheet insolvency
- Having negative net assets – in other words, liabilities exceed assets.

A business may be 'cash flow insolvent' but 'balance sheet solvent' if it holds illiquid assets, particularly against short term debt that it cannot immediately realise if called upon to do so. Conversely, a business can have negative net assets showing on its balance sheet but still be cash flow solvent if ongoing revenue is able to meet debt obligations, and thus avoid default for instance, if it holds long term debt. Many large companies operate permanently in this state.

Insolvency is not a synonym for bankruptcy, which is a determination of insolvency made by a court of law with resulting legal orders intended to resolve the insolvency.

Insolvency is defined both in terms of cash flow and in terms of balance sheet in the UK Insolvency Act 1986, Section 123, which reads in part:

> *123. Definition of inability to pay debts*
>
> *(1) A company is deemed unable to pay its debts - [...]*
>
> *(e) if it is proved to the satisfaction of the court that the company is unable to pay its debts as they fall due. This is known as cash flow insolvency.*
>
> *(2) A company is also deemed unable to pay its debts if it is proved to the satisfaction of the court that the value of the company's assets is less than the amount of its liabilities, taking into account its contingent and prospective liabilities. This is known as balance sheet insolvency.*

Consequences of Insolvency

The principal focus of modern insolvency legislation and business debt restructuring practices no longer rests on the liquidation and elimination of insolvent entities but on the remodeling of the financial and organizational structure of debtors experiencing financial distress so as to permit the rehabilitation and continuation of their business. This is known as Business Turnaround or Business Recovery. In some jurisdictions, it is an offence under the insolvency laws for a corporation to continue in business while insolvent. In others, the business may continue under a declared protective arrangement while alternative options to achieve recovery are worked out. Increasingly, legislatures have favored alternatives to winding up companies for good.

Debt Restructuring

Out-of court debt restructurings, also known as workouts, are increasingly becoming a global reality. Debt restructurings are typically handled by professional insolvency and restructuring practitioners, and are usually less expensive and a preferable alternative to bankruptcy.

Debt restructuring is a process that allows a private or public company - or a sovereign entity - facing cash flow problems and financial distress, to reduce and renegotiate its delinquent debts in order to improve or restore liquidity and rehabilitate so that it can continue its operations.

Government Debt

Although the terms bankrupt and insolvent are often used in reference to governments or government obligations, a government cannot be insolvent in the normal sense of the word. Generally, a government's debt is not secured by the assets of the government, but by its ability to levy taxes. By the standard definition, all governments would be in a state of insolvency unless they had assets equal to the debt they owed. If, for any reason, a government cannot meet its interest obligation, it is technically not insolvent but is "in default". As governments are sovereign entities, persons who hold debt of the government cannot seize the assets of the government to re-pay the debt. However, in most cases, debt in default is refinanced by further borrowing or monetized by issuing more currency (which typically results in inflation and may result in hyperinflation).

Insolvency Law in Individual Countries

Insolvency regimes around the world have evolved in very different ways, with laws focusing on different strategies for dealing with the insolvent corporate. The outcome of an insolvent restructuring can be very different depending on the laws of the state in which the insolvency proceeding is run, and in many cases different stakeholders in a company may hold the advantage in different jurisdictions.

South Africa : In South Africa, owners of businesses that had at any stage traded insolvently (i.e. that had a balance-sheet insolvency) become personally liable for the business' debts. Trading insolvently is often regarded as normal business practice in South Africa, as long as the business is able to fulfill its debt obligations when they fall due.

United Kingdom: In the UK, the term bankruptcy is reserved for individuals. A company which is insolvent may be put into liquidation (sometimes referred to as winding-up). The directors and shareholders can instigate the liquidation process without court involvement by a shareholder resolution and the appointment of a licensed Insolvency Practitioner as liquidator. However, the liquidation will not be effective legally without the convening of a meeting of creditors who have the opportunity to appoint a liquidator of their own choice. This process is known as creditors voluntary liquidation (CVL), as opposed to members voluntary liquidation (MVL) which is for solvent companies. Alternatively, a creditor can petition the court for a winding-up order which, if granted, will place the company into what is called compulsory liquidation or winding up by the court. The liquidator realises the assets of the company and distributes funds realised to creditors according to their priorities, after the deduction of costs.

It can be a civil and even a criminal offence for directors to allow a company to continue to trade whilst insolvent. However, two new insolvency procedures were introduced by the Insolvency Act 1986 which aim to provide time for the rescue of a company or, at least, its business. These are Administration and Company Voluntary Arrangement:

- **Administration** is a procedure to protect a company from its creditors in order for it to be able to make significant operational changes or restructuring so that it could continue as a going concern, or at least in order to achieve a better outcome for creditors than via liquidation. In contrast to Chapter 11 in the US where the directors remain in control throughout that restructuring process, in the UK an Administrator is appointed who must be a licensed Insolvency Practitioner to manage the company's affairs to protect the creditors of the insolvent company and balance their respective interests. Unless the company itself is saved by this process, the company is subsequently put into liquidation to distribute the remaining funds.
- A **Company Voluntary Arrangement (CVA)** is a legal agreement between the company and its creditors, based on paying a fixed amount lower than the outstanding actual debt. These are normally based on a monthly payment, and at the end of the agreed term the remaining debt is written-off. The CVA is managed by a Supervisor who must be a licensed Insolvency Practitioner. If the CVA fails, the company is usually put into liquidation.

One particular type of Administration that is becoming more common is called pre pack administration (more information under administration (law)). In this process, immediately after appointment the administrator completes a pre-arranged sale of the company's business, often to its directors or owners. The process can be seen as controversial because the creditors do not have the opportunity to vote against the sale. The rationale behind the device is that the swift sale of the business may be necessary or of benefit to enable a best price to be achieved. If the sale was delayed, creditors would ultimately lose out because the price obtainable for the assets would be reduced.

In addition to the above-mentioned corporate insolvency procedures, a creditor holding security over an asset of the company may have the power to appoint an insolvency practitioner as administrative receiver or, in Scotland, receiver. The process, latterly known as administrative receivership or, in Scotland, receivership, has existed for many years and has often resulted in a successful rescue of a company's business via a sale, but not of the company itself. Since the introduction of the collective insolvency procedure of Administration in 1986, the legislators have decided to set a shelf life on the administrative receivership or, in Scotland, receivership procedure and it is no longer possible to appoint an administrative receiver or, in Scotland, receiver under security created after 15 September 2003.

In individual cases the bankruptcy estate is dealt by an official receiver, appointed by the court. In some cases the file is transferred to RTLU (OR Regional Trustee Liquidator Unit) that will assess your assets and income to see if you can contribute towards paying costs of bankruptcy or even discharge part of your debts.

United States: Under the Uniform Commercial Code, a person is considered to be insolvent when the party has ceased to pay its debts in the ordinary course of business, or cannot pay its debts as they become due, or is insolvent within the meaning of the Bankruptcy Code. This is important because certain rights under the code may be invoked against an insolvent party which are otherwise unavailable.

The United States has established insolvency regimes which aim to protect the insolvent individual or company from the creditors, and balance their respective interests. However, some state courts have begun to find individual corporate officers and directors liable for driving a company deeper into bankruptcy, under the legal theory of "deepening insolvency."

2

Disclosure of Security Laws

Introduction

Disclosure is required in each registration statement filed under the Securities Act, as well as in the various reports that must be prepared and filed in order to comply with the requirements of the Exchange Act. Also, even when the transaction is exempt from registration under the Securities Act, as might be the case when the issuer chooses to rely upon one of the so-called private placement exemptions that are available under Section 4, it may be necessary to prepare a disclosure document containing information that is similar to that required for registered offerings.

Integrated Disclosure under the Federal Securities Laws

A. Overview

In 1982, the SEC adopted a program of "integrated disclosure" that was intended to reduce burdens on companies while at the same time insuring that security holders, investors, and other marketplace participants had access to meaningful and timely information with regard to the company upon which they could base their own individual investment decisions. The SEC's actions were intended to eliminate the substantial overlap that previously existed between the information that might be required under the transaction-oriented framework of the Securities Act and the status-oriented framework of the Exchange Act by standardizing many of the disclosures on the registration forms, periodic reports, and other documents issuers must file and distribute pursuant to the federal securities laws. The desired standardization of information is accomplished by:

- setting out all of the non financial disclosure items (including exhibits) required in the integrated disclosure system in either Regulation S-K or, in the case of "small business issuers," Regulation S-B;
- setting forth substantially all of the accounting statement requirements for documents to be filed under either of the federal statutes in Regulation S-X;
- providing for uniform financial statements in each of those disclosure documents that require the preparation and filing of financial statements; and
- reducing the burden of potentially duplicative filings by authorizing incorporation by reference of previously filed information into documents that might be filed for other purposes under the securities laws.

B. Forms and Documents Used in the Disclosure System

1. In General

The forms and documents used in the integrated disclosure system include the Securities Act registration forms, the Exchange Act registration forms, the forms upon which information is to be disclosed in response to the reporting requirements included in the Exchange Act, the annual report companies registered under the Exchange Act must deliver to their shareholders, and the proxy statement materials generally required for meetings of the shareholders of reporting companies.

2. Securities Act Registration Forms

The main Securities Act registration forms are as follows:

Form S-1. Form S-1 is the general registration form available to all issuers for primary offerings. Form S-1 requires full disclosure of all required information in the registration statement, without incorporation by reference from documents that may have previously been filed pursuant to the Exchange Act.

Form S-2. Form S-2 is available to issuers that have been reporting companies for at least three years immediately preceding the filing of the registration statement and have timely filed all reports during the past twelve calendar months and the portion of the month in which the registration statement is filed. Form S-2 is not available for exchange offers or to issuers that have recently defaulted with respect to obligations to make any dividend payment or sinking fund payment on preferred stock. If available, Form S-2 permits extensive incorporation by reference, generally from the issuer's annual report to shareholders; however, it will be necessary to disclose certain information relating to the terms of the specific offering.

Form S-3. Form S-3, as to a primary distribution, can be used by issuers that satisfy, specified "registrant requirements" for transactions that satisfy the "transaction requirements" included in the form. The registrant requirements are essentially identical to those that apply for the use of Form S-2, except that the period during which the issuer must have been subject to the reporting requirements is reduced from three years to one year. The transaction requirements for primary and secondary offerings for cash will be satisfied if the aggregate market value of the voting stock held by the non affiliates of the issuer equals or exceeds $75 million. Form S-3 relies almost exclusively upon incorporation by reference to the issuer's Exchange Act reports and is usually considered to be the simplest method of registering securities under the Securities Act.

Form SB-2. Form SB-2 replaced Form S-18 for registration of securities under the Securities Act and is available to any "small business issuer" (SBI). An SBI is defined as an "entity" (1) that had revenues of less than $25 million during its last fiscal year; (2) that is a domestic or Canadian issuer; (3) that is not an investment company; and (4) with an aggregate public float (i.e., the aggregate market value of the issuer's outstanding securities held by nonaffiliates) of less than $25 million. Form SB-2 may be used by reporting and non-reporting issuers alike, and SBIs may register an unlimited amount of securities on Form SB-2. Form SB-2 may be used for both primary and secondary distributions of any type of securities offered for a cash consideration.

Other Securities Act Registration Forms. In addition to the above-referenced registration forms, the issuer may utilize various other forms to register securities in certain contexts. For example, Form S-4 is available for the registration of securities issued in business combination transactions, including; mergers and exchange offers for securities of the issuer or some other entity, and Form S-8 can be used to register securities to be offered to employees pursuant to an employee benefit plan. Also, Form SB-1, which was adopted by the SEC in June 1993, can be used by certain "transitional" SBIs to register up to $10 million of securities to be sold for cash, provided that the SBI has not registered more than $10 million in securities offerings in any continuous twelve-month period, including the transaction being registered.

3. Exchange Act Registration Forms

Form 10 is the basic form for registration of securities under the Exchange Act and calls for extensive disclosure relating to the registrant presented on an item-by-item basis. However, in those cases where the registrant has previously registered its securities under the Securities Act, Form 8-A, a simplified form that relies largely upon information included in the Securities Act filings, can be used to register certain securities under the Exchange Act. SBIs may register securities under the Exchange Act by filing Form 10-SB, which allows the registrant to use any one of three alternative disclosure formats. Two track the disclosures that might be made in a Regulation A offering, and the other sets out certain items in Regulation S-B that must be addressed.

4. Exchange Act Reporting Forms

The annual report on Form 10-K must be filed by reporting companies with the SEC within ninety days after the end of each fiscal year. Form 10-K requires extensive disclosures relating to the financial condition, business, and properties of the issuer. The quarterly report on Form 10-Q which must be filed by reporting companies with the SEC within forty-five days after the end of each of the first three fiscal quarters. It includes uncertified financial statements for the quarter and year to date presented on a comparative basis with corresponding periods of the prior fiscal year. Finally, current reports on Form 8-K must usually be filed with the SEC within fifteen days after the occurrence of the event the form requires be reported.

SBIs meeting their Exchange Act reporting obligations by using Regulation S-B disclosures can make their filings on Form 10-KSB, which is an annual report for SBIs analogous to Form 10-K, and on Form 10-QSB, which is a quarterly reporting form corresponding to Form 10-Q. For an SBI entitled to use the abbreviated forms, the items under Form 10-KSB and Form 10-QSB are identical to those in

Forms 10-K and 10-Q; however, the relevant items in the abbreviated forms are referenced to the simplified requirements of Regulation S-B rather than to Regulation S-K.

5. Annual Report to Shareholders

The annual report to shareholders must be distributed by companies with a class of securities registered under the Exchange Act in connection with the annual meeting of shareholders at which directors are elected. It must contain the standard financial statements and other basic information but is largely an unstructured document in which management is free to report what it chooses. The SEC has amended the annual-report-to-shareholder requirements as they relate to SBIs to permit the use of information prepared within the SBI disclosure system.

6. Proxy Statement Materials

Proxy statements must be filed with the SEC and delivered to shareholders by companies with a class of equity securities registered under the Exchange Act in connection with the solicitation of proxies. The content of the proxy statement is prescribed by Schedule 14A adopted by the SEC pursuant to Section 14(a) of the Exchange Act. As with the annual-report to-shareholder requirements, the SEC has amended the proxy rules as they relate to SBIs to permit the use of information prepared within the SBI disclosure system.

7. Disclosures in Non-Registered Transactions

As noted above, an issuer engaged in a financing transaction otherwise exempt from the registration requirements of the Securities Act may nonetheless prepare and distribute to potential investors some form of disclosure document. For example, offerings made to non accredited investors under Regulation D may require delivery of certain information determined by reference to the requirements of Securities Act registration forms. In such cases, the manner of presentation will vary substantially, and no real standard exists, since the SEC does not review any such disclosure documents. However, it is generally prudent for an issuer to adhere to the disclosure requirements of the integrated system. In particular, a reporting company involved in a private placement can usually satisfy its disclosure obligations by providing copies of its Exchange Act reports, supplemented by any additional information regarding the specific transaction.

C. Regulation S-K

1. In General

Regulation S-K sets forth the "Standard Instructions for Filing Forms Under Securities Act of 1933, Securities Exchange Act of 1934 and Energy Policy and Conservation Act of 1975" and is the core of the informational requirements of the integrated disclosure system. The contents of Regulation S-K can be broken down as follows: the Securities Act "standard items," which dictate the disclosures regarding the offering and future obligations that may be relevant to purchasers of the offered securities; various items designed to insure that the business and properties of the issuer have been fully described, including any legal proceedings material to the issuer; a description of the securities being offered, as well as any other outstanding securities; financial information; information regarding management of the issuer, as well as certain significant security holders; and various exhibits and other items.

2. Securities Act Standard Items

Items 501 through 510 of Regulation S-K are common to Securities Act registrations on Forms S-1-2-3. These so-called "standard items" include a summary section and a discussion of any risk factors associated with the registrant and/or the offering itself, a statement of the anticipated use of proceeds, a description of the dilution to the new shareholders, a brief description of the securities being offered and the methods used to determine the offering price, a computation of the ratio of earnings to fixed charges in debt offerings, a description of the plan of distribution, information pertaining to any selling security holders, disclosures relating to any interest in the issuer of named experts and counsel, and, in certain limited situations, specified statements relating to the indemnification of directors and officers.

3. Description of Business, Properties, and Legal Proceedings

Items 101 through 103 of Regulation S-K require a full description of the issuer's business and properties, as well as a description of certain specified legal proceedings relating to the issuer. As noted below, the description of the issuer's business is extremely broad, covering aspects of the issuer's products and services, customer base, research and development activities, and manufacturing and sales functions, as well as material competitive factors confronting the issuer.

4. Description of Securities

Pursuant to Item 202 of Regulation S-K, each issuer must supply a description of the securities being offered, as well as any of its other outstanding securities of the issuer. In addition, Item 201 of Regulation S-K requires the disclosure of information regarding the market for, and dividends on, common equity of the issuer. In the case of a first-time issuer (i.e., an initial public offering), such disclosure typically is limited to a statement that no public market has previously existed for the offered securities and a description of the issuer's past and expected future policies regarding the payment of dividends.

5. Financial Information

Items 301 through 304 of Regulation S-K set out the basic requirements for the disclosure of financial information. As a general rule, issuers must provide certain standardized financial statements and five years of comparative selected financial information, which allows the reader to compare key financial indicators such as net sales, gross profit, and net income or loss. The required information becomes the basis for the Management's Discussion and Analysis (MD&A) which must be prepared pursuant to Item 303 of Regulation S-K. In addition, the issuer must provide information relating to any change in accountants during the last two fiscal years resulting from a disagreement on accounting and financial disclosure.

6. Management and Certain Security Holders

Items 401 through 404 of Regulation S-K require certain information regarding the management of the issuer (e.g., its directors and officers) and certain transactions between the issuer and its managers, executive compensation, and information regarding the security ownership of management and significant security holders.

7. Exhibits

Item 601 of Regulation S-K lists the various exhibits that must be filed with the registration statement and that would be available for review by the public, including members of the investment community and competitors of the issuer. Among the requirements of Item 601 is disclosure of the contents of each material contract or agreement relating to the issuer's business or the terms of the offering. The documents disclosed in accordance with these requirements supplement the requirements of Item 101 of Regulation S-K relating to the description of the issuer's business and operations.

8. Miscellaneous Items

Certain additional disclosures must be included in the registration statement, but not in the prospectus, depending upon the circumstances. For example, a first-time registrant will be called upon to provide a variety of information regarding all of its securities issued in non-registered transactions within the prior three years. All registrants must include information relating to the expenses of the offering, and various disclosures and undertakings will be required if any arrangement (e.g., statutes, charter provisions, by-laws, or contracts) exists to insure or indemnify officers or directors against liabilities associated with the offering.

D. Regulation S-X

Regulation S-X sets forth the requirements with respect to the form and content of the financial statements to be filed with the SEC in connection with all filings under the Securities Act, proxy and information statements filed under Section 14 of the Exchange Act, registration statements filed under Section 12 of the Exchange Act, and annual and quarterly reports filed under the Exchange Act. The requirements of Regulation S-X are in addition to, and not in lieu of, the procedures required by "generally accepted accounting principles." They are supplemented by other requirements found in various provisions of Regulation S-K, as well as in the SEC's own Financial Reporting Releases, Accounting and Auditing Enforcement Releases, and Staff Accounting Bulletins, which contain opinions regarding accounting questions, administrative interpretations, and policies with respect to financial statements.

E. Organization of Disclosure Information

The various disclosure items included in Regulation S-K are organized and packaged in a specified manner in order to facilitate compliance with the specific requirements of each form and report that must be filed under the federal securities laws. In general, the integrated disclosure system works through the following: the "basic information package," or BIP, which is included in all of the Securities Act registration forms and many of the required Exchange Act reports; the in-depth disclosure items relating to the issuer's business, properties, management, and security holders, which is included in some form in all of the Securities Act registration forms and in Forms 10 and 10-K; and the Securities Act standard items. In addition, each form and report has its own exhibit requirements, and certain other disclosures may be required depending upon the filing.

The BIP includes all the business and financial information the SEC considers important to the investment community. Among the items included in the BIP are the financial information required by Items 301 through 304 of Regulation S-K, including the MD&A, a brief summary description of the issuer's business and certain segmental information; various market and dividend information; and, for certain issuers, supplementary financial information. The in-depth disclosures build upon the BIP by providing a full description of the issuer's business, properties, and legal proceedings, as well as detailed information regarding management and significant security holders.

F. Regulation S-B

In 1992, the SEC adopted a series of small business initiatives designed to facilitate capital raising for small businesses and reduce the costs of compliance with the federal securities laws. Among the most important developments was the creation of a simplified integrated disclosure system for SBIs through the promulgation of new Regulation S-B. Regulation S-B is the counterpart to Regulation S-K and works in conjunction with a new series of forms for registration under the Securities Act, particularly Forms SB-1 and SB-2, and registration and reporting under the Exchange Act. The SB forms incorporate the disclosure requirements of Regulation S-B in exactly the same way that the forms used in the general integrated disclosure system incorporate the items expressed in Regulation S-K.

The disclosure standards set forth in Regulation S-B generally follow those of Regulation S-K and even use identical item numbers (e.g., Item 402 under both relate to executive compensation). However, there are a limited number of Regulation S-K items, such as Items 301 and 302 which relate to selected and supplemental financial information, that do not appear in Regulation S-B. Moreover, there are differences between the disclosures required by Regulation S-B and the counterpart items in Regulation S-K in certain areas, including the description of the issuer's business and properties, market and dividend information, description of securities, and the MD&A.

Regulation S-B adopts and continues the significantly less stringent financial reporting requirements of former Form S-18, which was replaced by new Form SB-2. As noted above, Regulation S-B does not include any counterpart to Regulation S-K Items 301 and 302. Instead, Item 310 of Regulation S-B sets out, in narrative form without reference to Regulation S-X, the financial statement requirements that must be satisfied by SBIs. While the financial statements of SBIs using Regulation S-B must still be prepared in accordance with generally accepted accounting principles, they do not have to conform with the requirements of Regulation S-X, except as to the accountant's report and independence.

PREPARATION OF THE REQUIRED NONFINANCIAL DISCLOSURES

A. Overview

Preparing the required non financial disclosures in any registration statement or report to be filed under the Securities Act or the Exchange Act requires it full understanding of the business activities and corporate structure of the issuer. As a result, a good deal of attention must be paid to the due diligence process of collecting the necessary information. Thereafter, the specific disclosure requirements must be reviewed in order to begin preparation of the description of the issuer's business, the risk factors associated with the issuer and the offering, management compensation, and certain transactions and other disclosure items.

B. Description of the Issuer's Business

1. In General

The most important non financial element of disclosure in any of the documents filed within the integrated disclosure system is the detailed description of the issuer's business. Obviously, the issuer must address the requirements set forth in the registration and report forms and in Regulations S-K or S-B. Moreover, particularly when the discussion appears in a prospectus used for a registered securities offering, it must communicate to the investment community a clear statement of the issuer's business strategy, including a recognition of the issuer's strategic advantages, a knowledge of the proven needs of the issuer's customer base for its products and services, and an understanding of the basis upon which other companies will seek to compete with the issuer in the marketplace.

2. Introductory Paragraph

The first paragraph in the business description in the prospectus should briefly describe the activities of the issuer and the major industry segments in which the issuer competes or proposes to compete in the future. Reference should be made to the current products and services of the issuer, including the manner in which such products and services are delivered to the relevant markets, and any plans for future development and expansion of the business. If possible, reference should be made to the issuer's own particular strategic advantage with respect to the manufacture and distribution of its products. Finally, any significant financial milestones should also be mentioned, such as a material increase in dollar or unit sales.

3. Industry Overview

It is important to provide the prospective investor with the issuer's own sense of the industry in which it operates, its historical evolution and perceived future trends, as well as the role that the issuer is expected to play within the industry. Accordingly, the issuer should provide a general overview of each of its industry segments and the various business, commercial, and social problems the industry, and the issuer in particular, is seeking to address in the conduct of its business activities. For example, a health-care company might attempt to describe the breadth and severity of the particular health problems the issuer feels will support a market for its products. Also, with respect to each market problem, reference should be made to the various solutions that may have been offered by existing products and services.

If necessary, significant industry definitions and classifications should be introduced to the reader at this point, and the reader should be given a sense of the development of the industry and its technology, the needs and demands of the base of customers, pricing and costing characteristics in the industry, future trends regarding the overall size of the industry, and any changes in the markets and applications for the issuer's products and technology. Finally, even though it may otherwise be covered in the discussion of competition, it is important to state initially the basis for competition within the industry and the various factors (e.g., cost, manufacturing efficiencies, product reliability, technology, breadth of products, capacity, capital, distribution, service) the issuer believes may influence competition within the industry in the future.

4. Products and Product Strategy

The issuer should clearly and concisely articulate its strategies regarding the development of specified products and services. In particular, the issuer's disclosures should focus on material aspects of its products and services, characteristics that distinguish the issuer's products and services from those offered by its competitors, and if appropriate, a historical description of the development and introduction of the issuer's products and services. Also, reference should be made to the issuer's research and development projects, including the manner in which the issuer's products were developed or acquired.

Several different approaches can be used in the course of describing the issuer's product strategies. For example, an issuer may be seeking development through new technologies, the improvement of production efficiencies, cost reductions, quality enhancements, or the creation of reliable documentation. While these strategies focus on the production process, another issuer may be focusing upon extending its existing product lines and developing new distribution channels through joint ventures, reciprocal development agreements, and other strategies designed to facilitate the acquisition and distribution of new products. Allied strategies might also include enhancements to existing products, warranties, and service capabilities.

5. Manufacturing and Production

Depending upon the nature of its business, manufacturing and production can be an important component of the issuer's ability to bring its products promptly to market and fulfill the demands of the customers. The section should begin with an explanation of the manufacturing process and the definition of the crucial components thereof. In particular, attention should be paid to the following matters: facilities, testing, production line arrangements, packaging, raw materials, and government regulations with respect to environmental and quality-control matters. Also, research and development relating to manufacturing processes and technologies should be explained, as well as any dependence on vendors or suppliers.

If backlog is important in the context of the issuer's industry and production processes, appropriate disclosures should be made. The amount of the backlog, and any significant customers included in the backlog, should be discussed, and any plans the issuer might have to correct the situation should also be set forth. If the backlog may not be representative of actual sales for any succeeding period due to customer changes in delivery schedules or cancellations, disclosure should be made regarding scheduling and booking practices within the industry. In many cases, the rate of booking new orders varies from month to month, and the release of shipping dates and quantities against purchase orders may also fluctuate over time.

6. Marketing, Distribution, and Customers

The issuer's ability to identify the markets and customers for its products, and to develop the proper distribution channels for introducing those products to those markets, are the focus in this section. A typical introductory paragraph would include a listing of those markets the issuer has identified as targets for the sale of its products; the significant needs, in terms of product and service characteristics and the manner of delivery, of the projected customers; the appropriate uses for the issuer's products; and the various applications for the issuer's products. Clearly, significant customer relationships should be identified, including all customers that account for 10 percent or more of net product sales. Thereafter, reference should be made to the distribution channels, be they direct or indirect sales through Original Equipment Manufacturers (OEMs), Value Added Resellers (VARs), and systems integrators. Significant sales and distribution agreements should be discussed in detail, including the term of the agreement, any minimum quantity of products that must be purchased, the number of products purchased to date under the agreement, ordering procedures, any agreement with respect to scheduling, increasing or decreasing the amount of orders, charges for changes in delivery, product mix, and any agreement whereby the distributor could acquire the right to manufacture products. In the event that distributors meet significant competition themselves, this should be discussed, as should any factors that might affect the distributor's own customer base or product strategies. Finally, the issuer's own internal sales and marketing organization should be described, including such things as the number of members of the issuer's sales force, the location and coverage of the issuer's sales offices, trade show, and print advertising strategies, service and technical support capability, and warranty terms and coverage. Should the issuer be planning any significant modification in its marketing strategies, perhaps through the engagement of a third-party marketing partner, it should be discussed in this section.

7. Competition

Disclosures regarding competition begin a series of sections dealing with the issuer's external environment and non product-related resources. Typically, the registrant should discuss the following items:

1. The historical development of competition within the industry, including any cyclical variations and pricing factors, in order to provide the reader with a sense of the environment in which the issuer must develop, produce, and distribute its products or services.
2. The identity of specific competitors should be disclosed, as well as the basis upon which such entities compete with the issuer. If competition exists with respect to specific products, it should be identified in that manner. Remember that competition may come from specialized firms, as well as from larger companies with divisions capable of competing in the industry.
3. Future competitors and the resources they will bring to the marketplace should be identified.
4. The principal elements of competition, including price, performance, product quality and reliability, financial stability, adherence to standards, marketing, distribution, technical resources, production capacity, manufacturing efficiencies, and production yields.
5. The issuer should explain how effectively it is able to compete with respect to the elements of

competition referred to above, and any plan to improve the issuer's performance should be explained. Any competitive disadvantage with respect to the issuer due to the lack of breadth in its product line or otherwise should also be explained.

7. If the issuer expects significant changes in the competitive environment in the future, the nature of those changes should be explained, and any plans for remaining competitive should be discussed. These might include additional plans to lower manufacturing costs, introduce new products, and improve production yields.

The issuer should consider appropriate cross-references to risk factors within the competition discussion.

8. Government Regulation

The development, testing, and marketing of an issuer's products may be subject to regulation by a variety of federal, state, local, and foreign agencies. Such agencies, including the Food and Drug Administration and the U.S. Department of Health and Human Services in the case of pharmaceutical and biotechnology companies, regulate the product introduction, advertising, manufacturing, labeling, distribution, and record-keeping activities and practices of industry participants. Typically, before a product can be marketed, it must go through a number of stages of clinical studies and testing. The issuer should describe the stages of pre marketing development and identify where each of the issuer's current and developing products stand in the process. An attempt should also be made to describe the issuer's views as to how the regulatory process will evolve over time and the effect that any transition might have on the issuer.

9. Intellectual Property

The issuer should discuss its own intellectual property position, including any significant patent rights, as well as the relative strengths and weaknesses of competitors in this area. If the issuer has any material licensing arrangements, they should be fully described, including the scope of the licensed rights (i.e., products, territory, and exclusivity) and the economic terms of the license, such as the royalty rate and any other payment obligations. The issuer should include a description not only of agreements under which it has been granted licenses by others, but also of any arrangement that permits third parties to use the issuer's technology.

10. Research and Development

Research and development activities may have been discussed in the context of the issuer's future products. Disclosures should cover the following items:

1. The amount of technological change that has occurred within the industry in the past and the direction of emerging technology the issuer believes will dominate competition within the industry in the future.
2. The issuer's principal research and development activities and the type of product development efforts undertaken in the past.
3. Any research and development activities devoted to improving the issuer's process technology.
4. Any research and development activities aimed at enhancing existing product offerings and developing new offerings based on advanced technologies.
5. The amount of research and development expenses and any independently financed research and development contracts, including partnerships.

11. Properties and Facilities

Disclosures regarding the issuer's properties and facilities are specifically required under Regulation S-K. Typical descriptions will refer to the issuer's principal business and manufacturing facilities, the amount of square footage and degree of utilization, plans for future expansion, and a statement as to whether or not such facilities are properly maintained and adequate for their purposes. Significant lease arrangements should also be included. The location of the issuer's properties and facilities may have an effect on its ability to attract and maintain its pool of human resources, utilize university research facilities, and rapidly move finished products into the distribution channel.

12. Human Resources

The issuer's human resources may have already been discussed in the context of competition, intellectual property, and research and development. Basic disclosure will include the number of employees, including a breakdown of the number of employees active in the areas of marketing and sales, research and development, engineering, manufacturing, production and facilities support, and general management, including finance and administration. Any plans for hiring additional personnel in particular areas should be disclosed, particularly as they relate to strategic plans for product development and distribution that might already have been discussed. Significant factors relating to the recruitment and retention of key personnel should also be included in the discussion.

C. Risk Factors

1. In General

A discussion of various risk factors is often included in prospectuses used in a primary offering of securities. Also, many issuers have included risk factors in their Exchange Act reports, although the referenced items will necessarily exclude matters that are particular to a securities offering (e.g., dilution).

2. Financial Risks

One of the most typical risks arises from the issuer's limited operating history, which may include a prior record of operating losses or recent adverse trends in sales, earnings, margins, and backlog. In such cases, the prospectus should discuss whether or not the issuer's historical financial results are relevant to a consideration of its future prospects. Moreover, as discussed below in the context of preparing the MD&A, risks associated with the issuer's future liquidity and ability to meet its obligations with respect to any fixed obligations should also be described, as should the effect of any covenants under existing credit arrangements which might inhibit the issuer's future operations and flexibility.

3. Product Development Risks

The issuer may not yet have a track record of commercially accepted products and services. Accordingly, an effort should be made to identify any market and/or product development uncertainties, including the time period and costs required to achieve commercial success. For example, are the needs of the marketplace sufficiently defined so as to insure acceptance of the issuer's new products? Alternatively, is the issuer's success dependent upon its ability to develop or acquire new products in the future? In those cases where the issuer has already completed the development of one product, attention must be paid to whether or not that product can fully support the issuer as it seeks to develop new and additional products.

4. Technological Risks

Technological uncertainties can affect the issuer's ability to complete its product development efforts on a timely basis as well as the likelihood that the issuer can achieve and maintain an advantage based on its research activities and obtain legal protection with respect to its technology and related intellectual property rights. Moreover, research can often prove to be very costly, particularly in those industries subject to significant government regulations and approvals, and the issuer must be certain of its ability to obtain the funds necessary to complete any required projects.

5. Production and Distribution Risks

A significant risk associated with the actual distribution of the issuer's products is its reliance upon one or more customers, since the loss of a major customer may have a material adverse effect on the issuer's financial situation as well as its overall image and perception in the marketplace. Also, as noted above, the issuer may be dependent upon one or more key suppliers, licensors, researchers, or distributors with respect to its products, and therefore, attention should be paid to the consequences of any disruption or termination of those relationships. Finally, to the extent that the issuer is involved in foreign distribution activities, any particular risks associated with activities in foreign markets should be discussed.

6. Regulatory Risks

Is the issuer subject to regulatory risks that could affect its products, marketing efforts, pricing strategies, service routes or areas, and the timing of product introduction? Antitrust considerations are certainly important in those situations where the issuer is expected to be a dominant firm in a definable market area or may wish to conduct cooperative research and development activities. However, more important with respect to issuers in the health-care and biotechnology industries is the effect of the various regulatory approvals necessary to commence testing and distribution of various products. As noted above, an effort should be made to explain any relevant regulatory procedures in the business section of the prospectus.

7. Competitive Risks

Competitive uncertainties are of tremendous importance in analyzing the prospects of any issuer. The issuer should candidly assess whether or not it lacks one or more significant production functions or support services that might be necessary to compete effectively in the marketplace or to realize the expected breadth and volume of distribution of its products. Moreover, it is no longer sufficient for the issuer merely to take note of the uncertainties with respect to competition from larger firms. Instead, the issuer should carefully analyze the direction from which competition might come and any plans that it might have to establish a countervailing advantage.

8. Management and Employee Risks

A number of key risks and uncertainties are associated with the issuer's dependence on one or more key managers and employees, the issuer's ability to recruit and retain qualified employees, and the operational experience of the issuer's current management to provide the leadership to manage a growing company in the issuer's industry. Again, this risk factor tends to be included without a great deal of thought to the issuer's own plans regarding recruitment of key employees. An attempt should be made to understand the issuer's future plans with regard to available cash and equity compensation for new employees, including the effect of future financing and expansion efforts.

9. Litigation Risks

For any issuer involved in technology-driven activities, actual or threatened litigation regarding material elements of its technology portfolio or asserted intellectual property rights can be disastrous, severely impairing the viability of the proposed offering and significantly depleting its financial assets. For example, competitors may assert that rights used by the issuer infringe upon their technology rights or, alternatively, that the technology actually arose out of the activities of current employees of the issuer who had previously worked at a competitive firm.

10. Environmental Risks

Consistent with the notion that the issuer should conduct an overall scanning of its competitive environment, no risk factor section would be complete without an attempt to discern those uncertainties that might arise out of general social, political, and economic conditions. For example, long-term trends with respect to the nation's health-care payment system might have a significant effect upon the pricing structure for issuers involved in the health-care industry. Also, political uncertainties in foreign markets might adversely affect the issuer's ability to obtain reliable low cost labor for its future manufacturing activities. If these risks are known and have been factored into overall business planning, consideration must be given to mentioning them in the prospectus.

D. Management, Certain Transactions, and Compensation

1. In General

A description of management, including certain transactions between the issuer and its controlling persons and the amount and type of executive compensation, is an important part of Securities Act registration statements, Exchange Act reports, and the annual proxy materials which typically include the solicitation of proxies relating to the election of directors.

2. Management

Item 401 of Regulation S-K requires certain information about each executive officer and director of the issuer, including name and age, all positions held by such person with the issuer, his term as an officer and/or director and the period during which he has served as such, a description of his business experience during the past five years, any arrangement with another person (who must be named) pursuant to which such person has been selected to act as an officer and/or director, and any family relationships among the officers and directors. If the issuer is a non-reporting company, employees who are not executive officers but are expected to make significant contributions to the business of the issuer should be identified, and information must be given concerning their backgrounds. If any director serves as a director of another reporting company, such services should be disclosed. Finally, information must be provided regarding certain legal proceedings relating to officers and/or directors.

3. Certain Transactions

Item 404 of Regulation S-K requires various disclosures relating to certain transactions and relationships between the issuer and persons affiliated in specified ways with the issuer. Among the items to be discussed are the following:

1. Transactions (or a series of similar transactions) between the issuer and any director or executive officer, any nominee for election as a director, 5 percent beneficial owners of any class of voting stock, and any member of the immediate family of any of the foregoing, in which the amount involved exceeds $60,000.
2. For issuers organized within the last five years and filing a registration statement on Form S-1, disclosure must be made of certain prior or contemplated transactions between any "promoter" and the issuer, including the nature of the transaction, the name of the promoter, the nature and amount of what was received by the promoter and the consideration received by the issuer. The principle (and by whom determined) followed in valuing any asset acquired from the promoter must be described, and if assets transferred by the promoter to the issuer were acquired by the promoter within two years prior to their transfer, the promoter's cost.

Any indebtedness owed to the issuer in excess of $60,000 at any time during the fiscal year by any director or executive officer, any nominee for election as a director, or any member of the immediate family of such persons, as well as indebtedness in similar amounts to the issuer of certain corporations, organizations, trusts, and estates, in which any director, executive officer, or nominee is an executive officer or partner or beneficial owner of 10 percent or more of a class of equity securities (as to corporations or other organizations), or, as to a trust or estate, has a substantial beneficial interest or serves as a trustee or in a similar capacity.

In addition, the following information must be disclosed as to anyone who is a director at the time of the filing (or in the case of a proxy or information statement, as to any director who will continue as such after the meeting) or a nominee for election as a director:

1. Whether such persons have been an executive officer or owner beneficially or of record in excess of 10 percent equity interest in a company to or from which the issuer and/or its subsidiaries sell or buy property or services involving the receipt (in the case of sales) or the payment (in the case of purchases) in excess of 5 percent of (i) the registrant's consolidated gross revenues for its last full fiscal year, or (ii) the other entity's consolidated gross revenues for its last full fiscal year.
2. Whether such persons have been an executive officer or owner beneficially or of record in excess of 10 percent equity interest in a company to which the issuer or its subsidiaries was indebted at the end of the issuer's last full fiscal year in an aggregate amount in excess of 5 percent of the issuer's total consolidated assets at the end of such fiscal year.
3. Whether such persons during the last fiscal year have been a member of or counsel to a law firm that the issuer has retained during the last fiscal year or a partner or executive officer of any investment banking firm that has performed services for the issuer (other than as a participating underwriter in a syndicate) during the past fiscal year.
5. Any other relationship substantially similar in nature and scope to the foregoing.

If an affirmative response is required to any of the foregoing items, disclosure must be made of the name of such persons, the identity of the entity with which the relationship existed, the affiliation of such persons with the entity, the relationship between the issuer and the entity, and the amount of business done. In the case of relationships with law firms or investment bankers, the amount of business needs to be disclosed only to the extent that such amount is 5 percent or more of the law firm's gross revenues for the last full fiscal year or 5 percent of the investment banking firm's consolidated gross revenues for that firm's last full fiscal year.

4. Executive Compensation

Item 402 of Regulation S-K requires a "Summary Compensation Table" that reflects all compensation paid to the issuer's chief executive officer and other four most highly compensated executive officers whose annual compensation exceeds $100,000, as well as the compensation paid to all executive officers as a group. Information must be presented in tabular format for each of the following categories: (1) salary; (2) bonus; (3) other annual compensation; (4) restricted stock awards; (5) accrued dividends on restricted stock; (6) long-term incentive payouts; (7) stock options; (8) stock appreciation rights; and (9) other compensation. "Other *annual* compensation" includes items such as perquisites, annual contributions by the issuer to pension and other retirement plans, annual compensation under deferred compensation plans, and annual premiums on insurance funded deferred compensation arrangements. "Other compensation" includes compensation that does not fit any of the other categories, such as termination or severance awards (i.e., golden parachutes) in excess of $60,000.

In addition to the information in the compensation table, the issuer must deliver a report by the compensation committee of the board of directors that indicates the factors relied upon in setting the amount of executive compensation. The report should cover the specific performance criteria used to set the compensation paid to the issuer's chief executive officer, including such things as profitability, sales growth, return on shareholders' equity, and market share. The report must include a supplemental discussion of its general compensation policies for other key executives. The information in the compensation table and report can be placed in perspective by reference to a line graph the issuer must provide which compares the issuer's stock price over the past five years to a broad stock market index, such as the Standard & Poor's 500, and to an industry or peer-group index chosen by the issuer. Issuers must also provide detailed information regarding executive stock options, including estimates of the value of any unexercised stock options or similar rights held by executives.

PREPARATION OF THE REQUIRED FINANCIAL DISCLOSURES

A. Introduction

Securities Act registration forms require a substantial amount of financial information regarding the issuer. For example, when Form S-1, the basic Securities Act registration form, is used, the issuer must supply the following information:

- Financial statements meeting the requirements of Regulation S-X, as well as any financial information required by Rule 3-05 and Article 11 of Regulation S-X;
- Information required by Item 301 of Regulation S-K, selected financial data;
- Information required by Item 302 of Regulation S-K, supplementary financial information;
- Information required by Item 303 of Regulation S-K, the MD&A discussion;
- Information required by Item 304 of Regulation S-K, disagreements with accountants on accounting and financial disclosure; and
- Financial statement schedules required by Regulation S-X.

B. Financial Statement Requirements

1. In General

Article 3 of Regulation S-X requires that SEC filings governed by the regulation contain a consolidated balance sheet and consolidated statements of income changes in financial position. However, Rule 3-13 provides that the SEC may, upon the informal written request of the issuer, permit the omission of one or more of the required financial statements or the filing in substitution of appropriate statements of comparable character. The SEC may also by informal written notice require the filing of other financial statements in addition to, or in substitution for, the statements required by Regulation S-X.

2. Balance Sheet Requirements

Specifically, Rule 3-01 requires the filing, for the issuer and its subsidiaries, of audited consolidated balance sheets as of the end of each of the two most recent fiscal years of the issuer; provided that the filing is made within forty-five days after the end of the issuer's fiscal year and audited financial statements for the most recent fiscal year are not available, the balance sheet may be as of the end of the two preceding fiscal years, and the filing shall include an additional balance sheet as of an interim date at least as current as the end of the issuer's third fiscal quarter of its most recently completed fiscal year. For filings made 134 days subsequent to the end of the issuer's most recent fiscal year, Rule 3-01 (e) requires that the filing shall also include a balance sheet as of an interim date within 135 days of the date of filing. Any interim balance sheet may be unaudited and condensed.

3. Statements of Income and Changes in Financial Position

With respect to consolidated statements of income and changes in financial position, Rule 3-02 requires the filing of audited statements for each of the three fiscal years preceding the date of the most recent audited balance sheet being filed pursuant to Rule 3-01. In addition, for any interim period between the latest audited balance sheet and the date of the most recent interim balance sheet being filed, and for the corresponding period of the preceding fiscal year,

Rule 3-02(b) requires that statements of income and of changes in financial position be provided. As in the case of interim balance sheets, interim income statements may be unaudited and condensed.

4. Additional Financial Statement Requirements

In addition to the financial statements of the issuer that are required under Rules 3-01 and 3-02, it may be necessary to provide additional financial statements for the following entities:

- ❐ Historical financial statements of a predecessor corporation (Rule 3-01);
- ❐ Historical financial statements of businesses acquired or to be acquired (Rule 3-05);
- ❐ Separate financial statements of subsidiaries not consolidated and 50 percent or less owned persons (Rule 3-09); and
- v Financial statements of guarantors and affiliates whose securities collateralize an issue registered or being registered (Rule 3-10).

C. Management's Discussion and Analysis

Perhaps the most meaningful portion of the prospectus, other than the financial statements, the business summary, and the description of any risk factors, is the MD&A, which includes a narrative discussion of such things as the results of operations, liquidity, capital resources and the impact of inflation. The MD&A brings the financial and non financial portions of the registration statement together, and the SEC has stated:

> *The management discussion gives the registrant an unusual opportunity to articulate its objectives and financial policies; to describe where it is headed and how it hopes to get there; and to establish and maintain credibility. Included in the management discussion should be factors about the particular business which management is in the best position to know. For each business, there is a limited set of critical variables which presents the pulse of the business.*

While the instructions for preparation of the MD&A in Item 303 of Regulation S-K are somewhat self-explanatory, care must be taken to insure that the following items have been considered and adequately explored:

- *Liquidity Analysis.* Liquidity is the ability of an issuer to generate sufficient cash or other working capital to fund the ongoing operations of its business. The issuer should identify trends, demands, commitments, events, or uncertainties that are both presently known to management and reasonably likely to have a material effect on the issuer's short-term and long-term liquidity.
- *Fixed Commitments.* Any discussion regarding liquidity should be related to an identification and description of known material fixed commitments for capital expenditures.
- *Expansion and Acquisitions.* Liquidity is also relevant with respect to the issuer's ability to implement and complete any future plans with regard to debt repayments, capital expansion, acquisitions and divestitures, and the overall restructuring of credit arrangements and borrowings.
- *Segment Disclosures.* The financial performance and operations of the issuer should be discussed in segments if subdivision of the issuer's business into groups representative of different industries is appropriate.
- *Revenue and Sales Analysis.* Should the financial statements of the issuer disclose material increases in net sales or revenues, the issuer should provide a narrative discussion and analysis of the extent to which such increases are attributable to increases in prices, to increases in the volume or amount of goods or services being sold, or to the introduction of new products or services. Also, reference should be made to the impact of inflation and changing prices on the issuer's financial performance.

- *Key Performance Indicators.* The analysis of revenues and sales should be accompanied by an analysis of such other items of revenue or expense, as well as balance sheet items, that serve as key performance indicators of the issuer's overall financial condition and results of operations.
- *Analysis of Period-to-Period Changes.* Material changes in the issuer's financial condition and performance from year to year and during any interim periods, as reflected in financial statement line items, should be discussed.
- *Extraordinary Events.* The issuer should describe any unusual or infrequent events or transactions and any other items that it feels may not be indicative of future operations. For example, the issuer should discuss the impact of discontinued operations and extraordinary gains and losses when these items have had, or are reasonably likely to have, a material effect on the issuer's reported or future financial condition or results of operations.

3

Fragmentation's Costs in Financial Costing

Introduction

The costs fall into three categories: problems with managers, problems with securities markets, and problems with organizing industry. Problems with managers are obvious. Dispersion in small holdings creates a collective action problem for shareholders, making managers less accountable in a way that can hurt performance, particularly when the firm faces unusual problems. Senior managers in the large public firm are among the least directly accountable in American society. While other groups also have low direct accountability tenured faculty at solvent universities come to mind few of them have tasks as important as those of senior managers at leading firms.

Problems with securities markets arise from the difficulty of transmitting complex, proprietary, and technological information from inside the firm to the American securities market. If scattered shareholders cannot understand complexity, and if managers cannot be rewarded for what shareholders cannot understand, firms may abandon some long-term, technologically complex projects.

Overlapping ownership a financial institution that owns a big block in both a supplier and its customer can sometimes improve the organization of industry. Firms, suppliers, and customers all need to coordinate their activities, and in the United States often do so in big, vertical firms. Overlapping ownership could allow them to stay separate. It could help keep firms smaller and nimbler, reducing the number of slow-moving vertically integrated behemoths. Flat organization at the top might work better when technological change quickly makes many managers' training obsolete. Psychological and sociological theories indicate that nonhierarchical forms may function better in some new industries in today's world.

My point is not that we have theory or data to prove the superiority of other organizational forms, but that there is just enough data, and just enough theory, to tantalize. Had there been a contest between organizational forms, concentrated ownership might have had enough going for it to have been *one* of the survivors. Alternative forms such as those prevailing in Germany and Japan seem, despite their own distinctive defects, able to do just about as well as the American forms.

Complaints are heard that shareholders fail to monitor managers. Managers build empires and pursue bad strategies without shareholder intervention until matters are so out of hand that the ultimate outcome is the violence of the hostile takeover or the bloodshed of a fired CEO or the instability of the leveraged buyout or the waste of a bankruptcy. Many 1980s takeovers targeted firms grown too large, which the takeover entrepreneurs then broke up. In other 1980s takeovers, empire-building firms sought to extend their grasp. Either way, persistent shareholder involvement could have led to intervention before bloodshed.

It is not just that with stockholders scattered, a few managers could pursue their own agendas: building bigger empires, pursuing quieter lives, or persisting in failed strategies because they were familiar. It is also that in trying to do well, some managers did not adopt the best technologies and strategies for the future. That most managers do well is both a tribute to their being professionals and a sign of the other constraints on managers' doing badly, of the adequacy of existing structures. The question is whether different ownership structures in some firms could have induced even better performance.

Weak boards have historically been a debility of the large American firm. Board membership has come via invitation from the CEO, who typically invited insiders and CEOs from other firms. CEOs as directors have disadvantages: their time is constrained, they lack the financial incentive to be inquisitive, and, psychologically, they do not want the board to intrude on the CEO's authority any more than they want their own boards to intrude on their own authority. Board members are typically neither large stockholders with an independent base and interest in the firm nor representatives of large stockholders, owning, say, 5 or 10 percent of the firm, because such stockholders rarely exist in American firms.

Weak monitoring and low shareholder involvement depend partly on Berle-Means fragmentation. It's just not worthwhile for a shareholder with a small block to incur the expenses of involvement. It's easier to sit the crisis out, or sell off the stockholding. To implore an owner of $10 million of the stock of a $10 billion industrial firm to be active may do no good. Such a shareholder can capture only one-thousandth of the corporation's gain. The shareholder should rationally decline to invest $100,000 of his or her time and wealth, even if that $100,000 would yield a $100 million gain for the corporation.

The blocks must be big enough to give the shareholder both the incentive and the means for action. The large shareholder, able to capture a bigger part of the gains than can fragmented shareholders, would have a greater incentive to act. A $100 million shareholder would spend more than a $10 million block holder, because it could capture a tenfold greater part of any gains. And incentives are not enough. Although even a $10 million stockholder has some incentive, it may lack the means to bring about change. Managers can, and often do, deflect the activist, who needs a large holding as a percentage of the firm's stock either by itself or in alliance with other large holders to get the power to be effective.

But, one must ask, since most intermediaries are themselves Berle-Means corporations, why should they not succumb to the same agency problems that affect the Berle-Means corporation? While I'll deal with this in more detail in Part V (and there's no sure answer to this), let me sketch out a few possibilities. As long as the intermediaries' debilities are not the same debilities afflicting the industrial firms in which they own stock, as long as the industrial firm's and the financial firm's weaknesses lie in different dimensions, then there might be improvements. For instance, outside auditors search for managerial fraud in a firm; at times they do succumb to temptation and become part of the fraud. But the outside auditor without daily operational involvement is independent often enough to provide a valuable although not foolproof check. Specialization among agents is a common organizational improvement for principals. A rudimentary management technique is to divide a task: one person does the job, another person checks the work; this can improve results over only assigning the job to the doer *even if* the checker is no better than the doer. She only has to catch a few of the doer's mistakes, and not reverse the doer when he does the job right. Here, I can categorize three potentially beneficial forms of monitoring: hierarchal, collegial, and crisis.

Hierarchal monitoring is specialization. Financiers specialize in getting a financial return; operating executives run firms. Both have their defects, but if we combine the two in the boardroom, but not in the same person, we could hope to reduce their defects, keep their strengths, and improve performance.

Collegial monitoring depends on directors' having the financial incentive to be involved and well informed. No financial institution *commands* the operating managers, but the two groups seek consensus. The operating managers are better informed about the firm and its business prospects; the collegial monitors from financial institutions should have a broader financial picture. Between the two, they might make better decisions at the top than either would alone. Operating managers would take the lead, but have even better financial colleagues in the boardroom than they have now.

Crisis monitoring, the third type, requires neither that the monitors manage day to day nor that they even understand the industry well; they must only be able to identify poor results and evaluate whether these results were due to poor management. If they were, the crisis monitors motivate the responsible executives, or replace them. Even if outsiders with big stock positions were usually passive, they would think about intervening earlier, when results first turn down; managers, aware of that potential, might get better results.

It would be foolish to think that institutions could run firms better than managers. Institutions will not be systematically better than operating managers, and they need not be. As long as the institutions knew to defer to operating managers, as long as they did little when results were good, they would do little harm and be ready to make a contribution when results were poor. That some institutions, like some managers, may not be savvy enough to know their limits is not a trivial problem; but ex ante we cannot tell whether institutions would systematically intrude too much to waste away whatever gains they might make.

Institutions would also not be entrepreneurial enough for many firms. But firms and monitors should sort themselves out: firms that would benefit from institutional monitoring would tend to have it; firms needing entrepreneurial leaders should tend not to be institutionally controlled. The two forms would then compete.

Difficulty of Building Long-Term Financial Relationships

Maybe managers are not the problem, but shareholders are. Managers complain that shareholders are transients, uninterested in the firm's long-run health. Institutions' trading mentality means that when managers need steadfast investors, the traders are gone. And with small blocks the norm among institutional investors, if they discover a problem early, they have an incentive to dump the stock and run, rather than hanging in to help fix the problem. Big blocks should up the incentives for fixing the problem rather than running. Managers could better depend on the institutions' being there when managers needed them, which at least in the managerial rhetoric is what managers want.

Maybe there's no systemic problem with managers at all. Some succeed, some fail, and in a competitive market that's just what one would expect. But perhaps there's another problem to be remedied, a systemic defect that undercuts managers. Perhaps securities markets are the weak link, transmitting their debilities into operating firms, weakening them by pushing managers into simple short-run strategies, because operating managers cannot transmit proprietary, complex, and technological information well to distant, atomized shareholders. If this happens, senior managers who expect to retire in a few years and cash in their stock options by then could shun long term investment, and industry would under invest in research and development as well as human capital, because these investments are too difficult for distant shareholders to understand.

These informational problems are highly speculative, cut against the usual belief that American securities markets are informationally efficient, and so far lack strong empirical backup. For these reasons, mandated change to end a speculative, unproven problem isn't sensible. But there is just enough suspicion in the business world that securities markets induce short-term behavior, and just enough plausibility to link this to the American scattered ownership structure, that there is a basis for inquiry here.

Industrial Organization as the Problem

Organizing industry is complex and subtle. When separate business firms invest in factories that relate to one another the engine company makes auto engines for the auto assembler and the auto assembler makes auto bodies into which the engine will fit the relationships governing these separate steps in production cannot all be written down in a perfect contract, because too many unexpected things can happen over the lifetime of the contract. To reduce the conflicts that can arise here, American industry has often brought these different steps in production into a single, vertically integrated firm.

Vertical integration in a single firm has costs, sometimes creating a stultifying bureaucracy and a sluggishness in responding to market signals. Separate firms could avoid bureaucracy and be fast, but the arms'-length contract they would need to govern their relationship over a number of years could be too hard to figure out and write down. A loose ownership relationship between the supplier and customer might work better than either contract or vertical integration alone. Instead of one firm's being a division or subsidiary of the other, each would be partially owned by an overlapping group of financial institutions. Neither would be a controlled subsidiary, but there would be connections, information exchange, and, if there were disputes, a financial "escrow agent," a mediator, to settle those disputes. When financial institutions cannot take big blocks and help to coordinate these relationships, the likely result seems to be more vertical integration and bigger, perhaps slower firms.

Productivity and Fragmentation

These three costs of fragmentation less accountable managers, short-term securities markets, and weaker industrial organization would show up in lost productivity in American history. A debater might observe here (correctly) that U.S. productivity is generally the highest in the world, and then urge us (mistakenly) to ignore fragmentation's costs. The debater would observe (also correctly) that American ownership is fragmented, and the voting blocks of the largest firms in Germany and Japan are not fragmented. Since the United States is generally more productive, big blocks do not induce greater productivity.

That kind of analysis would help us little. Improving U.S. corporate governance would still be worth pursuing if it could be done cost-effectively. Even if it is the best there is on the planet, improving it further would make Americans better off; it does not matter whether an improvement would let the United States "catch" up with, or pull further ahead of, foreign firms. Either way, the United States would be better off. Foreign successes and foreign differences alert us that there are other possibilities for corporate ownership, but a productivity gap disfavoring the United States doesn't tell us if governance produced the gap (there are too many other factors), nor does a productivity gap favoring the United States end the inquiry just because the United States is "ahead." We should not, then, be content to rest on our productive laurels, but ask whether we can improve what is basically a sound system.

The evidence from abroad comes in two packages, one clear, one not. The clear one is that ownership structures that contrast starkly with American fragmentation can exist and survive. None of the fifteen largest American firms has an institution or group holding 20 percent of the firm's stock not GM, not Exxon, not IBM. None. In Japan, every large firm has a financial group holding an aggregate of 20 percent of the company's stock: Toyota, Fujitsu, Mitsubishi every one.

The differences and persistence of the different structures are clear, but it's unclear whether the different corporate governance structures overall helped or hurt the foreign firms. The weaknesses that arise when lenders are major stockholders conflicts of interest, institutions protecting errant managers who "buy" them off are not trivial. Moreover, key tests of foreign governance are only now beginning. Whether those at the top of foreign firms will be better than U.S. boards at reacting to crisis and avoiding misspending on capital projects when the firm's franchise deteriorates is yet to be seen, because the industrial crises that hit a mature competitive economy are only now coming to afflict Germany and Japan. The early evidence from the problems at Volkswagen, Daimler-Benz, and Metallgesellschaft indicate that boards dominated by institutions are far from perfect. The task of seeing whether they are better that is, institutional voice only had to cut two years off of GM's ten-year delayed reaction to crisis to have made an improvement, even an imperfect one is still ahead.

There is another debater's point here. Governance cannot explain some shortfalls in American industry, because the United States more or less had the same corporate governance system fifty years ago, and was then the world's dominant economy. Changes in governance cannot explain the relative decline. Does the fact that the United States had the same corporate governance system decades ago, when it led in productivity by a mile, and in the 1990s, when it leads by less, mean that governance is irrelevant?

Governance is only one contributor to productivity and profitability. Until recently, American industry had two big advantages over much industry abroad: economies of scale and competitive structure. The American market was (and still is today) so large that it could support two or three firms, and hence workable competition, at the highest economies of scale in even the heaviest of industries; no other market in the world could do both. Economies of scale in a small nation meant monopoly, but competition often meant inefficient scale. American industry had both scale and competition, so if some details of organization at the top and in the boardroom were not perfect, no matter, because scale and competition were so important and might allow for profits that would hide a few defects in organization.

Thus the United States' huge lead was at least partly based on these advantages (and perhaps not on any corporate governance advantages); and these advantages of scale and competition are no longer exclusive to the United States. A common market in Europe and a globalized marketplace allow foreign firms both economies of scale and a competitive market. Competition is fiercer, and it is at least possible that competition between corporate governance systems and methods of organization are one dimension of international competition, with each system having a distinctive set of advantages and disadvantages.

Costs and Benefits

To assert that there are costs to fragmentation is neither to assert that these costs outweigh benefits nor that policymakers can eliminate those costs without creating other problems. The benefits of the Berle-Means corporation in managerial specialization, capital-raising ability, and organizational flexibility especially in raising capital for new entry into many industries are quite high. Those benefits may exceed any of the costs.

Moreover, managers work in several markets and social structures. The internal organization of the boardroom and its relationship with institutional shareholders is only one. Professional pride makes managers and directors try hard even if the organizational constraints acting on them are weak. The embarrassment of media attention (or fear of it) will help correct egregious errors. Product markets, capital markets, managerial labor markets, employee labor markets, and corporate takeover markets constrain managers. This is all another way of saying that corporate governance is only one dimension of competition.

The question then is whether fragmentation sometimes has enough costs whose elimination could pay for the costs of concentration. Had a GM board with representatives from five or six institutional owners of GM reacted strongly in 1982, instead of 1992 (when the board did react strongly), the gains might have been measured in billions of dollars, paying for more than a few institutional errors. Even if most firms are better off the way they are (and I think most probably are, and the costs of change for many would be too high), some firms might be better run if they had concentrated owners. Other nations have them sometimes; the United States, rarely. While our prescriptions will, when we get to Part V, not be to remake the American system, we now have several reasons to want to know why the American firm turned out as it did. First, we would like to know as a matter of academic curiosity whether it was inevitable. Second, we'd like to know if law and history played a big role. And third, if they did play a big role, then the prescriptive question becomes more urgent. That is, to say that one wastes energy from the heat of a light bulb does not tell us much. We have a cost, but if it's a technological requirement, it's a necessary cost of getting light. But if we learn that we can use alternative technologies to make light, and that the choice of technologies depends on non engineering factors (such as a nation's politics) then the possibility of avoiding waste becomes a real one.

While disadvantages would afflict heavy institutional ownership the restrictions were reactions to conflicts of interest, financial abuses, cartelization, banking instability, politically intolerable accumulations of power we shall hold off until Part V a fuller evaluation of whether to let organizational forms compete. Rather than prescription, we want first to understand how politics helped to determine corporate structure.

4

Public Company Status and its Trading

Introduction

There are certain situations where secondary trading can only occur if the securities are included on a registration statement or sold in strict compliance with regulations designed to insure that the seller is not an underwriter with respect to the securities. If the issuer has completed a registered primary offering of its securities, or has otherwise become subject to the reporting provisions of the Exchange Act, secondary transactions will take place in the context of the integrated disclosure system's formal requirements of annual and periodic reporting. Public company status can become quite burdensome to the company; however, the ability to access the public capital markets carries with it the responsibility to adhere to the SEC's guidelines with respect to disclosure and protection of shareholder rights.

Trading Markets

Trading markets are concerned with transactions in previously issued and outstanding securities which are bought and sold on a routine basis without any of the special selling efforts that are required when a large block of shares is sold by the issuer or any major shareholder. While secondary transactions can certainly take the form of an isolated purchase and sale that does not involve a broker-dealer, most of the regulatory activity under the federal securities laws focuses upon trading in organized markets, such as the various national stock exchanges and the over-the-counter markets, and transactions involving broker-dealers that are subject to the various rules and regulations imposed at the federal and state level.

Trading procedures will vary depending upon whether the securities are traded on a national stock exchange or in the over-the-counter market. In those cases where the securities have been listed for trading on a national stock exchange, a specialist will be assigned to establish and maintain an orderly trading market for the security. The specialist, who is subject to regulation by the exchange and the SEC, matches buy and sell orders and attempts to maintain some degree of liquidity in the security, perhaps by purchasing shares for his own account. Specialists are subject to minimum capital requirements that have been established by each of the exchanges and the SEC.

In contrast, the NASDAQ allows market-makers to submit their quotations electronically for specified securities, which quotations are then made available to all subscribing broker-dealers who simply make a query to the system for quotations that then appear on TV-like consoles. In order to effect a trade, the executing broker-dealer queries the system for the best available quotation in the security. With this information, the broker-dealer immediately contacts the appropriate market-maker to complete and affirm the purchase or sale, depending on the circumstance, of the required number of shares.

As to actively traded over-the-counter securities not quoted on the NASDAQ either because they are not eligible for quotation or no market maker has elected to register the security for quotation quotations are likely to appear in the privately published National Daily Quotation Sheets often referred to as the "pink sheets." Market-makers who subscribe to the National Daily Quotation Service pay to have their quotations reflected in the pink sheets. The pink sheets are disseminated, albeit on a somewhat delayed basis, to other dealers who use them to determine the market in a quoted security. In order to effect a trade, a broker-dealer contacts by private wire, or other means, the market-maker with the apparent best market in the security. Once the latest quotation has been determined, the broker-dealer can complete execution of the customer's order.

LEGAL FRAMEWORK FOR SECONDARY TRADING ACTIVITIES

A. Overview

1. In General

As a general rule, secondary trading activities with respect to outstanding securities following their original issuance can be accomplished without the need to register the transaction under the provisions of Section 5 of the Securities Act. However, there are two notable exceptions to this principle. First, securities originally issued in an exempt, or non-registered, transaction may not be resold to the public without some means for insuring that the purchasers are sufficiently informed or that the original sale was not simply a means for circumventing the requirements of Section 5. Second, a sale of a large block of securities by certain persons deemed to be "in control" of the issuer may also be subject to various limitations, since the position of the seller in such cases raises potential disclosures issues similar to those that exist when the issuer itself distributes securities.

2. Statutory Framework

Secondary trading transactions are addressed by Section 4(1) of the Securities Act which provides that the provisions of Section 5 relating to registration shall not apply to "transactions by any person other than an issuer, underwriter or dealer." In turn, most dealer transactions are exempted under Section 4(3), subject to certain exceptions that generally apply during the period that a public distribution of securities is occurring. Accordingly, the availability of an exemption for a non-issuer transaction turns on whether or not an underwriter is involved. Section 2((11) of the Securities Act defines an "underwriter" as follows: "The term 'underwriter' means any person who has purchased from an issuer with a view to, or offers or sells for an issuer in connection with, the distribution of any security, or participates or has a direct or indirect participation in any such undertaking." Section 2(11) goes on to expand the term "issuer" for purposes thereof to include "affiliates" thereof as follows: "As used in this paragraph [that is, for purposes of defining an underwriter] the term 'issuer' shall include, in addition to an issuer, any person directly or indirectly controlling or controlled by the issuer, or any person under direct or indirect common control with the issuer." The manner in which the term "underwriter" is defined in Section 2(11) has the following effect:

- A person who purchases shares from an issuer with a view toward "distribution," which is generally considered to be a resale of such shares to the public, would be deemed to be an underwriter, and any such resale would not fall within the exemption provided by Section 4(1). Persons purchasing from an issuer in an exempt transaction are at risk of being statutory underwriters with respect to any future resale.
- In addition to the considerations that apply to any person who purchases shares from an issuer, an affiliate making a distribution of any shares,

including shares that may have been purchased in the open market, may not be able to rely upon the Section 4(1) exemption since the persen purchasing shares from the affiliate may be deemed to be an underwriter if such shares are being purchased for distribution.

Persons purchasing shares in the trading market from someone other than an affiliate are free to resell such shares without registration, since there is no danger that underwriter status will be assigned to the seller.

As a result of the foregoing, careful attention must be paid to insuring that persons involved in secondary transactions do not unwittingly become underwriters and, as a result, engage in sales that violate the registration requirements. In the case of shares purchased from an issuer in an exempt transaction, procedures will be implemented to demonstrate that the shares are being purchased for investment, not for distribution. Moreover, the SEC's own Rule 144 was adopted as a form of "safe harbor" which can be relied upon for the public resale of securities in circumstances that may otherwise run afoul of Section 4(1).

B. Rule 144 Transactions

1. In General

Rule 144 is a "safe harbor" applicable both to the sale of restricted securities and to securities sold for the account of an affiliate (controlling person) whether or not such securities are restricted securities. Restricted securities are defined as securities acquired directly or indirectly from an issuer or an affiliate in a transaction not involving a public offering. Therefore, Rule 144 is available for shares issued in reliance on the exemption under Section 4(2) for transactions not involving a public offering, as well as for resale of securities subject to the resale limitations of Regulation D.

2. Definition of "Affiliate"

The rule defines an affiliate of the issuer as "a person that directly, or indirectly through one or more intermediaries, controls, or is controlled by, or is under common control with, such issuer." The SEC staff has determined that the following individuals are affiliates: (1) an officer or director of the issuer; (2) a person owning more than 10 percent of the issuer's outstanding common stock; (3) a person whose spouse is an officer and director of the issuer; and (4) a corporation with an officer or director serving as a director of the issuer.

3. Current Public Information Requirement

As a general rule, Rule 144 can be used only when there is adequate current public information available about the issuer of the securities. The test can be satisfied in two ways. First, the issuer must be subject to the periodic reporting requirements of the Exchange Act and be current with respect to the filing of such reports. Alternatively, the current information requirements can be satisfied by proof that "Rule 15c2-11 information" has been made publicly available.

4. Holding Period Requirement

When Rule 144 is being used for the resale of restricted securities, a minimum of two years must have elapsed between the later of the date of the acquisition of the securities from the issuer or from an affiliate of the issuer and any resale of such securities in reliance upon the rule. For purposes of determining when the two-year holding period begins in the case of a purchase, the rule provides that it shall not begin until the full purchase price or other consideration has been paid or given by the acquiror. There are detailed tacking rules applicable to the holding period of donees, trusts, and estates that permit in some instances the holding period of the donor, settle or, or decedent, as appropriate, to be used in determining the two-year period. In those cases where Rule 144 is being used by an affiliate to sell shares acquired in open market transactions, the holding period condition does not apply.

5. Limitations on Amount of Securities Sold

The amount that can be sold by any person pursuant to Rule 144 during any three-month period cannot exceed 1 percent of the outstanding class of securities, in the case of over-the-counter securities, and that amount or the average weekly reported trading volume over the appropriate four week period, if greater, in the case of listed securities and over-the-counter securities traded through the NASDAQ. In determining the Rule 144 quantitative limitations, the effect of detailed attribution and aggregation rules must be taken into account.

6. Manner of Sale Requirements

Other than transactions made pursuant to Rule 144(k), as described below, securities sold in reliance on Rule 144 must be sold to a market maker or in *unsolicited* agency transactions in which the broker acts as agent for the seller and receives only the usual and customary brokerage commissions. If the shares being offered pursuant to Rule 144 by the seller exceed five hundred in number, or $10,000 in aggregate sales price, Form 144, primarily setting forth information relevant to determining the availability of the exemption, must be filed with the SEC and, if listed on an exchange, the appropriate exchange.

7. Removal of Certain Conditions for Shares Held by Nonaffiliates for Long Periods

Rule 144(k) allows a person who has been a nonaffiliate of the issuer for at least ninety days and who has held securities for three years (determined in the same manner as the two-year holding period) to sell such securities in unrestricted quantities without regard to the nature of the transaction, commissions, or discounts paid, the filing of a Form 144, or whether the requirements regarding the availability of information regarding the issuer have been satisfied. A seller pursuant to Rule 144(k) may simultaneously sell other restricted securities held for less time and as to which the seller must comply with volume limitations. Sales under Rule 144 (k) are not aggregated with sales of restricted securities for purposes of such volume limitations.

C. Rule 144A: Resales by Qualified Institutional Buyers

1. In General

Rule 144A provides an exemption from registration for persons (other than the issuer) who reoffer and resell certain unregistered securities to offerees and purchasers that are (or which the seller reasonably believes to be) "qualified institutional buyers." Rule 144A is intended to facilitate the development of an orderly and liquid market among large institutional investors with respect to securities issued in private placement transactions. A related development was the creation by the NASD of the PORTAL market for the purpose of providing a computerized, screen-based quotation, trading, settlement, and clearing system for securities that may be sold in reliance upon Rule 144A.

2. Qualified Institutional Buyers

A "qualified institutional buyer" is generally defined as an entity that satisfies both of the following requirements: (1) In purchasing the unregistered securities, the entity is acting for its own account or for the accounts of other qualified institutional buyers (the account requirement); and (2) the entity, in the aggregate, owns and invests (on a discretionary basis) at least $100 million in securities, excluding securities of its affiliates (the securities held requirement).

Types of entities that may be qualified institutional buyers include, among other organizations, any insurance company, registered investment company, employee benefit plan (private or governmental), or registered investment adviser, and any corporation, partnership, or business trust. In order to be a qualified institutional buyer, in addition to satisfying the account requirement and the securities held requirement, a bank or savings and loan must also have a net worth of at least $25 million as shown in its latest audited annual financial statements.

3. Excluded Securities

Rule 144A does *not* apply to the offer or sale of securities that, when used, are of the same class as securities of the issuer already listed on a registered national securities exchange or quoted in the NASDAQ. Eligibility is determined at the time the security is issued; therefore, eligibility is not affected if a class of securities that was not publicly traded or quoted at the time of issuance subsequently becomes publicly traded or quoted. In addition, certain securities that, when issued, are convertible or exchangeable into other securities publicly traded are treated as part of the same class as the underlying securities, as will certain warrants exercisable for other securities publicly traded.

4. Information Requirements

There are no informational requirements under Rule 144A if the issuer of the securities to be resold is a reporting company under the Exchange Act. However, if the issuer of the securities is not a reporting company, the seller, and any prospective purchaser designated by the seller, must have the right to obtain certain information from the issuer upon the request of the seller, and the prospective purchaser must receive that information from the issuer, the seller, or a person acting for either of them, at or prior to the time of sale, upon the request of the prospective purchaser to the holder or the issuer. The information that must be made available to the seller and prospective purchasers of the securities includes a brief statement of the nature of the issuer's business, products, and services as they exist as of a date within twelve months prior to the date of resale and specified financial information (e.g., balance sheet and profit and loss statements).

5. Resales of Rule 144A Securities

Securities purchased by a "qualified institutional investor" in reliance on Rule 144A are restricted securities which may be resold in reliance on Rule 144 or Rule 144A.

D. The "Section 4 ½ "Exemption

There may be other situations where the purchaser of securities in an exempt transaction subsequently wishes to sell the securities other than pursuant to a registration statement or Rule 144. Ordinarily, in making such a sale, the person would risk being deemed an underwriter, since the transaction may be used as evidence that the securities were originally acquired for resale and not for investment. However, underwriter status will attach only if the person acquired the shares with a view to distribution, which generally means a public offering. If the subsequent sale essentially takes the form of a private placement, as might be the case when the sale is made to persons who would have satisfied the requirements of Section 4(2) if they had purchased the shares directly from the issuer, the sale will be exempt under Section 4(1) on the theory that an underwriter was not involved.

These secondary private placements have been referred to as Section 4 ½ transactions, since while the exemption claimed falls under Section 4(1), the criteria utilized are more akin to issuances made in accordance with the Section 4(2) exemption, which can only be used by issuers. Securities sold in such transactions are deemed restricted securities for purposes of Rule 144. The sale of securities in such transactions starts a new holding period for the purchaser for purposes of Rule 144, and the purchaser cannot tack the holding period of the person from whom the securities were acquired.

E. Registered Secondary Transactions

Obviously, one way to insure that a secondary distribution of securities is made in compliance with the registration requirements is to register such shares for public sale. A number of the forms for Securities Act registration can be used for resales, including Form S-1 and, if available, Form S-3, which essentially consists of incorporating certain Exchange Act filings by reference. Only the issuer can file a registration statement, even if it pertains only to secondary sales. Accordingly, persons who acquire shares in an exempt transaction, such as a private placement under Section 4(2), will bargain for a contractual agreement by the issuer to register such shares on the terms and conditions agreed to by the parties.

F. Secondary Trading under State Securities Laws

In contrast to the exemption for trading transactions included in Section 4(1) of the Securities Act, Section 301 of the Uniform Act subjects all sales of *nonexempt* securities, including trading transactions, subject to the registration of securities provisions. However, securities listed on the principal stock exchanges are exempt and, in most jurisdictions, an exemption is available for securities as to which appropriate information is included in a recognized securities manual (primarily *Moody*'s and *Standard and Poor*'s). Many jurisdictions also have an exemption for isolated non-issuer transactions which may or may not be broad enough to cover the typical trading transaction. The state Blue Sky laws permit the administrator, on appropriate grounds, to revoke the manual and isolated transaction exemptions as to any particular security.

PUBLIC COMPANY STATUS

A. Overview

Issuers become subject to the continuous disclosure requirements of the Exchange Act as a result of either of the following: (1) the registration of an offering of securities pursuant to the Securities Act or (2) the registration of a class of securities under Section 12 of the Exchange Act. In either case, the issuer must file with the SEC the following reports:

- The annual report of Form 10-K or the counterpart form available for use by SBIS, which must be filed within ninety days after the end of the issuer's current fiscal year;
- Quarterly reports on Form 10-Q or the counterpart form available for use by SBIs, which must be filed within forty-five days of the end of the appropriate quarter for each quarter other than the year-end quarter; and
- Form 8-K, which must be filed as to certain items within fifteen days of the earliest event to occur and, as to other material developments relating to the issuer, within ten days after the end of the month in which the event occurs.

In addition, issuers which have become subject to the continuous disclosure requirements because they have actually registered a class of securities under the Exchange Act must also comply with the following provisions of the Exchange Act:

- The rules relating to the solicitation of proxies pertaining to the class of registered 7 securities, including the requirement that an annual report be prepared and distributed to shareholders;
- The rules regulating tender offers for registered securities; and
- The "going private" rules relating to disclosures which must be made in certain transactions initiated by issuers or affiliates thereof which would have the effect of deregistering the issuer's securities under the Exchange Act or causing the issuer's securities to be delisted by an exchange or over-the-counter market.

In addition, the "short-swing profit" rules will impose liability upon insiders of the registrant for any profits which they may realize in specified trading transactions involving equity securities of the registrant.

B. Disclosure Obligations under the Exchange Act

1. In General

Issuers subject to the disclosure obligations of the Exchange Act will need to prepare and file an Annual Report on Form 10-K, quarterly reports on Form 10-Q and, if required, reports on Form 8-K to cover specified events. SBIs have the option of complying with the Exchange Act reporting obligations by using special report forms adopted by the SEC which incorporate the simplified form of disclosure under Regulation S-B. In addition, issuers subject to the proxy rules must prepare and distribute an annual report to their shareholders, which differs in form and content from the Form 10-K.

2. Form 10-K

Part I of Form 10-K consists of Item 101 (description of business), Item 102 (properties), and Item 103 (legal proceedings) of Regulation S-K, as well as specified information with respect to any matter submitted to a vote of security holders during the fourth quarter of the fiscal year. The information regarding developments of the company business included in the description of business in the Form 10-K need cover only those which have occurred since the beginning of the last fiscal year.

Part II of Form 10-K includes the BIP. Part III of Form 10-K consists of Item 401 (officers and directors), Item 402 (management remuneration and transactions), and Item 403 (security holders of management and 5 percent beneficial owners) of Regulation S-K. Part IV of Form 10-K consists of schedules to the financial statements and separate (as distinguished from consolidated) financial statements of the registrant to the extent appropriate, a list of the financial documents and exhibits, and a statement as to whether any reports on Form 8-K were filed during the last quarter of the fiscal year covered by the Form 10-K. The exhibits include the articles of incorporation and bylaws, and all material contracts, although, to the extent such documents have been previously filed with the SEC, they may be incorporated by reference.

A registrant is permitted, but not required, to incorporate Annual Report information (see below) into Part II of the Form 10-K. However, since the Annual Report must include only a portion of the information called for by Item 101 of Regulation S-K, the Annual Report may not include all the information required in the Form 10-K relating to the company's business. A registrant may also incorporate by reference information from its definitive proxy statement relating to its annual meeting into Part III of the Form 10-K, but only if the proxy statement will be available within 120 days of the end of the fiscal year. If the proxy statement is not filed with the SEC within 120 days from the end of the fiscal year, the Part III information must be filed as an amendment to Form 10-K under cover of Form 8 within 120 days of the end of the fiscal year.

3. Quarterly Reports on Form 10-Q

Form 10-Q requires condensed profit and loss statements, balance sheet and source and application of funds. The profit and loss statements have to be for the last quarter presented on a comparative basis with the comparable quarter for the prior year and on a year-to-date basis also presented on a comparative basis for the comparable period during the prior year. Balance sheet information is presented as of the end of the quarter and is presented on a comparative basis at the same date for the previous year. The condensed statement of source and application of funds is presented on a year-to-date basis for the current and prior year. The statements do not have to be certified, nor do they have to be reviewed by an independent public accountant; however, they must be prepared in accordance with Accounting Principles Board Opinion No. 28 relating to a change in accounting principles.

The Form 10-Q must also include an MD&A discussion which covers material changes from the end of the last fiscal year to the date of the balance sheet included in the 10-Q as well as material changes from the date of the corresponding balance sheet for the previous year to the date of the most recent interim balance sheet. The MD&A should also discuss material changes in results of operations between the most recent quarter and the comparative quarter for the prior year and as between the year-to-date results with the results for the comparable period of the prior year. Part II of the Form 10-Q must include information relating to:

- Legal proceedings (item 1) initiated during the quarter or with respect to which there were material developments during the quarter;
- Modifications in and limitations (including working capital restrictions and other limitations on the payment of dividends) on the rights of security holders of a class of registered securities (item 2);
- Changes in the collateral securing a registered class of securities (item 3);
- Any material default with respect to senior securities in the payment of principal, interest, or sinking fund installments not cured within thirty days (item 4);
- Increases in the amount of outstanding securities (including debt securities) if the aggregate amount of all such increases not previously reported exceeds 5 percent of the outstanding securities in the class including as to securities which were not registered a statement as to the exemption relied on and the basis for claiming the exemption (item 5);
- Decreases in outstanding securities the aggregate amount of which not previously reported exceeds 5 percent of the class (item 6); and
- The results of any matter submitted to a vote of shareholders (including as to the election of directors the name of directors elected and those continuing

in office) must be set forth (item 7) except an uncontested election of directors does not have to be reported if proxies were solicited pursuant to the proxy rules, and matters which are procedural and the selection or approval of auditors do not have to be reported.

4. Form 8-K

Form 8-K needs to be filed only if one of the events which the form requires The reported occurs. Such events include:

- Changes in control of the registrant (item 1);
- The acquisition or disposition of a significant amount of assets other than in the ordinary course of business (item 2);
- The appointment of a receiver and certain material orders issued in a bankruptcy or reorganization proceeding (item 3);
- The resignation or dismissal of the certifying accountant (with information relating to any disagreement over accounting principles), and a confirming letter from the accountant to the SEC (item 4); and

The resignation of a director if the director has furnished registrant with a letter describing a disagreement on any matter relating to registrant's operations and the director requests that such matter be disclosed (item 6).

The registrant may also include, at its option, any other matter the registrant regards as of material importance to security holders and elects to report on in the Form 8-K (item 5).

The Form 8-K is to be filed within fifteen days of the event reported on except as to item 5 (other material events) which can be reported on at any time since it is optional. Registrants, however, are encouraged to file promptly after occurrence of the event and are urged in this context to take into account accuracy and currency of information in a Securities Act registration statement which incorporates Exchange Act reports by reference, such as Form S-3.

5. Exchange Act Reporting by SBIs

SBIs meeting their Exchange Act reporting obligations by using Regulation S-B disclosures can make their filings on Form 10-KSB, which is an annual report for SBIs analogous to Form 10-K, and on Form 10-QSB, which is a quarterly reporting form corresponding to Form 10-Q. For an SBI entitled to use the abbreviated report forms, the items under Form 10-KSB and Form 10-QSB are identical to those in Form 10-K and Form 10-Q. However, the relevant items in the abbreviated forms are referenced to the simplified requirements of Regulation S-B rather than to Regulation S-K. The SEC also has adopted corresponding amendments to the proxy rules and annual report to shareholder requirements insofar as they relate to SBIs.

6. Annual Report to Shareholders

An annual report must be sent to shareholders before or with the proxy statement relating to the annual election of directors, and seven copies must be filed with the SEC concurrently with its distribution to shareholders. The annual report includes the BIP, certain segmental and geographic financial information, limited narrative information relating to the company's principal products and/or services, and a brief description of the business done by the company during the most recent fiscal year so as to indicate the general nature and scope of its business. Also, all of the directors and executive officers must be identified with the principal occupation or employment of each such person together with the name and principal business of the organizations by which such persons are employed.

The annual report may include any other information that the issuer wishes to include (e.g., a letter from the registrant's chief executive officer). The annual report may be in any form deemed suitable by management.

All of the structured portions of the annual report other than the financial statements may be included in an appendix or a separate section provided attention is called to such presentation. Some issuers follow the practice of utilizing the Form 10-K (typically without those portions [Part III] that will be included in the proxy statement) wrapped around the letter from the chief executive officer and an attractive cover as their annual report.

C. Regulation of Corporate Governance

1. In General

The federal securities laws, particularly various provisions of the Exchange Act, can have a significant impact upon corporate governance with respect to issuers having securities registered under the Exchange Act. Among the areas in which special rules and regulations have been adopted are the procedures relating to the solicitation of proxies, tender offers with respect to securities of registered issuers and "going private" transactions. Issuers with securities listed on national securities exchanges or in the over-the-counter market, particularly the NASDAQ, must also take into account corporate governance rules which may be imposed as a listing condition.

2. Proxy Solicitation Procedures

Section 14(a) of the Exchange Act makes it unlawful to solicit proxies in violation of the rules and regulations adopted by the SEC. Pursuant to Section 14(a), the SEC has adopted extensive regulations controlling the solicitation of proxies from shareholders in connection with the election of directors, approval of compensation plans, extraordinary corporate actions (e.g., mergers, consolidations and acquisitions), and shareholder proposals. In particular, if a proxy solicitation (or other form of consent or authorization) pertaining to a security registered under the Exchange Act is directed to more than ten persons, a proxy statement and proxy form complying with the proxy rules must be filed and used. With some exceptions, the proxy statement must be filed as preliminary proxy material with the SEC at least ten days prior to the mailing of the definitive proxy statement.

3. Tender Offer Regulation

A tender offer generally involves an attempt to acquire a substantial portion of the outstanding stock of a company by making an offer to purchase all shares, up to a specified number, tendered by shareholders within a specified period at a fixed price, usually at a premium above the market price. Since a successful tender offer can, in effect, result in a change in control with respect to the underlying company, they have been made subject to extensive regulation in Regulations 14D and 14E. The Regulation 14D rules, all of which begin with a 14d prefix, are applicable to tender offers pertaining to equity securities registered under the Exchange Act and equity securities of certain insurance companies. The Regulation 14E rules, all of which begin with a 14e prefix, are applicable to all tender offers.

A person making a tender offer (bidder) must file with the SEC, "as soon as practicable on the date of the commencement of the tender offer," a "Tender Offer Statement" on Schedule 14D-1. The Tender Offer Statement must identify the bidder, set forth the source of the bidder's funds, the bidder's purpose (including future plans) in making the tender offer, any securities of the target company that have previously been acquired by the bidder and, if the bidder is not a natural person, appropriate financial statements if the bidder's financial condition is material to a decision by the security holders of the target company.

Rule 14e-1(a), which is applicable to all tender offers, requires that any tender offer must remain open for at least twenty business days from the commencement thereof, and for ten business days from the date the bidder first gives notice of any increase or decrease in the percentage of the class of securities being sought or the consideration offered or the dealer's soliciting fee to be given in the tender offer. In connection with a tender offer for securities for which a Schedule 14D-1 must be filed, any person who has deposited securities may withdraw them any time prior to the expiration of the tender offer. In the event that a tender offer is for less than all shares tendered, the bidder must purchase shares tendered pro rata if a greater number of shares are deposited than the bidder is willing to purchase. The bidder is also required to disclose the extent to which it presently intends to purchase shares if its offer is over tendered.

The tender offer rules are supplemented by the reporting provisions of the Williams Act, which require a person or group in the process of acquiring a substantial block of equity securities of a company to notify the SEC and the subject company about the acquisition, and to disclose, among other things, their ultimate intentions regarding control of the company. The Williams Act provisions become applicable when a person or a group acquires 2 percent of the outstanding shares of a class of equity securities registered under the Exchange Act and, as a result, becomes the owner of 5 percent of the outstanding shares. Once the aforementioned threshold is met, the person or group must file a Schedule 13D with the SEC and transmit a copy to the company within ten days.

4. Rule 13e-3: Going Private Rules

The so-called "going private" rules may be applicable to transactions which involve a purchase of, or a tender offer for, the equity securities of a reporting company by the issuer or an affiliate of the issuer which would result in the issuer no longer being subject to the Exchange Act registration requirements. The going private rules may also apply to a merger of a reporting company with, or the sale of all of the corporate assets of the company to, an affiliate, if the resultant company is not subject to the Exchange Act registration requirements. Since, in each case, the business of the reporting company ends up in the hands of a small group of former shareholders, Rule 13e-3 was adopted to insure full and fair disclosure to the public shareholders in order to mitigate the potential for self-dealing and misuse of inside information which exists in these types of transactions.

5

Mutual Funds in Corporate Finance

Introduction

The cutoff's timing is ironic, because Berle and Means had just published their finding that the atomization of shareholdings had shifted power from shareholders to managers. Key political players then wanted to ban mutual fund (and other banker) control of industrial firms. Explanations for their preference for passivity include popular mistrust of large financial institutions, public-spirited rules to foster stable, honest mutual funds for the average investor, the accidents of tax doctrine, and a faint interest group story as some political actors favored local managers over Wall Street.

Investment Company Act of 1940

Mutual funds pool investments from many investors, who get diversification and buy expert management from the fund's managers. Even when the Investment Company

Act of 1940 was passed, cognoscenti recognized that mutual funds offered a third function: "The investor may be able to join in the purchase of control of one or more other corporations." Mutual funds could have evolved into the missing link between dispersed investors and large operating firms.

Power of Control

Congress disliked funds that controlled industry; passivity was best. Unscrupulous financiers and industrialists sometimes used investment companies to get control "of the wealth and industries of the country." To stop concentrated control, Congress had to "prevent the diversion of these [investment] trusts from their normal channels of diversified investment to the abnormal avenues of control of industry," perhaps by "completely divorcing investment trusts from investment banking." Congress then directed the SEC to draft legislation regulating mutual funds.

The SEC declared in its proposed bill that "the national public interest is adversely affected when investment companies [have] great size [and] excessive influence on the national economy." In 1935, 56 investment companies controlled 187 portfolio companies. Little good could come out of control over portfolio firms. The investment company could lack diversification and fail. It might pump money into the portfolio firm to protect its large position. It might unwisely change the financial policy or capital structure of the portfolio firm, or unwisely force out high dividends. Finally, it might force a merger on terms disadvantageous to minority interest in the controlled company.

The SEC conceded that fund control could reduce the informational and organizational problems of scattered shareholders; with its specialized personnel, the fund would have expertise, the motivation to improve managerial performance, and the clout to do so. But the downside of powerful funds offset the upside. The SEC wanted mutual fund directors and employees off the boards of all portfolio firms; they wanted a Glass-Steagall type of severance. They also wanted to cap fund size at $150 million in assets. Eventually the SEC compromised with the mutual fund industry, but it achieved substantial severance.

Diversification

First, a mutual fund cannot advertise itself as diversified if it owns in the regulated part of its portfolio more than 10 percent of the stock of any company. Three-quarters of the portfolio is subject to this fragmentation rule, even if that influential block of stock is a small portion of the fund's portfolio. (Several states have had more severe rules, banning a fund from selling its shares to state residents if the fund owned more than 10 percent of any firm; many mutual funds conformed to the most severe restrictions.) The SEC wanted that restriction to disable control.

To be sure, these portfolio limits allow for some, perhaps even substantial, corporate governance activity, particularly for the very large mutual funds that have arisen in recent years. But the smaller funds that prevailed until recently could not build large blocks without devoting a big part of the fund's portfolio to a few firms in a way that the 1940 Act made harder than it had to be. Even today the very biggest funds cannot take big blocks in the largest firms without bumping into these portfolio rules. (And the portfolio rules cumulate with other restraints to raise the cost of activity.) Whether mutual funds should be able to offer undiversified portfolios to investors is a question about which policy-makers may disagree. But the point here is that the portfolio rules make that kind of a big-block fund difficult, or illegal.

Second, a fund calling itself diversified has 75 percent of its portfolio restricted; for that portion, it can have no more than 5 percent of its assets in the securities of any one issuer. As a diversification standard, this provision is crude but understandable. Many mutual funds are designed for unsophisticated investors who cannot assemble a diversified portfolio or evaluate the mutual fund's portfolio. By requiring some standard of fragmentation if the fund chooses to call itself diversified, the 1940 Act helps make sure that investors get what they were promised.

But this crude standard justifies only the 5 percent restriction (no more than 5 percent of the mutual fund's assets in any single company). The 10 percent restriction (no more than 10 percent of the *portfolio* firm's stock) adds nothing to diversification. Obviously, an investment company could have a small portion of its assets in a single firm, but if the firm were middling-sized, the investment company could have an influential block of stock. The goal seems to have been to disable control, not to promote diversification.

Networks and Affiliates

Although the 1940 Act exempts a quarter of the "diversified" fund's portfolio from the fragmentation rules, and theoretically the fund could choose not to call itself diversified and then be free of the portfolio rules entirely, it could not escape the similar tax portfolio rules I discuss below.

Other restrictions apply. True, as enacted, the act does not stop a fund or its employees from sitting on the board of a portfolio firm. But if a fund either owned 5 percent of a portfolio firm's stock or sat on its board, the portfolio firm would become a statutory affiliate of the fund and of the mutual fund's principal underwriter. This would trigger transactional prohibitions, many of which are quite sensible safeguards against the risks of insider self-dealing, and these prohibitions would deter the relationship. A buyout, exchange of shares, conversion of shares from one class to another, and sale of shares by the portfolio firm to the fund all seem to be covered and to require special SEC exemption. And without SEC exemption, the fund cannot act jointly with another financial institution to go onto a portfolio firm's board of directors, or otherwise exert control. Until recent years, banking law was interpreted to bar banks from close affiliation with a mutual fund, further reducing the prospect of joint influence.

The 1940 Act bars cross-ownership between a portfolio firm and its mutual fund, meaning that a portfolio firm's managers could oust an active mutual fund by buying up enough of the mutual fund's stock. No fund may buy a firm's voting stock if both would own more than 3 percent of the voting stock of the other. I understand that target firms have neutralized mutual fund ownership in a hostile takeover via the cross-ownership ban.

If the fund wanted to act jointly with an affiliate to exercise control, it would need prior SEC approval. Imagine an incipient network of institutional investors: An investment bank, an insurance company, or a commercial bank could become the investment adviser to a mutual fund. The adviser might take 4.9 percent of the portfolio firm's stock, as does the mutual fund, and combine it with a holding of the investment bank, the insurer or the commercial bank's trust department. That block would be big enough to be influential, to get a representative into the boardroom. Perhaps SEC approval of activities, control actions, and control changes would be easy for the mutual fund and the other institutions to obtain, but in the absence of a blanket SEC authorization more expansive than that now given, the rules are at least another cost to joint activity.

ORIGINS IN THE 1936 REVENUE ACT

A mutual fund controlling portfolio firms would risk being taxed on its entire portfolio, since tax law allows only diversified funds to pass income up to shareholders, untaxed to the conduit fund. The 1936 Revenue Act notion of diversification, like that of the Investment Company Act, was not a notion found in a modern textbook on corporate finance: no investment in a firm constituting either more than 5 percent of the portfolio *or* more than 10 percent of the *portfolio firm's* stock. Later, in 1942, Congress eased up, allowing half of the portfolio to be more concentrated. Witnesses at the hearings on the 1940 Act said that the diversification rules were not tax policy but regulatory policy, to distinguish "good" mutual funds (those that did not exert control), which were left untaxed, from the others, which would be taxed.

If a mutual fund could not get pass-through status, its income would be taxed, resulting in a triple taxation, which would destroy the fund. The portfolio firm would pay taxes on its earnings, and then the fund would pay taxes on dividends it received from the portfolio firm, at an effective tax rate of about 10 percent on dividends; it would pay capital gains at a higher rate. This income would be taxed again when paid to shareholders of a non diversified fund, yielding three tax events for the same income, one in the portfolio firm, one in the fund, and one for the owner of the fund. The tax rules, like the 1940 Act rules, don't stymie all mutual fund activity, but they eliminate one important financial product the big-block fund and make other kinds of action less likely.

People knowledgeable about the multiple taxation of inter corporate dividends view the rule as merely technical. But it is not. Dig into the legislative history, and one finds that the New Deal Congress taxed dividends to discourage complex corporate structures. It is part of a pattern from antitrust and financial regulation that seeks fragmentation and arm's-length dealing and has continuing effects today. Not only does it help explain the path of mutual fund regulation and taxation the funds needed some doctrinal hook to free themselves from the intercorporate dividend tax, and the "passive" trust was the handy hook but it stops nonfinancial interlocks. Suppliers and customers might take blocks of stock in one another, in ways similar to what often occurs in Japan. The intercorporate dividend tax discourages this, not just as a technicality but because Congress used tax rules to discourage the complex structure itself.

Let's see in more detail why taxes deter most ordinary corporations from large long-term ownership blocks, because even if financial intermediaries cannot take big blocks, one might ask why ordinary corporations do not. Part of the answer is that to get pass-through tax treatment, the business probably has to qualify as one of these financial institutions. A corporation might accept the unfavorable tax status in the short run, as a prelude to a takeover and restructuring. But a firm asserting long-term influence would need acute skills to make up for the taxes. If it received half of its income in capital gains and half in dividends, it would pay approximately 20 percent of its income in taxes. Nor could it organize itself as a partnership, which usually can pass through its income to owners without itself paying a tax. To get pass-through status, a publicly traded partnership must comply with subchapter M's portfolio rules. Private partnerships with under one hundred investors can get pass-through treatment without conforming to the tax law's portfolio rules; these private partnerships in fact exist, suggesting that some public mutual funds, with their wider access to capital, might have developed similar big block portfolios.

Thus if a fund wished to sell services as a monitor, by dividing its portfolio into three or four stocks, it could not get the advantage of pass-through tax treatment. Such organizations do arise elsewhere. In Sweden, for instance, large mutual funds own big blocks of five or ten companies; they would be taxed out of existence here.

ARE MUTUAL FUNDS TAXABLE AS CORPORATIONS

A persistent tax problem is determining which entity has to pay the separate tax levied on a "corporation," a term which, said the Revenue Act of 1926, includes "associations, joint-stock companies and insurance companies." Were trusts and mutual funds taxable as corporate associations, and not as pass-through, untaxed entities?

A trust that did not carry on a business (and met other requirements) did not have to pay the corporate tax. But "common law trusts which act or do business in an organized capacity" did have to pay the corporate tax.

When trustees merely hold property for the collection of the income and its distribution among the beneficiaries of a trust, and are not engaged in the carrying on of any business no [taxable] association exists. When the trustees are not restricted to the mere collection of funds and their payment to the beneficiaries, but are associated together with similar or greater powers than the directors of a corporation for the purpose of carrying on some business enterprise, the trust is taxable as an association within the meaning of the statute.

Was controlling an operating firm and affecting its policies a business? Probably But trusts said that when they assembled a passive portfolio of diversified stocks and did no more, they were not taxable corporations.

Morrissey

The IRS then responded that providing diversified investments was itself a taxable business, making all trusts and mutual funds taxable at corporate rates. In 1935, the Supreme Court decided *Morrissey v. Commissioner of Internal Revenue*, in which it agreed with the IRS.

The *Morrissey* decision left the unit investment trust as the only tax-free fund left. That kind of trust puts together a portfolio, sells interests in it, collects the earnings, and returns them to the beneficiaries. The trust usually does not trade the securities in its portfolio; it is passive.

These passivity doctrines persist in today's tax law. Not only does portfolio fragmentation induce passivity, but pass-through treatment is available only to funds that derive 90 percent of their income from investment in stocks, bonds, and other securities. On the statute's face, it is dubious whether a fund making more than 10 percent of its income from management, as opposed to passive investment, would be untaxed.

Liberalization in the 1936 Tax Code

The 1936 tax code "liberalized" tax law for mutual funds by exempting fragmented funds. Yes, such funds were carrying on a business. But it was not a "real" business. It was the business of picking stocks and bonds, not of making operating decisions. As the president of a leading mutual fund said: "The tax code now recognises us as being, for purposes of taxation, *not a productive agency* in itself which should shoulder a heavier tax burden, but in effect merely a managing agency to collect dividends and gains for distribution to its shareholders."

Proponents said that "another safeguard that the amendment contains is to prevent an investment trust or investment corporation being set up to obtain control of some corporation and to manipulate its affairs." The safeguard could have been against the "evil" of Wall Street control of industry or the deterioration of tax doctrine in not allowing the investment trust to carry on a true business.

Consistency with the Political Paradigm

The American public mistrusted accumulations of economic power, as we have seen; bankers and the mutual funds they sponsored were not politically popular, especially if they were perceived as out to control industry. As we have also seen, FDR thought that political stability depended on a dispersal of economic power. Whether the issue was rechartering the Second Bank of the United States or interstate banking or insurer ownership of stock or mutual fund control of industry, American politics usually opted for fragmentation of financial power.

A standard move in public choice analysis is to look for interest groups that "bought" legislation at the expense of a diffuse and disorganized citizenry. In financial regulation of banks and takeovers, commentators see strong elements of this public choice, interest group approach. But this approach is less useful for the 1940 Act, because mutual funds just were not important enough then to provoke much interest group intervention. Rather, politicians were operating at the symbolic level, creating via regulation and taxation a framework in accord with their concept of what a mutual fund ought to be. Thereafter mutual funds had to grow up within that framework.

Anti–Wall Street Sentiment

In the early 1930s, Congress held widely-publicized hearings into the ways Wall Street affected the Great Depression. These hearings, called the Pecora hearings, after Ferdinand Pecora, its leading counsel, reflected the public's anti–Wall Street sentiment and, through publicity, heightened that sentiment. These hearings and the popular sentiments they reflected were factors in the New Deal confirmation of a fragmented financial structure generally, and of the mutual fund regulation specifically. As we saw earlier, Wall Street bankers were defensive at these hearings, with Morgan claiming that the bankers were not really the national danger Pecora claimed they were. Popular opinion, such as that also seen in Father Coughlin's widely heard speeches, was virulently anti banker and anti–Wall Street. To understand the sudden rise to national prominence of Huey Long and Father Coughlin, one must, concludes one historian, see that while the two men had their repulsive, demagogic side, they also tapped deep-seated, sensible sentiments of popular protest against distant financial institutions:

> *The most troubling feature of modern industrial society, Long and Coughlin maintained, was the steady erosion of the individual's ability to control his own destiny. Large, faceless institutions;*

> *wealthy, insulated men; vast networks of national and international influence: all were exercising power and controlling wealth that more properly belongs in the hands of ordinary citizens. These same forces had created the economic crisis of the 1930s and threatened, if left unchecked, to perpetuate it. Power, they argued, should not reside in distant obscure places; the individual should not have to live in a world in which he could not govern or even know the forces determining his destiny. Instead, the nation should aspire to a set of political and economic arrangements in which authority rested securely in the community, where it could be observed and, in some measure, controlled by its citizens. Concentrated wealth and concentrated power had damaged the nation's social fabric; a system of decentralized power, limited ownership, and small-scale capitalism could restore it.*

Bankers in general and Wall Street bankers in particular caused the Depression; they had to be punished. Certainly, bankers were too powerful. Both Huey Long and Father Coughlin extolled the virtues of small business and small banks:

> *Essential to the survival of the community, therefore, was an economy of small scale, local enterprise. How important such an economy was to Long and Coughlin was apparent in the frequency with which both men lamented its disappearance. One by one, they complained, the autonomous local institutions that sustained a meaningful community life were vanishing in the face of distant, impersonal forces. Local financial institutions what Long described as "the little banks in the counties and the parishes" and what Coughlin termed the "small bankers outside the great ring of Wall Street" were in dire peril. So were the "small industrialists," who had, Coughlin claimed, "been bought out or ... destroyed by questionable competition."*

Roosevelt had reason to coopt Long (who had in 1933 led the fight on behalf of the local bankers to prevent widespread bank branching) and Coughlin:

> *It was that possibility that Long and Coughlin would not only continue to gain support, but that their movements would begin to complement each other and to merge that politicians like Franklin Roosevelt and James Farley found particularly alarming.*

> *Separately, Long and Coughlin were formidable foes; together, many feared, they might mobilize a popular following of truly remarkable proportions.*

The politics of the "Second" New Deal, begun in 1935, tried to co-opt the less ugly elements of Long's and Coughlin's program. Against that background, the next year's Revenue Act fragmented mutual funds. When the mutual fund provisions of the 1936 Revenue Act were discussed in committee, Senator La Follette argued specifically against mutual funds that facilitated investment banker control of industry and generally against the concentration of control of the public's money in the hands of a few financiers.

William O. Douglas, chairman of the SEC and a key player in New Deal financial legislation, such as the 1940 Act, articulated a general goal of fragmenting economic power. People who dominate financial markets have "tremendous power," he said. "Such [people] become virtual governments in the power at their disposal. Sometimes it is the duty of government to police them, at times to break them up, to deter their further growth." Wall Street bankers should provide and direct the flow of capital, but not control the enterprise after the capital has flowed to it, he said.

In 1935 Long seemed likely to seek the presidency the next year; the 1935 tax proposals, coming before he was assassinated, were said to steal his thunder, and to shock both Congress and the business community. They were "a stick to beat off the storm troops of Senator Long and Father Coughlin." FDR said tax change was needed because the tax code had "done little to prevent an unjust concentration of wealth and economic power." The later 1936 provisions that fragmented mutual fund portfolios should be seen as a residue of this populist, anti–Wall Street feeling.

Public Interest Perspectives

For most of the New Deal financial legislation, looking only at populism, federalism, and interest groups, as we have been doing, distorts the picture. I emphasize them not because they are the only explanations, but because they have been neglected as causes of corporate ownership fragmentation. They are not a full explanation, but they are an important and neglected partial one. Many political players also had public interest goals and these helped motivate the legislation.

Protecting Unsophisticated Investors

Congress feared that unsophisticated investors would expect diversification but be unable to evaluate a portfolio to see whether it really was diversified. And since the SEC thought, as it said, that a fund's only positive function was to diversify there was little reason not to require diversification; anything more risked thievery, anything less had no positive purpose. Keeping mutual fund managers out of controlling positions kept them free from conflicts of interests; prohibiting insider transactions kept retail shareholders from being bilked. The serious question here was where to draw the line, not whether to draw one. The funds' investment adviser, an investment bank, would use the fund's control to get securities underwriting business from the portfolio firm. Or the investment bank would unload bad securities onto a gullible public that owned the fund. Or the fund would force a transaction with a portfolio firm that was favorable to the fund, so that the fund could report high earnings to its own shareholders.

The mutual fund industry did not strongly oppose the restrictions. It was interested in selling its product and felt it needed a code of conduct that would certify it to the general public. Indeed, one type of mutual fund the Massachusetts trust preferred that Congress require all mutual funds to use a structure that it had already adopted, which prohibited control over industry. When the 1936 tax act was considered and passed, one key player, the chair of the Senate Finance Committee, was from Massachusetts; he advocated that all mutual funds conform to the Massachusetts trusts' structure. Massachusetts trusts could comply without a change in operation; others would have to bend.

Promoting Political Stability

The political stability perspective also has a public-regarding dimension. As we saw, FDR himself said:

> *It is time to reverse that process of concentration of power which has made most American citizens, once traditionally independent owners of their own businesses, helplessly dependent for their daily bread upon the favor of a very few,* who by devices such as holding companies, *have taken for themselves unwarranted economic power. I am against private socialism of concentrated economic power as thoroughly as I am against government socialism. The one is equally as dangerous as the other;* and destruction of private socialism is utterly essential to avoid government socialism.

If Roosevelt was right, then political stability in the United States surely a worthwhile objective was dependent in the 1930s on fragmenting finance.

One way to fragment finance at least symbolically was to eliminate investment banker control of industry through mutual funds.

The financial reality of the mutual fund industry in the 1930s was that destruction of mutual fund power was symbolic. Sure, the funds had taken some first steps toward influencing industry, and, yes, mutual funds had the potential to be big players in finance and industry. But their aggregate assets were then too small to threaten political stability directly; in 1940 there were only sixty-eight mutual funds, with total assets of only $400 million. It was not the immediate prospect of "unwarranted economic power," to use Roosevelt's words, but the symbolic potential, or, at best, the prospect that in alliance with other financial institutions, the mutual fund would play a serious role.

Fighting Cartels

Blocking control also blocked cartelization. A mutual fund could be the means by which an investment banker controlled several companies in a single industry to promote and police a cartel.

The anticartel theory is still in the tax law. Although Congress liberalized the fragmentation rules in 1942 at the behest of the mutual fund industry, it still restricted control, barring a fund from putting more than a quarter of its portfolio into two or more controlled firms "engaged in the same or similar trades or businesses or related trades or businesses." Owning 20 percent of the stock of a portfolio firm gave the mutual fund control for purposes of this rule. In Germany and Japan, one function of bank ownership is industrial organization, loosely linking vertically related firms. In the United States neither banks nor insurers can help this linkage, and the intercorporate dividend tax makes partial, loose linkage costly. Tax rules help to deter mutual funds from linking vertically related firms.

The antilinkage rule produces odd results. If the fund fragments its entire portfolio, it can put it all into one industry. A few do this Fidelity's "Select" funds come to mind giving their investors lots of company but no industry diversification. Because the fund managers are investing in a single industry, they might get the expertise to second-guess some firm managers every now and then. They might feel comfortable with a few influential stock positions. After all, the shareholders are not getting much diversification from the fund anyway: its portfolio is all in one industry. But the fund cannot put more than 25 percent of its assets into control blocks in a single industry; the fund *cannot* make big-block investments in a single industry without tax penalty.

Interest Groups

Did managers support mutual fund fragmentation? Although they benefited, the evidence does not show that managers directly lobbied or even testified in 1936 or 1940. Although they probably did not bother to exert their influence in the 1930s because mutual funds were then minor financial players, and the political action was mostly symbolic, we should not dismiss a managerial public choice story completely. Some politicians promoting the 1940 Act appealed to managerial freedom from Wall Street control, and the fragmentation rules of the 1936 Act and 1940 Act had survival strength because they did not threaten managers.

During William O. Douglas's days as commissioner, the SEC proposed the Investment Company Act and formulated rules limiting joint action. Douglas's statements show a displeasure with Wall Street, which corresponds to our populist principle, and with bankers controlling managers, which corresponds to our managerial interest group story. He surely wanted to destroy Wall Street control of Main Street, saying in 1937, as I've noted before, that investment bankers would be "restricted to underwriting or selling" and stripped of "the financial power [they had] exercised in the past over [industrial policy]." The power of Wall Street must be held at bay: "Finance moves into the zone of exploitation whenever it becomes the master rather than the faithful and loyal servant of investors and business. To make finance such a servant rather than a master becomes a central plank in any platform for reform."

Members of Congress applauded calls to limit the power of bankers, who, members said, were responsible for many great industrial failures. Bank directors who lived "remote from the properties operated have no understanding of the industry they direct. Congress must make it unlawful for any person to act as a director who shall also be an investment banking partner.

Survivorship

Even if managers were not crucial to passage of the legislation, one can still see a managerial interest group picture, although a dimly lit one. If the rule had seriously impinged on managers' authority, they would have objected, and the evidence suggests that they could have killed it; a rule threatening management would have been unstable, challenged, and probably reversed.

Contrast the fifty-year persistence of fragmentation in the 1936 Revenue Act which has been watered down only once, in 1942 with the tax on accumulated corporate income in that same tax act. A firm was taxed, at up to 27 percent of undistributed income, if it failed to distribute its income to its shareholders. That tax made managers more dependent on capital markets than they had been in its absence, because the tax pushed them to distribute all profits, forcing growing firms to go back to capital markets to get back these funds. When the firms went to the capital markets, bankers and securities buyers would scrutinize the managers' results, and penalize them (via higher capital costs) if the results were poor. Firms whose prospects for profit suggested contraction would find it harder to raise funds than to retain earnings. During the Depression, many firms merited contraction; once they dividend out their funds, they would have to shrink. Managers would unhappily find themselves controlling a smaller enterprise.

While this view of capital markets and managers has a modern ring, it was intuitively understood during the 1930s. A representative of management said during the 1936 hearings that the undistributed profits tax will cause conflict "between those engaged in the management of a business and those who are purely investors." Berle and Means recognized and advocated finding ways to subject managers to the capital markets:

> Only one general protection beside the power of active revolt remains to guarantee a measure of equitable treatment to the several classes of security holders. The enterprise may need new capital. The management must, therefore, maintain a situation in which additional capital is forthcoming. This need for new capital sets a very definite

limit on the extent to which those in control can abuse the suppliers of capital.

Rexford Tugwell, the Roosevelt administration's principal proponent of an undistributed profits tax, and at times an academic and administrative colleague of Berle, offered managerial discipline as a rationale. Although his principal goal was to reduce excessive corporate savings, a reduction he thought would increase consumer spending, he and others in the administration also thought the tax "would give the stockholders more influence in the formulation of corporation dividend and corporation saving policies."

"Few taxes," one analyst has written, "have evoked such a storm of passionate and partisan controversy. Spokesmen for corporations objected strenuously on the ground that the tax made for economic instability [and] interfered with corporate policies." In 1938, the Chamber of Commerce, the National Association of Manufacturers, the American Mining Congress, and the New York Board of Trade all opposed the tax. First they got Congress to cut its rate. The next year they got Congress to repeal it. The corporate tax would no longer be affected by managers' decisions on how much of the profit to pay out to shareholders; managers could retain earnings, freeing themselves from the discipline of the capital markets.

The survivorship argument should now be clear. Proposals can originate in the Treasury Department without any interest group pressure, based on what the Treasury thinks would be best for the country. But to survive, a proposal must not gore the ox of a powerful interest group. The tax on undistributed profits threatened managers; within a few years the tax was dead. The Treasury's simultaneous proposal to tax mutual funds with only fragmented portfolios did not incur the ire of managers; it survived.

Managers were not the moving force behind the mutual fund tax bill in the same way that they were the moving force behind some modern antitakeover legislation. This story suggests that managers might have killed mutual fund fragmentation if it threatened them. They did nothing about it either because they liked it or because they were indifferent to it. Since mutual funds were small players in the 1930s, managers may have cared little about the structure of mutual fund portfolios back then.

Current Prospects

Mutual funds may yet emerge as viable corporate governance players. In the early 1990s, Vanguard, one of the biggest mutual fund complexes, found itself with enough stock in Chrysler that the senior manager of its stock portfolio, John Neff, became interested in the succession and retirement of Lee Iacocca. Indeed, Neff led an unusually active mutual fund complex, "shipping a set of two-sentence 'pointed but not hostile' faxes to the Chrysler directors, who were gathering for a special meeting." Unlike most big stockholders of a public firm, neither Vanguard nor Neff went into the Chrysler boardroom, perhaps because of some of the considerations outlined here. They spoke through a fax machine, not from a boardroom seat.

For our purposes, investment companies can be seen as coming in two main varieties: the open-end mutual fund, which stands ready to turn its shares into cash overnight; and the closed-end investment company, which never redeems its shares. The two types have different business characteristics that bear on how well each can act in corporate governance.

The open-end mutual fund has liquidity problems, which will deter it from active involvement in corporate governance. Big blocks are illiquid, but if the fund must be ready to redeem overnight it cannot afford to be illiquid.

Law compounds this problem, because for an open-end mutual fund to raise cash if it is hit with heavy redemptions, it must sell some of its portfolio of investments. But section

16(b) of the Securities Exchange Act of 1934 requires that a shareholder with 10 percent or more of stock or any director must return any short-swing profits even if the trading was done without inside information. Stockholders that buy a big block and hold it will not find this rule more than a nuisance. But mutual funds, which must trade, will find section 16(b) a serious impediment, putting lots of big blocks out of the question.

The rule, which applies to a company's 10 percent–plus shareholders and to its directors, tends to keep a mutual fund from sending one of its people in to be a director of a portfolio firm; the rule also frays the fund's potential ties with other directors. If a court sees a portfolio firm's director as having been "deputized" by the mutual fund, then the fund's trading could be subject to 16(b) limitations, even if the fund never had inside information and never itself owned more than 10 percent of the firm's stock. Thus while the 1940 Act restricts each fund's portfolio, it does not directly restrict a group of affiliated mutual funds run by the same firm from taking stock positions that aggregate to a big, influential block. One fund might take 5 percent, a second one might take another 5 percent, and a third another 5 percent. But I understand that some mutual fund complexes have restricted themselves from taking a cumulative block of 10 percent, fearing that regulators might treat the stock in their different funds as a single block.

When Peter Lynch, the star manager of Fidelity's Magellan fund, joined the board of W. R. Grace in the early 1990s (just before he retired from Magellan), Magellan sold its Grace stock. Fidelity's general counsel said: "We do not [think] that institutional investors should be represented on boards. It causes a lot of legal problems."

Open-end funds must be liquid; regulations require that 85 percent of the fund's assets be liquid, a ratio most might approach anyway without the rule. The combination of 16(b) liability with a block of 10 percent or more or with a deputized director would render the influential portion of the portfolio illiquid, because then the only way to avoid 16(b) liability would be to avoid trading. But mutual funds must be ready to redeem out their investors quickly, and their resulting need for liquidity precludes carrying many big, difficult-to-sell blocks.

Keep in mind that section 16(b) would hit funds even if they did not trade on inside information; it applies if the big investor or the investor with a boardroom deputy trades in a short period. More general insider trading laws would deter some mutual funds; I do not analyze this problem here, because these rules against true insider trading are sound. Big blockholders should not be able to dump their stock when they learn of negative information. Indeed one might argue that in return for being permitted to take big blocks, the new big blockholders might be required to make even greater commitments to a long-term relationship than laws now require.

The closed-end fund does not have the liquidity problem that open-end funds have; indeed, there is at least one nation where closed-end funds are involved in corporate governance. In Sweden, where the portfolio rules do not bind as tightly as do the subchapter M and 1940 Act rules, a noticeable governance institution is the closed-end fund with big blocks of stock and boardroom influence. But they would have a different structural problem here in the United States, because they do not discipline fund managers as well as the open-end funds do. The nature of a closed-end fund is that the shareholders cannot redeem their shares and move their assets out easily. Persistent discounts the American closed-end fund's shares often sell for less than the value of the fund's assets in their share price also make the structure unpopular here.

Current U.S. regulation forces an extreme trade-off for investors, a tradeoff that makes "big-block" funds cumbersome. Either the investor must buy a liquid open-end fund or the investor must buy a closed-end fund. Liquid open-end funds that redeem overnight provide excellent discipline to mutual fund managers: if the fund managers err badly, they will find themselves managing funds with no assets, because investors can cash out overnight. But liquidity needs mean the fund cannot take big blocks easily. Closed-end funds do not stand ready to redeem overnight, but they provide poor discipline to their managers and have been unpopular. The statute and the rules do not contemplate hybrids.

Business entails trade-offs, trade-offs that the American rules here do not yet allow. An investor cannot yet buy a fund that takes big illiquid blocks with the investor allowed to redeem on only, say, three months' advance notice. Such vehicles would be particularly useful for retirement money, for which the investor has a long horizon, not expecting to withdraw it for decades.

Even though neither fund managers nor corporate managers were critical in getting the 1940 Act and the related tax rules passed, incumbent institutions might in the 1990s oppose even permission to change. They understand the current financial world in which they have succeeded, and often see no reason to change it. People's sense of the right way to do things is often shaped by the way things have usually been done in their lifetime. The general counsel to the largest American mutual fund complex recently examined the possibility of big-block mutual funds and concluded that "to implement their ideas on a broad scale, [those seeking big blocks] would have to persuade Congress to relax the current limits on institutional investors substantially." But although institutions and managers would then remain free to reject the big blocks if they found them inefficient, the mutual fund counsel predicted that "corporate executives would undoubtedly oppose such a relaxation as a threat to management control, *and they would find allies in most institutional investors*," whom he said are repelled by a German or Japanese model.

Summary

Just when Berle and Means were announcing the emergence of the public corporation with uncontrolled managers at the helm, Congress raised the cost of mutual fund influence. The restrictions in the 1936 tax code and the 1940 Act make it impossible to deploy a majority of the fund's portfolio in control blocks. The 1940 Act raised the cost of control even with the unregulated portion of the portfolio, but for genuinely public-regarding reasons. Still, the rules may cut wide, because stymieing any and all influence was then seen as valuable, not as a cost.

Each rule is a cost to big blockholding, not a complete show-stopper. But their sum is considerable, and can tip open-end mutual funds, which are not financially well-suited to take big long-term blocks anyway, into passivity. To avoid the corporate tax, an activist fund must build an odd portfolio. It could divide the portfolio in half, with one half in two firms and the other half in ten. None of the ten could have more than 10 percent of a portfolio firm's stock. And the two 25 percent blocks (if they yield 20 percent of the portfolio firms' stock) could not be in the same industry, or even in related industries. Even if a mutual fund used the most concentrated portfolio it could, it would usually have had to form alliances with other investors to be effective, especially because until recently equity mutual funds have been small. Those alliances are hard to bring off in any case, and the securities laws have historically discouraged them.

The fund could avoid these rules by holding very big blocks and then accept taxation that is high enough to wipe out the private gains from activity. And mutual funds, which must redeem stock regularly, cannot take too many illiquid big blocks; short-swing trading rules stymie funds from trading in big blocks, inducing greater illiquidity. And putting a director onto the portfolio firm board, or owning 10 percent of the portfolio firm also triggers 16(b), requiring disgorgement of any trading gains and embarrassing a financial business that needs to cultivate probity and avoid headlines of violations of even "technical" SEC rules.

And then there are the transactional rules, which prohibit joint transactions with affiliates (which two 5 percent owners of a portfolio firm would be), and prohibit (unless they got a SEC exemption) transactions with the portfolio firm. Intended to deal with transactions that hurt minority shareholders or fund beneficiaries, the rules also stymie innocuous financings and recapitalizations. The blanket SEC exemptions help, but may not work well when the mutual fund has a director in the boardroom.

Elements of a basic public choice story of interest groups buying favorable laws are present. And elements of a basic public-oriented, good regulation story are also present. But the interest group scenario did not drive the legislation, and some of the good regulation goals could have been accomplished through other means. Rather, the ideology of fragmentation seems paramount in tipping the balance. Key actors FDR and Douglas— thought that Wall Street control of industry was bad. The interest group story lies less in visible lobbying than in the appeals some political players made, sometimes favoring managers over bankers, and in the survival properties of the fragmenting legislation. Simultaneous with passage of the fragmenting tax legislation, Congress passed an undistributed profits tax, which threatened managerial independence. That tax was unstable, challenged, and eventually repealed.

Rather than an interest group story, we should think of the politics of mutual funds in the 1930s as creating mutual funds. Without tax exemption, the funds could not readily prosper. Politicians allowed tax exemption consistent with their conception of what a mutual fund should be and should not be. It should not control industry; it should not have concentrated investments; it should not be entangled in financial alliances that could create conflicts of interest. Politicians created a framework for mutual funds to grow, a framework that made it difficult or impossible for mutual funds to actively enter the governance structure of their portfolio firms.

6

Problem of Short Term Finance for Financial Institutions

Introduction

Managers complain that the short-term bias of a stock market of furious traders makes it hard for managers to concentrate on the long term. Hence, managers must spurn the long term and under invest in building up their organizations and their employees. While this sounds true to many, it has theoretical problems. Even furiously trading shareholders include buyers as well as sellers. Buyers are interested in what price they will get for their stock when they sell it. So, today's buyer is interested in what tomorrow's buyer will pay, who is interested in what the next day's buyer will pay, and so on. Since each buyer is dependent on the price to be garnered in some distant long run, each buyer is interested in the long run price, even if he or she will not be the long-run owner. There must be something more complex to support the short-term argument than furious trading alone.

And there is one, at least in theory, tied to fragmented ownership. Information does not always flow cost lessly and accurately from inside the firm to the firm's stockholders. When information is complex, proprietary, or "soft" (i.e., difficult to quantify), the insiders in the firm can understand it, yet be unable to explain it to the outsiders. Stockholders with small holdings cannot spend much in understanding complex, technological information, so they might ignore it. And managers with good but proprietary information would not want to reveal it to the stock market, and consequently to competitors, so the stock market never gets it.

That is, what if there are economies of scale in getting the information and judgment needed to accurately assess a firm's long-term outlook, because accuracy requires staff, expertise, and time spent inside the boardroom? If so, a large holding might be needed to spread the information costs.

Moreover, what if analytic evaluation required personal evaluation, from confidential conversations in the boardroom? Large blocks of stock would facilitate the flow of soft, technological information from the firm to the large block holder. If securities analysts sometimes undervalue long term research and development when they cannot understand it, then so might managers. "Soft" information about the quality of middle management may be available to those who sit regularly in the boardroom, but be hard for a distant stockholder to detect. If securities analysts undervalue long-term investments in the firm's employees' skills human capital because they cannot tell whether they are profitable or just a program to make managers feel good, then managers might avoid such human investments.

Consider how hard it is to convey soft long-term information to a distant market; dispersed investors cannot cheaply distinguish egoistic empire building from a high net present value project, a wasteful training program from valuable investments in employees' skills. And managers are wary of revealing proprietary information to many short-term shareholders; without good information, even highly paid, technically competent analysts cannot evaluate the long-term R & D policies. In contrast, financial analysts with generic skills can easily evaluate short-term financial data.

Managers might not get "credit" (salary raises in the last few years of their career, short-term stock options, etc.) if they improve the firm in ways that stockholders cannot see. Unable to get "credit," managers may forsake investments whose evaluation requires complex, proprietary, or "soft" information, and then they might blame the stock market and seek to insulate themselves from it. In theory, concentrated ownership structures could improve the flow of information from inside the firm to large shareholders, thus helping to deter such short-term possibilities. Size would give the stockholder an economy of scale over which to spread the costs of time and personnel in acquiring and evaluating complex information. Size and boardroom presence would give the stockholder a reason to keep proprietary information secret; it would be hurting its own large stock position to let the secrets out. The large shareholder would protect secrets and protect managers from outsiders who would second-guess truly profitable long-run investments. And some evaluations of technical, complex, long-term information need constant private interaction, in which a motivated board of stable stockholders asks for predictions and sees how they play out over years. Distant shareholders with small blocks cannot readily be part of that kind of an ongoing evaluation.

True, these informational problems challenge faith in the informational efficiency of American securities markets; the claim that these problems exist thus far lacks a strong empirical backup. But in theory the stock market could efficiently evaluate information already in the public domain, but be unable to accurately process soft, technological, and proprietary information not out there in public markets. Long-term investments could be especially susceptible to this problem, requiring inside evaluation of technological and proprietary information to allow the investor to form a good opinion of the payoff. If the investor is unable either to form a solid opinion or to diversify the risk, then the investor will need a higher return; a higher return will bias investors and managers toward shorter-term projects that outsiders can evaluate better (if only because they already show some returns and those returns will not change much during the remaining life of the project) than the informationally deficient long-term projects (over whose life returns might change a great deal). A financial system's lack of big block holders on the inside of those major firms susceptible to this problem could in theory be a reason for the short-term horizons said to afflict financial institutions and industrial managers.

I suggested this potential benefit of big blocks several years ago, and others have made similar and stronger analyses. But it is unproven, perhaps because current econometric techniques do not easily measure these problems. The potential, albeit unproven, benefits of concentrated ownership here is in reducing theoretical defects of the institutions, not of the managers.

Political Benefits of the Issue

Short-termism was a debater's weapon in the 1980s. Short-sighted financiers propelled takeovers, it was said, often by defenders of managers, compelling managers to manage for the short term; some managers' policy program was to stop takeovers, and they used the rhetoric (perhaps quite sincerely) of short-termism: for managers to manage for the long-term, they had to be free from takeover pressures, as, they said, were managers in German and Japanese industry. Major academic projects then sought to inquire into the causes of a short-term bias.

The antitakeover claim, and it is a plausible one, but only in some special settings, went that managers really knew that (1) the firm was best managed independently, and (2) projects in the pipeline had a high payoff that the market did not recognize and that managers, for proprietary reasons, could not disclose. A bidder, who might have known about the high value projects but not understood that the firm could be best run independently, would bid for the company, putting managers in a quandary about how to react. Their disclosure of the confidential information would not raise the price of the company's stock, because the effects would offset each other, disclosure would raise the price because the projects would be seen to be stellar, and lower it when analysts realized that competitors would now also take these projects on. Unable to defend against takeovers in such settings, managers might ditch these kinds of long-term projects.

Although the evidence, weak though it may be, is that the German and Japanese boardrooms are as sensitive to stock price and earnings movements as U.S. boardrooms, stopping short-termism as the rhetorical cover for reconstructing financial institutions has rhetorical, political advantages. Managers want to stop it; politicians do, too. Were reformers to rely on the rhetoric of managerial accountability, that rhetoric would induce opposition; the rhetoric of industrial hybrids would be too complex in a political debate. But the rhetoric of anti–short termism, like the rhetoric of patriotism, is simple and widely supported.

Improving Loan Markets

Concentrated stock ownership can improve financial markets by other means. Lenders may buy stock in their debtors to help protect their loans and provide a secondary information channel to support their loans. Lenders know that a crisis could arise and want to be able to influence the firm; stock may work more quickly than loan covenants and bankruptcy. Borrowers may also prefer that lenders own stock to reduce lender opportunism: First, a lender's threat not to roll over a short-term loan unless the debtor grants concessions is less credible when carrying out the threat would reduce the value of the stock the lender holds. Second, because lenders want loan repayment, and are less concerned with maximizing firm value, they tend to induce firms toward conservative strategies. When they also hold stock, they should tend to want "sensible" risk-taking, not unmitigated conservatism.

Similarly, when creditors also have large stock positions, workouts and recapitalizations to avoid a complicated and costly bankruptcy proceeding are probably easier. The lenders have multiple information channels, and in the right configurations, lender-debtor conflict is reduced if the lenders have stock positions, because they can "internalize" the conflict.

Monitoring by Multiple Intermediaries

"Improving" information has a dark role as well. Insider trading the trading of stock when the trader has special information helps to explain why German banks buy stock, or at least what happens once they own it, because without insider-trading laws, bank officers can and do trade on inside information from firms. Moreover, the influence from stock may yield mutual self-protection: The stockholding lender may induce the portfolio firm to borrow on terms unfavorable to the firm; in return the bankers promise to protect management from ouster.

One would have to measure whether these costs outweigh any benefits of enhancing accountability and deterring short-run finance. Since we have no such measurements now, we cannot know whether change will be good. But there are theoretical reasons why concentrated stockholding, if properly constructed, would not be highly risky. The easiest image of concentration is the concentration produced by a single large block holder, but the better structure may well be that produced by multiple intermediaries, who can deter opportunism by monitoring one another, impel action in a way that a single block holder might not, and facilitate power-sharing, not domination.

Multiple Blocks Checking One Another

Multiple intermediaries give managers the power to form a counter coalition against the opportunistic intermediary that is looking for side payments. A true managerial crisis inside the firm, however, should unite the stockholders all will want to end the crisis but the opportunist may have trouble acting alone, because it lacks enough stock to do so. True, a financial cartel might try to exploit the firm, but it would face several problems: because the members would have different financial interests (public pension plans would not try to exploit companies in the same way that insurance companies might), they would face bargaining problems in coming up with a common plan, they would attract legal attention, and if such financial cartels became common, they would attract political attention as well.

For this reason, some debate in the United States about public pension funds misses the mark. Critics of enhanced institutional voice argue that the most active institutions, public pension funds, have conflicts that will disable them in corporate governance. They will have a politicized agenda asking firms to invest in the pension fund's home state or to adopt social investing norms before there is a political consensus that will diminish the value of the firm. While these critics have identified a factor, they have not identified an important one, because they have not tied the debilities of public pension funds to ownership structure. Public pension funds now only own 10 percent of the American stock market. Generally a single public plan does not own a big block in a single portfolio company. They cannot themselves control a firm's actions even if they were to act in concert, because 10 percent is not enough; they must form a coalition with other investors, or at least be sure that a counter coalition will not form. Thus were a public pension fund to insist that a firm build unprofitable factories in the fund's home state, managers would have no trouble assembling a counter coalition. Since public pension funds would know that such a counter coalition could form, they would not often try to force decisions detrimental to the firm. Rather, they would usually have to seek corporate governance actions that appealed to a majority of all shareholders.

The more serious risk is not that the public pension funds will seek politicized decisions, but that managers can create conflicts to quiet them. That is, private pension funds will not lead, but they will sometimes follow if the public pension funds identify a serious firm malady. Incumbent managers may try to neutralize the activist public pension fund with a side payment, such as an extra factory in the home state (or a threat to close down the one already there), or by direct political attacks on the pension plan. Given today's ownership structure, the risk is more that managers could use home-state investments to neutralize useful governance forays than that public pension plans could alone foist a social action agenda on corporate America.

Multiple Blocks Impelling Action

Why don't American financial intermediaries, some of which can own some stock, go to the law's limits in stockholding? Isolated blocks, even big ones with 5 percent of the portfolio firm, are precarious because management may isolate, outmaneuver, and destroy them, as essentially happened when H. Ross Perot assembled a 6 percent block in GM and then became vocal in his criticism. (Perot's personality and maneuvering over the price of GM's buyout of Perot's stock were also factors.) In the United States a single 5 percent block does emerge here and there, but managers still have the upper hand in times of conflict. Even a half-dozen institutions with 5 percent blocks would have to coordinate their activities, which U.S. securities regulation has tended to deter. Thus, some "unleashed" American institutions should rationally refuse to hold the maximum permitted by American law because they know that in times of crisis they will need a critical mass of other large blockholders, a critical mass they lack.

This also shows some of the weaknesses in the German and Japanese ownership structures. The German banks' big voting blocks usually come from brokerage stock, for which the banks are unlikely to make heroic efforts in monitoring managers at the underlying firm. Each Japanese bank owns no more than 5 percent of an industrial firm's stock, a position that would be too weak to wrest control from managers in the United States. A German bank's typical directly owned position, while often larger than 5 percent, is usually alone still too small to yield control; only with brokerage stock or alliances with other stockholders can the bank get control. The German bank's motivation for involvement may come from the bank's directly owned stock; its means may require the brokerage stock. Directly owned stock gives the institutional owner a financial incentive to act; ancillary, backup stock bulks up voting power and provides the means. But as pressures, political and otherwise, mount on the German banks to unload their directly owned stock, the system may weaken further. For example, if political pressure on German banks leads them to reduce their amount of directly held stock while retaining their brokerage stock, they may face reduced incentives to act responsibly.

Multiple blocks may induce intermediaries to act in a way that a single isolated blockholder might not. The multiple blocks may solve the weakness problem without creating a dominating block that recentralizes authority in a dominating intermediary. Because the intermediaries have differing private agendas, a coalition for side payments may be difficult to maintain, but a weak firm could induce a coalition among a handful of powerful intermediaries.

Once again, we have theoretical, unproven benefits. Managers may not be the problem; institutions and their possible short-term propensities might be. With small blocks, far from the boardroom, the institutions might be unable to process complex, proprietary, and soft information.

Managers, knowing they will get little "credit" for projects with these informational problems, under invest, and American industry suffers. Multiple, powerful but not dominating, intermediaries might mitigate both the problem of institutional opportunism and the possible problem of short-term horizons.

7

Risk Aversion and Insurance in Company Financing

Introduction

We will see under what circumstances an individual trader might increase her positions in the market, be indifferent to her position, or wish to reduce certain risk exposures by purchasing insurance or hedging.

These issues may seem a bit abstract and far-removed from the subject of corporate risk management, but, in fact, most models of corporate hedging and risk management borrow liberally from this benchmark case of individual risk management. This jump from individual behavior to corporate behavior often produces models that fall flat empirically and are of little or no use strategically.

Risk Aversion and Utility Theory

In modern microeconomic theory, individuals are presumed to have a *utility function* that associates wealth or consumption with individuals' degrees of happiness.

Although the functional form of this utility function that all individuals are presumed to have is not always specified, most economists agree that it should exhibit several important characteristics for most individuals. The first behavioral feature of a normal utility function is that people prefer more to less. If utility is defined using consumption, more consumption is better than less. You can always give away or burn the excess, after all.

The second, related behavioral axiom is called nonsatiation. That simply means that people never reach a point where they have enough. More is always better than less. This makes some sense intuitively, because at a minimum it simply means that people derive some happiness from giving away what they themselves do not want or need.

A third important characteristic of the neoclassical utility function is called *diminishing marginal utility*. Although more is preferred to less, people tend to prefer more to less at a decreasing rate. So, the first steak consumed is better than the thousandth steak consumed in a year. Moving from a total wealth of $100,000 to $200,000 is more satisfying than moving from a net worth of $100,000,000 to $100,100,000, and so on.

If a typical individual's utility function is denoted *U (W)* where *W* is wealth (or consumption opportunities), then the nonsatiation and diminishing marginal utility behavioral axioms can be expressed mathematically:

$$U(W) > 0 \quad \forall W$$
$$U_W(W) > 0 \quad \forall W$$
$$U_{WW}(W) < 0 \quad \forall W$$

where the upside down A symbol, means "for all" and where subscripts denote partial derivatives—$U_W(W) = U/W$ and $U_{WW}(W) = U2/W2$. The first line represents the first assumption. It says that people get more units of happiness when they get more wealth, and that is true for all possible levels of wealth. The second relation (i.e., the first derivative is positive) means that for all levels of wealth people always prefer more to less. Finally, the second derivative of the utility function is negative, which means that people prefer more to less at a decreasing rate. In mathematical terms, this function is said to be concave. Economists also like to add some other technical restrictions to this utility function, like continuity and continuous differentiability, which merely guarantee that the above equations exist and are defined at all levels of wealth.

Figure 7.1 depicts a typical utility function. The *y*-axis reveals the units of happiness associated with the corresponding level of wealth. Note that the function never doubles back on itself, so all levels of wealth are associated with a *unique* level of utility. A wealth of $X is associated with *U (X)* units of happiness.

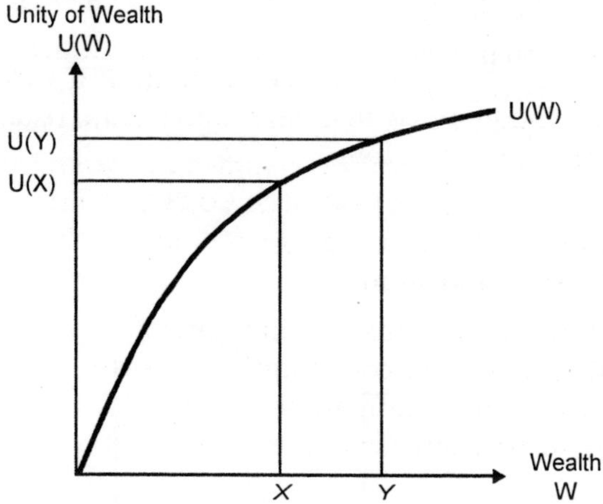

Fig. 7.1. A typical utility function.

Notice how the mathematical and economic properties of the utility function appear graphically. The assumption that more is better than less is reflected by the fact that the value of the utility function is positive for all positive levels of wealth and is increasing in wealth—if $Y > X$, then $U(Y) > U(X)$. The second assumption of nonsatiation is reflected by the fact that the line has a positive slope everywhere. For a small increase in wealth, the marginal utility gained is always positive, no matter what the level of wealth. Finally, the concave shape of the graph means that the slope of the line tangent to the function declines as the level of wealth gets higher. In other words, the marginal utility of an additional unit of wealth declines as the person gets wealthier.

Risk Aversion

The shape of a utility function dictates the degree to which an individual is risk-averse, risk-neutral, or risk-loving. Suppose the lottery ticket will award the individual \$0 or \$1,000,000 with equal probabilities. These payoffs and probabilities are known by all and are not in dispute, and the bet is fair so the price of the ticket is \$500,000—1/2 (\$0) + 1/2 (\$1,000,000).

Figure 7.2 shows the utility function of a risk-neutral individual. The increase in utility is the same regardless of how wealthy the individual.

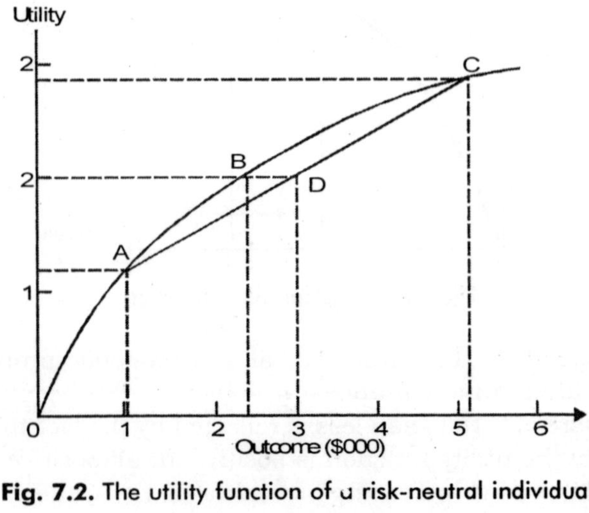

Fig. 7.2. The utility function of u risk-neutral individual.

In other words, this individual has a constant marginal utility of wealth. To determine whether or not the individual will buy the lottery ticket at the $500,000 price, a comparison must be drawn of the individual's utility of losing $500,000 for sure (i.e., paying for the ticket) with the individual's gaining $1,000,000 half the time and gaining nothing the other half. This comparison is thus a comparison of the utility of wealth of $500,000 with the expected utility of wealth, or the probability weighted utility of nothing and $1 million:

$$E[U(W)] = \tfrac{1}{2}U(\$0) + \tfrac{1}{2}U(\$1{,}000{,}000)$$

The comparison is shown graphically in Figure 7.2. The utility of $500,000 for sure is denoted *U*($500,000). Graphically, the way to find the point in the middle of two other points on a function is to run a straight line between those two points and then bisect the line. The bisection of the line corresponds to the equal-weighted average of the two endpoints. In this example, the utility function *is itself* a straight line, which tells us immediately that

$$U(\$5{,}00{,}000) = E[U(W)] = \tfrac{1}{2}U(\$0) + \tfrac{1}{2}U(\$1{,}000{,}000)$$

So, the loss of the utility of $500,000 in buying the lottery ticket is exactly the same as the gain in expected utility associated with an even chance of winning $1 million or nothing.

In general terms, a risk-neutral individual will be indifferent to taking a fair bet. The loss of utility paid for the fairly priced bet will always offset the expected utility gain from the lottery itself.

Figure 7.3 shows the contrasting situation of a risk-averse individual, whose utility function is concave rather than linear. In this case, the utility foregone from the lottery ticket purchase is *U*($500,000). Applying the same method as in the risk-neutral case, the expected utility of the lottery can be found by running a line between the two equally likely lottery outcomes, *U*($0) and *U*($1,000,000). Because the end points are equally likely to occur, the bisection of that line represents the expected utility of the lottery.

Unlike the case of the risk-neutral investor, the line connecting *U*($0) and *U*($1,000,000) in Figure 7.3 is no longer the same as the utility function *U (W)* itself. This time, the line is *below* the utility function. Consequently, E[*U (W)*] is *less* than *U (W)* for a *W* equal to $500,000. In other words, the utility of $500,000 *for sure* is higher than the utility of the *possibility* of $1 million or nothing, even though the expected value of the lottery is $500,000. Because the utility function is concave, the individual will reject a fair bet.

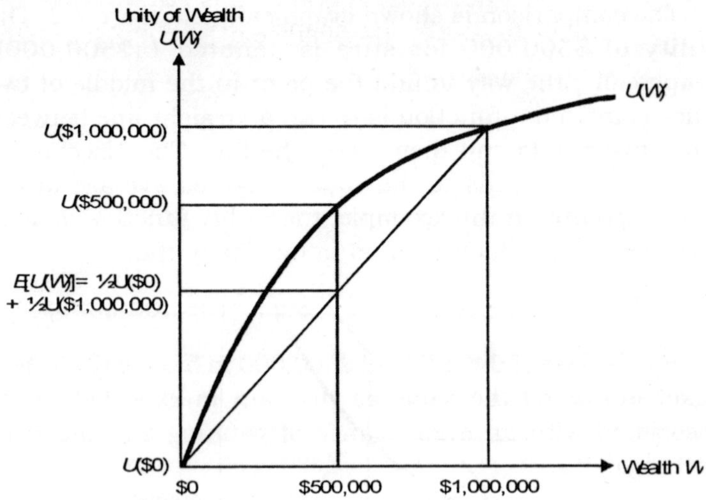

Fig. 7.3. The utility function of a risk-averse individual.

Now consider the final possibility, shown in Figure 7.4, that the individual is risk-loving. In this case, the individual's utility function has two of the same properties as the risk-neutral and risk-averse individuals more is still preferred to less, and the individual is still never satiated. The risk loving individual, however, has increasing marginal utility of wealth, so that the individual is happier for an incremental increase in wealth when she is already very wealthy than when she is poor. Mathematically, this means that the slope of the function *U (W)* is increasing over *W*. The function is convex, so that $U_W > 0$ and now also $U_{WW} > 0$.

As in Figure 7.2 and Figure 7.3, the utility of $500,000 with certainty is indicated as *U*($500,000). To determine whether or not the individual will pay that price for a fair bet with equal odds at $0 and $1,000,000, a straight line is again drawn between these two extremes and bisected. The point on the *y*-axis corresponding to this bisection point is the expected utility of the lottery ticket. In this case, *E*[*U (W)*] is *above* *U*($500,000). Not only will the individual buy the lottery ticket, but she will think it's a great deal. The utility foregone from the $500,000 paid is significantly less than the utility gained by the chance at winning a million.

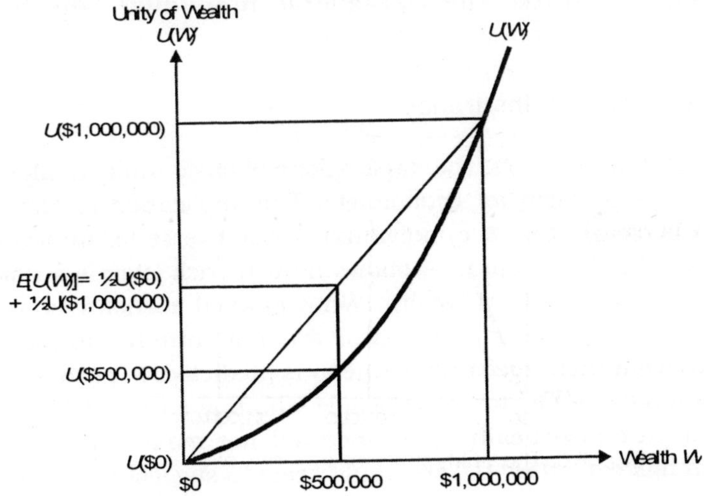

Fig. 7.4. The utility function of a risk-loving individual.

The critical distinction between the three cases lies in the dependency of the individual's marginal utility on her level of wealth. The risk-neutral individual has a constant marginal utility. The units of happiness derived from one more dollar or one more steak do not depend on the number of dollars or steaks she has. For a risk-averse individual, the satisfaction derived from more wealth or consumption declines as the level of wealth or consumption rises. The thousandth steak is still good and still makes the person happier than when she had only 999 steaks, but the jump from 999 steaks to 1,000 steaks yields less incremental happiness than the jump from 0 steaks to 1. Conversely, the risk-loving individual experiences a greater increase in happiness moving from 999 steaks to 1,000 than from 0 to 1.

These differences in marginal utility go a long way toward explaining individual behavior toward risk. Because the risk-averse individual has diminishing marginal utility of wealth, the chance at a big victory is not worth taking the risk of a big loss. Conversely, a risk lover will happily put her whole net worth at risk in order to chance a big win because, unlike the risk-averse individual, she has increasing marginal utility.

Gambling and Insurance

For many years, the implications of basic utility analysis posed a problem for economists. The implication of Figure 7.3 is clearly that the individual is risk-averse for all levels of wealth, and Figure 7.4 shows that the risk lover is a risk-taker at all levels of wealth. What puzzled economists was that people's observed behavior was not entirely consistent with what these nice utility functions predicted. In particular, the tendency for the same people who buy lottery tickets to also purchase health insurance did not make sense. The purchase of lottery tickets would seem to suggest risk-loving behavior, whereas the purchase of insurance implies clear risk aversion a willingness to pay some amount for certain in order to avoid the risk of a massive decline in wealth.

Friedman and Savage proposed a solution to this seeming paradox the now-famous *S-shaped utility function* shown in Figure 7.5. Over low levels of wealth denoted as the range from 0 to *B* on the figure the utility function is concave and demonstrates diminishing marginal utility.

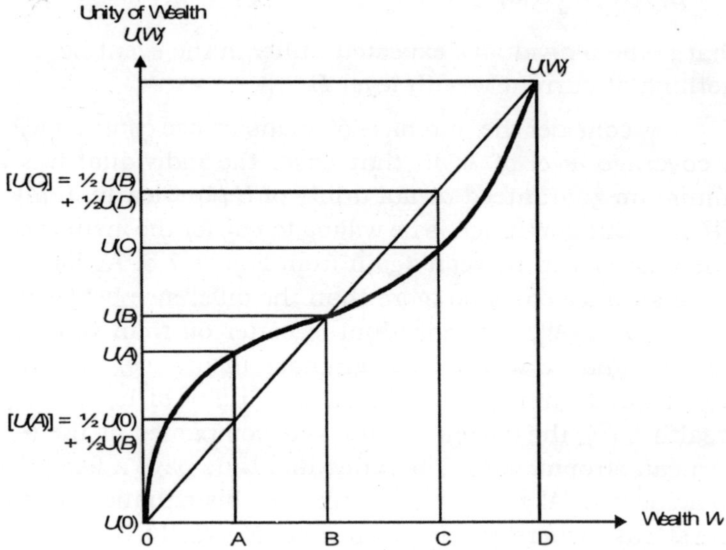

Fig. 7.5. The utility function of someone who both gambles and insures.

But for levels of wealth above *B*, the utility function reverses its shape and becomes convex, thus suggesting increasing marginal utility for levels of wealth above *B*. In other words, this individual is risk-averse at levels of wealth below *B* and risk-loving at levels of wealth above *B*.

Consider a person described by the utility function in Figure 7.5 with a current wealth of *B*. He faces some risk that a tragedy will occur that causes him to lose all of his money, and this tragedy will occur with probability one-half. An insurer approaches him and says he is willing to provide coverage for the individual so that his wealth is guaranteed not to fall below $*A*.

Without insurance, the individual's utility is described by the expected utility that he keeps his wealth $*B* half the time and that his wealth declines to $0 the other half of the time. This expected utility corresponds to the bisection of the line drawn between *U*(0) and *U* (*B*) on the graph, and the utility at this point is equal to

$$E[U(A)] = \tfrac{1}{2}U(0) + \tfrac{1}{2}U(B)$$

that is the individual's expected utility in the event he does nothing at current wealth level *B*.

Now consider the purchase of an insurance contract with a coverage level of *A*. In that case, the individual has a minimum guaranteed *actual* utility of *U (A)*. Clearly, *U (A)* > *E*[*U (A)*]. But how much is he willing to *pay* for the insurance? The answer can be seen again from Figure 7.5. As long as the insurance costs no more than the difference between *U (A)* and *E*[*U (A)*], the individual is better off than when he started, and he will indeed purchase insurance. Although the insured level *U (A)* is below the utility of his current wealth *U (B)*, the current wealth is accompanied by the risk of a catastrophic loss. The individual thus pays a fair price to achieve *U (A)* and actually improves his situation. In the worst case where the insurance costs exactly *U (A)* – *E*[*U (A)*], he is neither any better nor any worse off, but he has eliminated the stress of worrying about a loss. This is consistent with risk-averse behavior.

Now suppose the same individual is offered a lottery ticket. Half the time the ticket pays nothing, but half the time the ticket will pay *D* - *B* dollars, thus increasing his wealth from current level *B* to new level *D*. If the lottery ticket is fairly priced at $^1/2$ (*D* - *B*) = *C* - *B*, he will buy the ticket. Unlike the part of his utility function that exhibits diminishing marginal utility below wealth level *B*, he is now considering something that puts him in the part of his utility function where the marginal utility of wealth is increasing. He thus pays a fair price for a lottery ticket that has an expected utility of *E*[*U (C)*].

Utility Theory and Investments

Things that can cause a decreased utility are really what we mean by risk. The explicit link between changes in investor utility and probability theory can be seen if an investor who maximizes his expected utility of wealth with a utility function $U(W)$ is considered.

The investor's utility of wealth can be written as a function of the statistical properties of the random wealth variable using a Taylor series expansion around his utility of *expected* wealth:

$$U(W) = U[E(W)] + U_W[W - E(W)] + \tfrac{1}{2}U_{WW}[W - E(W)]^2 +$$
$$\tfrac{1}{3}U_{WWW}[W - E(W)]^2 + R$$

where R is a remainder term that reflects the fact that the expression could have been expanded further.

With wealth as a random variable, the individual in question maximizes his *expected* utility of wealth. This is slightly different than the utility of *expected wealth* shown in Equation 7.1. Expected wealth is the expected value of wealth given that it is subject to risk and random outcomes. Expected utility is the expected value of utility in the future, which is in turn dependent on expected wealth. But as it is now, Equation 7.1 for *actual* utility of wealth still depends in each term on W, a random variable.

Taking an expectation of Equation 7.1 yields:

$$E[U(W)] = U[E(W)] + U_W[W - E(W)] + \tfrac{1}{2}U_{WW}E[W - E(W)]^2 +$$
$$\tfrac{1}{3}U_{WWW}E[W - E(W)]^2 + E[R]$$

Applying the properties of the expected value operator gives us a simple version of equation 7.2

$$E[U(W)] = U[E(W)] + \tfrac{1}{2}U_{WW}E[W - E(W)]^2 +$$
$$\tfrac{1}{3}U_{WWW}E[W - E(W)]^2 + E[R]$$

Note also that several of these terms correspond to summary statistics with which we are used to dealing. In particular, recall the following definitions of statistics that summarize the distribution of the random variable wealth:

Definition	Abbreviation	Terminology	Measure of...
E(W)	μ	Mean	Location of the center of the distribution , or the average value of W
$E[W-E(W)]^2$	σ^2	Variance	Dispersion around the mean
$E[W-E(W)]^3$	γ	Skewness	Tilt of the distribution to one side or the other, or indication of asymmetry of extreme values relative to the mean
$E[W-E(W)]^4$	κ	Kurtosis	Thickness of tails and peakedness of center

In other words, the investor's expected utility of wealth can be written entirely as a function of known summary measures of the shape of the probability distribution from which wealth is drawn:

$$E[U(W)] = U[E(W)] + \tfrac{1}{2}U_{WW}\sigma^2 + \tfrac{1}{3}U_{WWW}\gamma + \tfrac{1}{4}U_{WWWW}\kappa + E[R]$$

Notice from Equation 7.4 that the investor's expected utility depends on all the typical summary measures of risk, and that the remainder term R captures an essentially endless sum of other measures of the shape of the distribution of W that do not even have a name. What remains to be seen, however, is how these measures impact the investor.

Investor Preferences and Known Statistical Measures

Assume in the spirit of traditional financial economics that investors have utility functions characterized by the three common behavioral axioms discussed earlier: (1) investors prefer more to less; (2) investors are never fully satiated; and (3) investors prefer more to less at a declining rate. For utility function *U (W)*, recall that this means mathematically that $U(W) > 0$, $U_W > 0$, and $U_{WW} < 0$ for all levels of wealth W.

Beginning with the obvious, the first behavioral axiom indicates that investors prefer more expected return to less. A security that has a higher expected return, other things being equal, thus is better.

Now consider variance, or the dispersion of wealth around its average value. Variance itself is always a positive number for risky securities and random variables such as wealth, because it is measured as the *squared* deviation of the variable from its mean. Looking at the second term in Equation 7.4, we also notice that variance enters expected utility as a multiple of U_{WW}. For risk-averse investors, the utility function is concave and U_{WW} is negative. So, the expression tells us that investors *dislike* variance. We can verify this by partially differentiating expected utility of wealth in Equation 7.4 with respect to variance:

$$\frac{\partial E[U(W)]}{\partial \sigma^2} = \frac{1}{2} U_{WW}$$

So, the higher the volatility of wealth or of a security, the less the risk-averse investor likes it—all else being equal. And conversely for the risk-loving investor, who has $U_{WW} > 0$ and thus derives utility from higher volatility.

Skewness and kurtosis are harder to address because no assumptions have been made about U_{WWW} and U_{WWWW}. So, the signs with which these terms enter the expected utility function are unknown. Unlike U_W and U_{WW} which have easy interpretations as marginal utility of wealth and rate of change in marginal utility, the higher ordered derivatives have no natural interpretation in microeconomics. They are basically just statistical constructs to describe how the function U behaves.

Behavioral finance has attempted to shed some light on what investors prefer. Figure 7.6 shows three different probability density functions for the random variable wealth.

The distribution labeled *A* is a *symmetric distribution* because any value above the mean has the same likelihood of occurring as the same value below the mean. This is not true for distributions B and C. Distributions B and C are asymmetric, so values equivalently far from the mean have different probabilities depending on whether the values are above or below the mean.

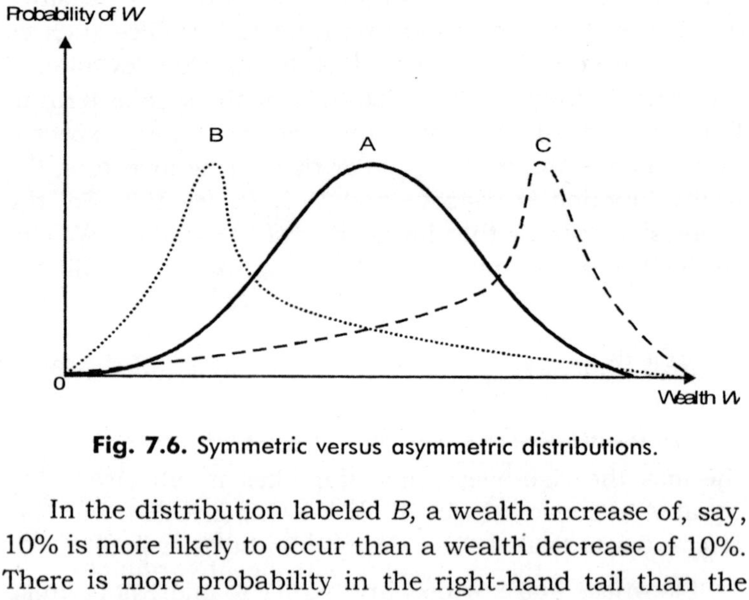

Fig. 7.6. Symmetric versus asymmetric distributions.

In the distribution labeled *B*, a wealth increase of, say, 10% is more likely to occur than a wealth decrease of 10%. There is more probability in the right-hand tail than the left, so that extreme increases in wealth are more likely than extreme declines. This is called a positively skewed distribution, and its coefficient of skewness γ would be a positive number.

The distribution labeled C, by contrast, is also asymmetric but is negatively skewed. For this distribution, γ would be a negative number, indicating that a large decline in wealth below the mean is more likely than a large increase.

Behavioral finance theorists argue that investors like positive skewness, or, more specifically, that expected utility of wealth is increasing in the coefficient of skewness γ. If the expected utility Equation 7.4 is differentiated with respect to γ, the result is

$$\frac{\partial E[U(W)]}{\partial \gamma^2} = \frac{1}{3!} U_{WWW}$$

So, for investors to derive units of happiness from skewness, this implies that $U_{WWW} > 0$, as was the case for U_W but not for U_{WW}.

As noted earlier, the third derivative of utility with respect to wealth has no natural interpretation. Nevertheless, Figure 7.6 does suggest why one might be inclined to buy off on the rationale that positive skew is "good" and negative skew is "bad." When focusing purely on extreme values, there is some plausibility to the notion that risk-averse investors are more worried about a catastrophic loss than they are thrilled by a correspondingly large gain.

Less well-documented is the impact of kurtosis on investor satisfaction. Kurtosis is a measure of the fatness of tails and peakedness of the center of a distribution relative to the tails and center of a normal distribution. The distribution labeled A in Figure 7.7 is a normal distribution of changes in wealth per period say, annually. Changes are used here instead of levels to allow the distributions to associate positive probability with negative values.

The normal distribution has several extremely useful statistical properties. First, it is symmetric, like distribution *A* in Figure 7.6 and unlike the other two. Second, it is easy to draw probabilistic inferences from the normal distribution using only mean and variance, which are completely sufficient to characterize the entire distribution.

The distribution labeled *B* in Figure 7.7 is *leptokurtic.* This means that the distribution has a coefficient of kurtosis ê above the kurtosis of the normal distribution. More usefully, that distribution *B* is leptokurtic means that it has fatter tails and a more peaked center than the normal distribution. Conversely, distribution *C* is *platykurtic,* or generally flatter than the normal distribution. More probability lies in the middle region of the distribution and less in the tails and center than the normal.

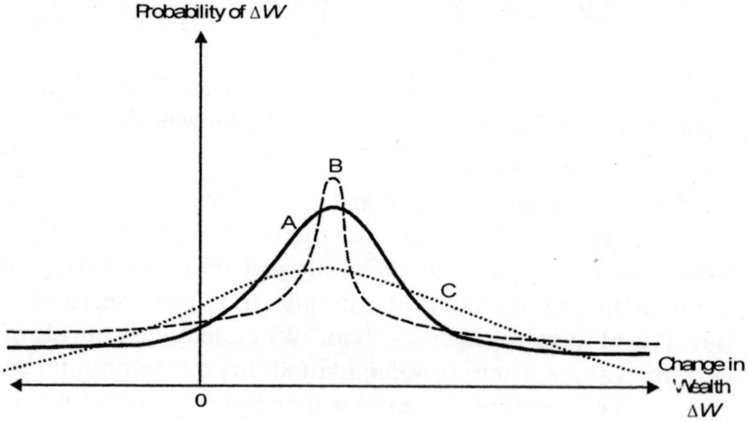

Fig. 7.7. Leptokurtic versus platykurtic distributions

Behavioral finance people argue that investors dislike kurtosis, or, more specifically, excess kurtosis which measures kurtosis relative to the kurtosis of the normal distribution. Like their arguments in the case of skewness, there is at least some intuition behind this. To see that intuition, imagine that Figure 7.7 is a distribution of returns on a portfolio of securities and not the change in wealth. The returns on the security drawn from distribution *B* would be characterized by long periods of stable, trending markets the concentrated peak around the mean followed by periods of extreme volatility and significant price changes the fat tails. This, behavioral finance tell us, is something we should dislike in an expected utility context.

8

Company Law for Transition Economies

Introduction

The alternative approaches that we consider include those currently used in OECD economies, as well as the Russian Federation, which recently adopted a new company law. The focus of this exercise is company law, i.e., legislation that regulates commercial organizations with limited liability and investments represented by shares: corporations in the US, aktiengesellschaften in Germany, societies acronyms in France, joint stock companies in Russia. Although legislation on joint stock companies is the object of primary focus, all countries will need to have legislation providing for other types of business organisations. This will not be discussed here however, except when their provisions are relevant to the assumptions underlying this document. It is nevertheless important to note that the legislation should exhaustively list all available forms of legal entities, and that registration procedures should ensure a clear identification of every registered legal entity. This is mainly because improper formation of a legal entity might have dire consequences for both investors and third parties.

Excluded from consideration are laws regulating securities exchanges and the rules for the general offering of securities to the public. It should however be noted that sometimes the boundaries between company and securities laws are blurred. Some countries will choose to regulate certain issues related to publicly-quoted companies and their shareholders through securities regulation while others include such provisions in the general company legislation. The principles that are discussed here and address these "grey-area" issues can be applied in either context. Regulations of the general relationship between joint stock companies and their employees, and special rules designed to handle the specific issues that arise for financial and industrial groups are also not discussed here. Finally, while the document considers the civil remedies for violation of the company law, it does not address criminal law issues related to joint stock companies and their behaviour.

Principle I. There are a number of important differences between transition economies and more developed market economies. These should lead to variances in the company law. Most importantly, market, reputational, and cultural constraints on self-dealing or mistreatment of minority shareholders are likely to be comparatively weak in transition economies. In response, the constraints on self-dealing and protections for minority shareholders imposed by the company law should be comparatively strict.

Transition economies are also likely to lack the legal infrastructure that allows them to address complex business cases. Thus, company law in a transition economy should strive for clarity, and for simple, bright-line rules that are easy to apply. The fine nuances that have developed over time in the company laws of OECD economies will sometimes be out of place in a transition economy, because they will add too much complexity to the law. An immediate corollary to this principle is that company law in transition economies should evolve as these economies develop. In particular, some of the strong shareholder protection provisions that are proposed here may reduce the flexibility of the joint stock company form. In a more mature market economy, the company law should probably strike a somewhat different balance between flexibility and shareholder protection, which is more favourable to the former.

There will also, of course, be important differences between different transition economies. Such differences arise from contrasting levels of economic development and national legal systems. It will, thus, rarely be appropriate for a transition country to simply copy the law of a mature market economy, or even the law of another country at a similar stage of economic development.

Principle II. There should be a clear separation between the property of a company and that of its shareholders.

The concept of a joint stock company as a separate juridical person includes a clear separation between the property belonging to a company and the property of the company's shareholders. The shareholders own shares; their shareholder status does not confer to them any direct claims or property rights on the company's assets after the latter is constituted and before it is liquidated. In principle, they can only influence the management of these assets through the mechanisms and institutions provided by the company law for the purpose of shareholder control and protection.

Similarly, the company may incur and pay its own obligations, but may not either incur obligations on behalf of its shareholders, nor pay obligations incurred by a particular shareholder. Only if the company's property is clearly separated from the shareholders' property, and the company's obligations are clearly separated from the shareholders' obligations, does the concept of limited liability become workable.

Principle III. The company law should not allow shareholders to withdraw their investments.

A central feature of company law is the permanence of the shareholders' investment: each shareholder cannot freely withdraw his/her investment, except through sales which is the primary means for exit. This permanence is one of the fundamental differences between the joint stock company form and other forms of business organisation, in which participants have much broader rights to withdraw their investment.

Exceptions to the general rule according to which shareholders cannot freely withdraw their investment do exist; they should be few, exhaustively enumerated, and clearly defined in the law, in order to give creditors the assurance that the shareholders' investment cannot easily be withdrawn. These exceptions address situations that create an especially high potential for some shareholders to profit at the expense of other shareholders.

Principle IV. The company law should have a unitary structure, not distinguishing between smaller and larger joint stock companies.

Law in most OECD economies provide for a number of different legal forms for business enterprises. The joint stock company is typically the principal legal form for an enterprise with a large number of investors. The limited liability company is designed for use exclusively by enterprises with a limited number of investors. Enterprises can also be created in the form of a general partnership or a limited partnership. The available forms are still evolving and additional forms may be available in some jurisdictions.

In some countries, the company law provides for two sets of rules: one designed for large joint stock companies with a large number of shareholders, and another for joint stock companies with a small number of shareholders. This gives investors an additional option; in addition to using the separate legal form of a limited liability company.

It seems, however, that a unitary structure for the joint stock company law which does not make a general distinction between joint stock companies with few and numerous investors is better suited for transition economies. On balance, such a streamlined approach serves better the goals of simplicity and legislative coherence, which are of great importance to the strengthening of the rule of law in transition economies. Moreover, adopting a unitary structure does not mean that the company law should treat all joint stock companies alike. Special provisions for joint stock companies with a limited number of shareholders may be included in certain articles of the law, when this is necessary for reasons of flexibility and efficiency.

Principle V. Protection of minority shareholders is important, especially in the context of transition economies.

The protection of minority investors from majority abuses is one of the objectives of company law in any market economy. It should be more so in economies characterised by a high proportion of companies that are controlled by a single shareholder or a small group of shareholders, or where substantial shareholding by managers is frequent. In addition to the above traits, transition economies are also often characterised by relatively weak non-legal constraints on the power of managers and controlling shareholders to act to benefit themselves at the expense of minority shareholders; such constraints are usually imposed by efficient capital and product markets. At the same time, companies in transition economies will often need outside investment, which may take the form of minority equity holdings by the "outsiders." The latter want to make sure that rights will not be abused.

Company law in transition economies should respond with strong rules that are designed to protect minority shareholders. This will encourage investment in these countries, by reducing the risk of expropriation of "outside" investment by managers and controlling shareholders.

Examples of such rules are: cumulative voting for election of members of the board of directors; a one (common) share, one vote rule; special rules for approval of transactions in which managers or large shareholders have a conflict of interest; requirements that a company issues and acquires its own shares only at market value; redemption and appraisal rights for shareholders who do not approve of reorganisations, major transactions, and changes in the company's charter that limit their rights; and takeout rights that allow investors to sell their shares to a shareholder who acquires a controlling block of a company's shares.

Principle VI. Many discrete rules included in the company law could be "default" rules that can be amended by agreement of the shareholders.

The needs of all companies cannot be met by a single set of rules. Also, in many cases, the participants in an enterprise will be in a better position than lawmakers to decide which rules are best in their particular situation. Many of the rules to be included in a company law should be "default" rules, that is rules which can be changed by decision of the shareholders in the company's charter. For example, the law could specify the minimum required to approve a merger or a charter amendment, and at the same time could allow a company's charter to require a higher vote. The law could also specify a minimum list of company actions that require approval by the shareholders, but allow this list to be expanded through the company's charter.

On the other hand, there are two important reasons to consider the adoption of mandatory, instead of default, rules: first, the need to protect minority investors, who cannot be expected in advance to anticipate all of the ways that a majority of shareholders can take advantage of their position; second, the need to protect creditors against actions by the joint stock company or the shareholders that improperly prevent the satisfaction of their claims. Often, deciding whether a rule should be a default rule or a mandatory rule will require balancing the flexibility advantages of a default rule against the shareholder or third party protection advantages of a mandatory rule.

Principle VII. The cost for establishing a company should be small.

One of the main aspects of transition is that a great number of productive assets are transferred to new entrepreneurial uses. Thus, transition economies generally need to encourage formation of new businesses. Allowing formation of such enterprises at a reasonable cost is important. The main costs are those related to drafting a corporate charter and other founding documents, those related to substantive review or certification of the charter which is required for registration, and those related to state registration of a legal entity.

The cost of forming a business enterprise would be greatly reduced if the company law contained default rules to govern almost the entire range of corporate actions; this would simplify the task of drafting a corporate charter. If this is the case a further certification of the charter by a notary or other public official might not be needed. In the event that a notary is required for the drafting or review of an extensive corporate charter, his/her fees should be controlled. Moreover, the process of state registration should be simple and fast, and the fees charged for registration should be low. Review of a company's charter by the state officials charged with registration of legal entities should be limited to confirmation that required information is included and that the most important mandatory provisions of law are complied with. On the other hand, it should be kept in mind that some necessary degree of procedurally transparent certification is unavoidable. Where this is lacking, an increasing amount of litigation on the validity of company formation might create serious enforcement bottlenecks.

Principle VIII. The company law should state the remedies for a breach of its provisions where possible.

Appropriate and specific rules of law are only one aspect of a well-designed joint stock company law. Provision for remedies and consequences in case of a breach of those rules is equally important. Business and legal professionals in transition economies are only recently becoming accustomed to the patterns of rights and remedies common to the organization of companies. In this environment, it is especially important for the law to make the consequences of a breach of legal requirements clear and specific, rather than relying on general principles of law, which may not provide for appropriate or effective remedies.

Principle IX. Third parties should have strong assurance that contracts in good faith with a company will be enforceable.

In an environment riddled with economic and legal uncertainties, reducing the costs and risks associated with entering into standard business contracts is very important. Transition economies should thus establish rules that provide for a high degree of assurance to third parties that their contracts with a company will be enforceable. For example, a company should generally be able to exercise the full range of civil rights and obligations, and to engage in a full range of business activities. If a company's charter restricts its range of permitted activities, this should not affect third parties, unless they had actual advance notice of this fact.

The law should specify the consequences of a company entering into a transaction with a third party without complying with the procedures for internal governance laid out in the company law or the company's charter. Invalidation of such transactions should be rare, and should be reserved only for cases of serious violations of the required procedures, in which the third party did not act in good faith. In any case, a judge should have the discretion not to invalidate a transaction. Thus, a company's managers will not be able to use their own failure to follow correct procedures as a reason to back out of a business transaction.

PART II : MAIN PROVISIONS

I. Legal Capacity of a Company

A company should be established for an unlimited period of time, unless otherwise provided for in the company's charter. In addition, the company should have full power to engage in any type of lawful business, i.e., any activity that is not prohibited to other persons and/or is not expressly limited to a certain specific category of legal persons. This latter category usually includes areas such as banking and insurance; enterprises involved in these activities are subject to special organisational and financial rules. The law should require their clear and unambiguous identification from other, general purpose companies.

The company should have available to it all civil rights, and the power to incur all civil obligations, necessary for carrying out its activities. Some countries permit a limitation on purpose of powers to be included in a joint stock company's charter. However, allowing limited purpose companies creates a risk that third parties will enter into a transaction with a company in good faith, only to discover later that the transaction is invalid because it exceeds the company's power.

In transition economies, the risk of harm to third parties if a company's charter can limit the company's powers may outweigh the potential benefits from allowing these limits. If such limitations are permitted, a duty to investigate whether a limited purpose company has the power to engage in any particular transaction should not be imposed on third parties. It may be best in this case to create a clear rule that a third party can enforce contractual rights against a limited purpose company unless it can be shown that the third party had actual knowledge that the transaction exceeded the company's powers. Such knowledge cannot be assumed on the basis of the company's registered charter.

II. Foundation of a Company Procedure for Creating a Company

The procedure for creating a company should be simple and fast. The documents required to be filed during state registration should be kept to a minimum. Review by the registration office of a company's application for state registration and the substance of a company's charter should be limited to basic matters such as whether the charter includes the company's name and location, payment of the required amount of charter capital and the required registration fee, and submission of the required documents. The registration office should not be permitted to demand submission of documents not required by the law. It should not be allowed to refuse registration unless one of the above formal prerequisites for company establishment has not been fulfilled. The principles of speedy registration and strictly limited power of the registration office should also apply to amendments to a company's charter. A country should have a single register system for juridical persons, to ensure that two companies do not register in two different offices under the same name. This should not preclude the possibility for a register of having multiple offices for the convenience of persons wishing to create legal entities.

The information contained in the company registry should in principle be public. Given, however, the law enforcement situation in some transition countries, its disclosure may be subject to specific authorization procedures aiming at the protection of company founders and shareholders from criminal elements.

Some countries have extensive licensing requirements for enterprises wishing to undertake certain activities (related, for example to public health). Such industry-specific procedures should be kept separate and distinct from the general registration procedures for the creation of companies. The contrary would result in additional administrative costs for companies in all sectors and might be the source of confusion on both the administrative and judicial levels.

With simple rules for the nation of companies, few cases of defective registration should occur. In any event, only directly interested parties should be given the right to file before the courts to request invalidation of a registration. The registration office should not have such a right, but the office of the procurator (or other equivalent, public interest institutions) might be given standing to sue. When cases of defective registration do occur, a company's contracts should be enforced to the maximum extent possible, as if the company had been properly registered. Where this is feasible, the company's shareholders should be given an opportunity to correct the defects of registration. If correction of the defects is not possible, the company should be liquidated, in the same manner as if it had been properly created. Creditors' claims should be satisfied out of the company's assets and out of the assets of founders or shareholders who were at fault for the improper registration.

Founders 'liability for obligations incurred before the company's state registration.

A rapid registration procedure will minimize problems of liability of the founders for obligations incurred on behalf of a company before it is officially formed, and the need for formal assumption by a company of obligations incurred by the founders on the future company's behalf. Nevertheless, such issues should be addressed in the company law.

A common rule is that the founders are jointly and severally liable for the obligations incurred by each of them on the future company's behalf in the interim period. This period starts with the decision to create the company and ends with formal registration. Once the company is formed, the founders can agree that the company should assume liability for obligations to third parties incurred by the founders before registration. This need not release the founder who incurred the obligation from liability; but the third party can agree by contract to release him or her from liability at the time that the company is registered and capable of assuming the obligation. Some countries provide for the automatic substitution of the company as debtor for debts incurred during the formation period. This rule however might be difficult to enforce in jurisdictions where the concept of a "company in formation", i.e., a legal person not yet constituted but pretty distinct as an economic entity, is lacking, in both statutory and case law.

Charter of a company. The charter of a joint stock company is the document defining the structure of the company, the internal patterns and rules of governance, the rights of shareholders, and other fundamental matters. Although certain systems provide for a second document governing some of the internal procedures of the company, for simplicity and clarity the charter should be the only required founding document and the definitive statement of internal rules and relationships. Each shareholder should have the right to receive free of charge a copy of the charter from the company. The company law should provide for a comprehensive set of default rules. This would help company's founders in the process of drafting the charter. The company law should also provide for a set of mandatory rules on the issues that must be addressed in the charter of every company such as: (1) the company's full and abbreviated name, which must indicate that it is a joint stock company; (2) the company's location; (3) the charter capital and the type and number of shares that may be issued; (4) the rights of shareholders for each type of preferred shares in the case of creation of preferred shares; (5) the procedure for holding shareholder meetings; and (6) the number of members of the company's board of directors, or if the law allows it, a statement that the company will not have a board of directors. The company's charter may contain other provisions which may specify more precisely the company's structure, and the powers of shareholders and of the company's management organs. However, company law provisions of an imperative nature will supersede anything contrary in the charter.

III. Limited Liability and Relations Between Parent and Subsidiary Companies

Limited liability of shareholders for a company's obligations and exceptions to limited liability: A central feature of a company, in every market economy, is the limited liability of shareholders. As a general rule, the creditors have no claim against the shareholders. For shareholders who are not involved in the management or control of company's actions, the principle of limited liability should be absolute. This principle makes it possible for companies to raise capital from a large number of investors who neither control the company's activities nor have detailed knowledge about the company's activities. However, limited liability should not exonerate shareholders from liability for their own actions. For example, if a shareholder deceives a creditor about the amount of a company's assets, the shareholder could be made liable to the creditor, on the basis of general fraud provisions.

The laws of every market economy provide for specific instances in which a shareholder may be liable for company obligations. One case of such exceptional circumstances may be when a shareholder is made liable to creditors if the shareholder has, through improper actions of some kind, caused the company to become insolvent and unable to pay its obligations to creditors. Exceptions to the general principle of limited liability of shareholders should be limited and defined as precisely as possible. Shareholder liability should be a subsidiary way for creditors to satisfy their claims. In accordance with this principle, it may be appropriate to require that the creditor exhaust other available remedies, such as avoidance of suspect transactions, through bankruptcy proceedings.

Controlling shareholders should be liable to creditors only in the case of serious fault on their part. Ordinary carelessness in determining a company's business decisions should be part of the risk that creditors bear. It is often important, in running a business, to decide to take a business risk quickly and based on limited information. The risk that courts will second-guess business decisions with the benefit of hindsight will discourage controlling shareholders from taking ordinary business risks that might produce large losses, but might also produce large profits. Exactly how the concept of serious fault should be defined and what degree of fault should be required to find liability will depend on a country's legal system. Often the issue of limited liability of shareholders is framed as a choice between no shareholder liability for a company's obligations and joint and several liability of shareholders. However intermediate positions are also legislative options, such as proportional liability (shareholder liability in proportion to share ownership).

Liability of a parent company for obligations of a subsidiary: An additional exception to the limited liability of shareholders is the liability of a parent company for the obligations of a subsidiary or dependent company. Some countries have special rules establishing instances where a parent company is liable to the creditors or shareholders of such a company. Other countries do not. Although there might be policy reasons to regulate groups of companies, regulation of the liability of parent companies should not be needed as a part of company law, in addition to regulation of the liability of controlling shareholders. From this perspective, it is better to view these issues on the same terms as the general issue of "piercing the corporate veil."

IV. Fundamental Changes to a Company: Charter Amendments, Reorganisations, Major Transactions, and Liquidation Amendments to a Company's Charter

Some countries allow charter amendments to be approved by a majority of votes of the shareholders who participate in voting, at a meeting at which an ordinary quorum exists. Others employ a stricter rule, under which approval by a majority of the votes of all shareholders, not just those who actually participate in voting, is required to approve a charter amendment. In any event, there should be a requirement for registration of every amendment to the company's charter.

In transition economies, a higher minimum vote for a charter amendment may be necessary as a means to protect minority shareholders. Assuming that the communication systems and voting rules make it possible for shareholders to vote by mail, there may be advantages to specifying the minimum vote required to approve charter amendments (and other fundamental changes) as a majority or supermajority of all voting shares, rather than a majority or supermajority of the votes of shareholders who participate in the voting. This prevents company's managers or controlling shareholders from manipulating the outcome by ensuring that only persons likely to support a proposal are able to attend a shareholder meeting (or vote by other means).

A number of company laws provide for special rules concerning amendments to the charter which limit shareholders' rights. An example of such an amendment would be the creation of another category of shares with higher priority than an existing class of preferred shares. Regarding such transactions, it may be appropriate for special voting rules to be provided. They would require a majority or supermajority of the affected class to approve the changes. In addition to this, shareholders who do not vote to approve the amendment should have an opportunity to have their shares redeemed at market value, as determined by an independent appraisal of the value of the shares.

Reorganisation of a company

Most company laws provide for mechanisms for the reorganisation of a company, such as a merger (two companies combining into a new company), an accession (one company acceding into another already existing company), a division (one company dividing into two new companies), a separation (a new company emerging from an existing company), and/or a transformation (a company transforming itself into another type of legal entity). The company law should list all available types of reorganization, and specify the procedure for completing them.

Often, different forms of reorganization can be used as substitutes for one another. Also, a transaction that is not considered to be a reorganisation can sometimes pursue the same business objective as a reorganization. For example, a sale of substantially all assets by Company A to Company B, which is not considered a reorganisation, can be a substitute for an accession of Company A into Company B. Thus, the company law should provide for similar shareholder protection for sales of substantially all assets to those that it provides for accessions.

A reorganisation can be a very large transaction or can greatly change the nature of a shareholder's investment, and involves a correspondingly high risk of harm to shareholders. Therefore, reorganisations should generally require approval by shareholders. In order to protect minority shareholders, a supermajority vote would be preferable. Shareholders who vote against a reorganisation or do not vote to approve a reorganisation should be given an opportunity to have their shares redeemed. Alternatively, the law could require that a shareholder must specifically vote against a reorganisation, rather than merely fail to vote, in order to receive redemption rights. This solution, however, depends on the level of the infrastructure available in transition economies (such as, for example, the mailing system), that is necessary for voting procedures to be effectively implemented and monitored.

An exception might be appropriate for a situation where a parent company owns more than 90 percent of the shares of a subsidiary company. An accession of the subsidiary into the parent company would be a conflict of interest transaction, which would normally require approval by the non-interested shareholders. However, in this case, the minority shareholders' redemption rights may provide for a sufficient substitute for voting rights, provided that the value of the shares is determined by a fair procedure.

Protection of Creditors during a Company's Reorganisation

An important issue concerning a company's reorganisation is to what extent the company law should contain mandatory protection rules for creditors. Some countries provide for very little creditor protection-generally only the assurance that some company will remain liable for a company's obligations following a reorganisation. Other countries provide creditors with the right to demand early repayment of the company's obligations for all forms of reorganisation.

Introducing financial discipline in market relations is an important prerequisite for a successful transition. Thus, creditors during reorganisations should be protected by company law in transition economies. For reorganisations that may generate important adverse effects to creditors, the latter should have the right to demand early repayment of the company's obligations. Reorganisations that have less potential for harm could be permitted to proceed with a simple prior notice to creditors. Such notice should be the minimum requirement for any type of reorganisation. This would allow the latter to exercise any contractual rights they may have, to inform themselves about the changes, and possibly demand early repayment where adverse effects can be reasonably foreseen. In certain cases, additional protection might be provided to creditors; for example, in the case of the division of a company into two legal entities, or of a spin-off (separation) of a new company out of the original entity, "old" debts can be covered by joint and several liability of both entities for a specified period of time.

Major transactions involving a company's acquisition or disposition of property. Large acquisitions and dispositions of property are similar to reorganisations in their potential to substantially change the nature of the shareholders' investment. In order to effectively protect minority shareholders, a class of major transactions that require shareholder approval is needed. Furthermore, in addition to a vote, a right of a shareholder to withdraw may be provided.

The type of transactions that fall within this class depends on the legislator's view of, on the one hand, the costs and delays from requiring a shareholder vote, and of, on the other, the increased shareholder protection resulting from shareholder review of very large transactions. One possible approach is to specify a threshold as a percentage of a company's assets (as valued in the most recent balance sheet available at the time that the company's board of directors approves a transaction). The board of directors would be required to obtain shareholder approval for an acquisition or disposition of property that exceeds this threshold. The threshold percentage prescribed in the law should be considered as a minimum protection; companies could provide for a lower, stricter threshold in their charter.

The threshold for approval of major transactions will not be useful if it permits a company's board of directors to evade the intent of the law by splitting what is in substance one transaction into more parts, each of which individually falls below the size threshold established in the law. A provision will likely be required which prevents this by defining closely related transactions as a single transaction, or by relating transactions in time. The managers should be made responsible for submitting adequate information on other related transactions to shareholders.

Another issue that arises for major transactions involves protection of the rights of third parties who conclude major transactions with a company. Third parties cannot be expected to know whether a transaction requires special approval based on the transaction's size relative to the company's assets. The law should protect the rights of bona fide third parties. If a company's board of directors fails to obtain shareholder approval, that is a matter of the internal governance of the company. In that case, shareholders will have a claim against the members of the board of directors. However, the company should be able to seek to invalidate a transaction when the third party knew that the shareholder approval was required and not obtained.

Appraisal and Redemption of Shares

Most company laws do not provide for a general right of shareholders to demand that the company redeem their shares. The relative permanence of a shareholder's investment is and should remain the general rule.7 Companies law should, however, provide for special rules ("appraisal and redemption right") if a company takes actions that will fundamentally change the nature of the company, or the shareholders' investment, of which the shareholder does not approve.

There are a number of exceptional instances where appraisal and redemption rights can be made available: (1) for a charter amendment that limits shareholder rights; (2) for a reorganisation; and (3) for a major transaction. A judge or an independent appraiser should determine the value of the redeemed shares. In case of an independent appraiser, a mechanism would be needed for the shareholder and the company to jointly select the appraiser: if a company's board of directors would be the only one to select the appraiser, the appraiser will be likely to reach a valuation close to the board of director's interests. Moreover, in case of a determination by an independent appraiser, a large shareholder should have the means to challenge this price and seek a higher price. The right to appraisal and redemption of shares should be available to shareholders who have voted against a proposed company action, and also to shareholders who did not vote on the action, but not to those who voted for it. The company law should prescribe a short period for exercise of the right.

If appraisal and redemption rights are limited in the ways described in the previous paragraph, there is in principle no reason to limit the fraction of a company's shares that can be redeemed as a result of an action by the company that causes these rights to arise. Nevertheless, in some countries, redemption and appraisal rights are limited to a specific percentage of the company's net assets. In any event, redemption of shares should be subject to limits based on a company's solvency and preservation of its charter capital. A company should be obliged within a period of time after it has redeemed shares, either to reissue the shares, to cancel them with a reduction of its charter capital, or to cancel them with an increase in the nominal value of its remaining issued shares sufficient to avoid a reduction in its charter capital.

To make it easier for shareholders to exercise appraisal and redemption rights, a company's board of directors should announce an offer price for the company's shares in the material sent to shareholders to solicit approval for the underlying transaction. That price, based on the market value of the company's shares as determined by an independent appraiser, should be paid promptly on shareholder demand.

Liquidation of a Company

Every company law provides for a procedure for a company to voluntarily liquidate. Voluntary liquidation should always requires shareholder approval. If the company law requires supermajority approval for charter amendments and reorganisation, it should require at least the same level of approval for a voluntary liquidation.

The question of voluntary liquidation is an issue that should be decided by the shareholders without the need for proposal by the board. This is because the members of the board might have vested interests in the continuation of the company, even when liquidation is desired by all of the shareholders.

V. Charter Capital

Minimum charter capital of a company and minimum paid capital: Most European company laws require a company to have and maintain a minimum level of charter capital, which is equal to the nominal value of all shares issued by the company. The principal purpose of this requirement is to ensure that a company has some assets available to pay its creditors. If the company's net assets fall below this minimum level, the company must raise additional capital or else liquidate. Company law in transition economies is likely to follow the European pattern and require a nontrivial minimum amount of charter capital to create a company. An important issue that needs to be addressed in this context is the adjustment of the minimum charter capital requirement for inflation, which might run considerably high during the first stages of transition. A number of indexing mechanisms have been devised for this purpose. It is important to note that the adjusted requirements should not be applied retroactively to companies already in existence; they should only apply to new companies.

Whatever the minimum level of charter capital required, the creditors should be able to rely on the amount of assets actually being contributed to the company. This means that only assets which could be available to creditors if a company were subject to liquidation should be eligible to be counted as charter capital. "In kind" contributions should, as a general rule, be subject to independent appraisal of their value, although an exception could be provided for contributions valued at very small amounts. Another option would be to subject the founders and/or the appraiser to liability to the creditors for a period of time after a company's creation if an inflated value is assigned to property. Non-saleable "assets," such as the business skills of the founders or the founders' promise to work for the company in the future, should not be eligible for inclusion in the charter capital.

In order to effectively protect creditors, the company law should require that a large portion of a company's charter capital be contributed close to the time of foundation. If the minimum required charter capital is relatively low, it might be feasible to require full payment of this amount at the time a company is created. If delayed payment is permitted, then at least 50 percent of the charter capital should be paid immediately and the balance due within a short period. In addition, the shareholders should be liable to creditors in the amount of their unpaid contributions.

Use of the concept of charter capital, and of the nominal value of shares, should not prevent a company from selling shares for a price higher than their nominal value. This power is necessary when a company issues shares at different times, and thus the market value of the shares is different. Such sales will not contradict the central understanding of charter capital as representing the minimum amount of property ensuring payment of a company's obligations to creditors. The creditors will have no objection if the company sells shares for a higher amount than their nominal value, since this can only increase the amount of the company's net assets.

Procedures for increasing or decreasing a company's charter capital: A company's charter capital is comprised of the total nominal value of its issued shares. Two techniques exist to increase a charter capital: to issue additional shares, and to increase the nominal value of previously issued shares. The company's total charter capital should not, however, be allowed to increase to a level higher than its net assets, as shown on the most recent balance sheet approved by the shareholders. The company has also two options to decrease its charter capital: by acquiring and then cancelling previously issued shares, and by decreasing the nominal value of previously issued shares. The nominal value of issued shares should be specified in the company's charter.

Consequences of a Decrease in Charter Capital

If a company has net assets less than its charter capital (but still higher than the minimum amount required by law), the company should be required to reduce its charter capital to the level of its net assets. A common rule to most countries that require companies to have a charter capital is that a company that reduces its charter capital must provide creditors with an opportunity to demand early repayment of the company's obligations. In practice, a reduction in charter capital often leads to liquidation. In order to avoid such a situation, the rule that a creditor has the right to demand early repayment could be only a default rule; creditors can agree to waive this right in their contracts with the company. In addition (or alternatively), a de minimise rule could be adopted (i.e., the amount of the increase/decrease as a percentage of the current amount of charter capital) below which changes in the charter capital would not alter the rights of creditors.

If a company's net assets are less than the minimum amount of charter capital required by the law, then it should be no longer possible for the company to reduce its charter capital. The common continental rule is that such a company must file for either bankruptcy or involuntary liquidation. If the company's managers fail to take this step then they can be held personally liable to the creditors for additional losses suffered by the creditors due to their failure to act promptly. This approach forces the preservation of some positive value in the company, which is thus more likely to be able to repay its creditors. The latter can agree, in the context of bankruptcy proceedings, to a re-organisation plan/compromise, if the debtor company's worth as a going concern is higher than its liquidation value.

However, the above approach assumes the existence of a flexible insolvency framework, which is not always the case in transition economies. An intermediate, more flexible legislative approach in the company law could be that if a company has inadequate capital, creditors would be notified about the company's situation; managers should be liable to creditors for failure to provide notice. The company (ie., its management) should not be required, however, to file for bankruptcy unless a shareholder, a creditor, or the public prosecutor (in the special cases he/she is allowed to file for bankruptcy of a company) would petition a court to this effect. This would provide an opportunity for a company to continue its activity, and perhaps to return to profitability, if all shareholders and creditors would agree, without having to enter formal bankruptcy proceedings; they risk to be (and, in many countries are) cumbersome and biased towards liquidation. However, if this approach is adopted, future creditors will not be aware that the company lacks the required minimum capital. The company should therefore be required to notify all new creditors of this. Management should be again liable for failure to notify.

VI. Types of Shares to be Issued by a Company

Company laws usually provide that a company must issue common shares. They also provide that the company has the power to issue one or more types of preferred shares, whose rights are generally specified in the company's charter.

A general issue is whether a company should be able to issue more than one class of shares with a general right to vote (for example, in the election of the company's board of directors). Some countries allow a company to have only one type of common shares and limit the circumstances in which a company can issue different types of voting shares, delivering different voting rights, or limit the creation of differences in voting rights between different types of voting shares. Other countries do not restrict issuance of different classes of voting shares.

Given the immaturity of their capital markets, transition economies might decide to choose a more shareholder protective approach by allowing only one class of common shares, i.e., one share, one vote. This rule better matches economic incentives with voting power, allows the market for control of companies to operate as a check on bad management and reduces the tendency for founders to retain control contrary to the interests of other shareholders.

Rights of Holders of Preferred Shares

Preferred shares usually have higher priority than the common shares in the receipt of dividends, and in payments during a company's liquidation. In transition economies, it might be better to adopt a relatively strict approach to preferred shares. These shares should be in principle non-voting. Preferred shares should be allowed to vote generally on election of directors in only two situations: (i) when the company has not paid the dividends of the preferred shares, and (ii) when preferred shares are convertible into common shares. In that case, preferred shares should be permitted to have a number of votes equal to the number of common shares into which they can be converted. The amount of dividends (as a percentage of profits) to be paid on the preferred shares, the type of the liquidation preference, and the other rights of holders have to be specified in the charter.

If the company law establishes a one share, one vote rule for common shares, it should also require that preferred shares are preferred over the common shares with regard to both dividends and payments during a company's liquidation. Otherwise, for example, preferred shares that have a liquidation preference but no preference during payment of dividends can be used as a near substitute for nonvoting common shares, in the common situation where a company is unlikely to be liquidated in the near future.

Some countries limit the percentage of a company's charter capital that can be represented by preferred shares. However, in practice, very few companies in OECD economies issue such a large amount of this special class of shares.

Registered versus bearer shares : Certain countries require that a company keep a registry of its shareholders (either actual or nominal holders of shares) and that all shares be issued in their name. Others allow the issuance of bearer shares, Le., certificates representing shares that are not registered to any specific holder or owner. For a bearer share, physical possession of the certificates themselves confers the rights associated with the shares. Such shares or certificates can be transferred freely without notice to the company.

The use of bearer shares presents special dangers in transition economies. Bearer shares involve four risks that can be substantially avoided with the use of registered shares: (1) the risk of fraud in the sale of forged certificates that purport to represent bearer shares; (2) the risk of theft of bearer shares; (3) the risk that controlling shareholders will use bearer shares to hide their control over a company; and (4) the difficulties of voting bearer shares, since voting by mail is not possible. Although the use of bearer shares eliminates the risk that a company will improperly refuse to register a transfer of shares, other remedies can be used for registration problems and the shareholder protection advantage of allowing only registered shares may significant outweigh any gain in flexibility from the use of bearer shares.

VII. Issuance and Transfer of a Company's Shares and other Securities Procedure for Issuance of Shares

In most countries, the maximum number of shares that can be issued is specified in a company's charter (authorized or announced shares). At the same time, a number of countries provide a mechanism by which the shareholders can authorise the board of directors to issue additional shares, within the limits of the number of announced shares.

The delegated power of the board of directors to issue additional shares provides important flexibility in financing the company. This power should however be specified and limited in the charter: the board of directors should not have power to issue shares similar to US "blank check" preferred shares, that is shares with whatever rights the board selects. In any event, no new shares should be issued unless the ones that have been already issued are fully paid-up. A company should be allowed to amend its charter to increase its charter capital only to the extent that the company has issued the shares that are announced in the charter. The mechanism for this could be, for example, a narrow delegation by the shareholders to the board of directors to amend the company's charter so that it reflects the number of shares actually issued by the company. This delegation should be given at the time the shareholders decide the amount of authorised shares. Preemptive rights during a company's issuance of shares.

In addition to the rights to authorise the number of shares that may be issued, shareholders may need additional protection during the issuance of new shares to prevent such shares from being issued at an unfairly low price to selected buyers, and to prevent the use of such issuance to reduce the influence of particular shareholders or groups thereof. The need for such protection may be especially strong in transition economies, where outside controls, such as market reaction, on majority or management abuses during issuance of shares may not yet be sufficiently developed. The joint stock company law may provide one or several types of shareholder protection during share issuance, including preemptive rights, a requirement that shares be issued at market value, and/or a requirement for special shareholder approval of large issuances.

Preemptive rights, i.e., the rights of shareholders to the first opportunity to purchase any newly issued shares, may protect shareholders against both "targeted" sales of new shares to others and general attempts to dilute the vote of existing shareholders. The law should require that such rights be provided to shareholders for any new issuance. Such requirement could be waived by shareholders in particular cases by majority (or qualified majority) vote. Small issuance of shares to managers and employees of the company should not be subject to the preemption rule. To protect shareholders who do not vote in favour of a waiver of preemptive rights, the law could provide for "participation rights," which allow the former to participate in a share offering by purchasing additional shares at the same price at which shares were sold in the main offering. In order to simplify charter preparation and provide clarity, it may be appropriate for the law to provide for a simple procedure for the exercise of these rights. The rules concerning preemptive rights that apply during a company's issuance of shares should also apply when a company sells its own shares that it has acquired or redeemed from shareholders.

Issuance of Shares at Market Value

A second valuable means of shareholder protection during issuance of shares is a requirement that shares be issued at a price no lower than their market value. Of course, the market value of shares may not be precise, especially for a company without an established trading market for its shares. Still, this rule may provide some protection against a company issuing shares to insiders or their friends at a very low price, because such an issuance could be challenged by other shareholders and might expose the members of the board to liability for acting in bad faith. 79. In some OECD countries, shares are sold at a below-market price as a form of incentive compensation to managers and employees. As a shareholder, the manager is expected to have a greater incentive to increase the value of the shares. Because of significant concerns in transition economies about the behaviour of manager shareholders, it may be best not to make any exceptions to shareholder protection rules for management compensation. Thus, managers and employees would be required to purchase shares at market value. Incentives could then be provided for in cash, linked to the purchase of shares at market value.

If the law is going to employ the concept of market value, it must define it. The market value could be defined as the price at which a seller and a buyer, having full information about the property's value and not obliged either to sell it or to buy it, would agree to sell and buy. More specific rules could be adopted for companies whose shares are publicly traded.

Shareholder Approval for Large Issuances of Shares

Another form of shareholder protection during issuance of shares is the requirement that an issuance that exceeds a threshold percentage of a company's previously issued shares be approved by a majority vote of the shareholders. Such a rule provides some additional protection to shareholders in the situation of large issuances. A large issuance, if made at too low price, could substantially dilute the underlying value of the company's previously issued shares.

When shareholders have preemptive rights, an ordinary majority should suffice to approve an issuance of shares. However, preemptive rights may not be available in certain circumstances. For instance, that will be the case when the shareholders vote to waive their preemptive rights. The future buyers of these shares and their affiliated persons should not be eligible to vote on the waiver of preemptive rights. Securities convertible into common shares and options to acquire common shares

Many company laws permit the issuance of securities which are convertible into shares and/or options to acquire shares. In OECD economies, their primary use is a form of compensation for the company's managers and employees, which is provided to them instead of ownership of the shares. In order to maximize the value of the option, those who receive them have an incentive to work to increase the value of the shares as much above the option price as possible. Because their fair price is very difficult to determine, in a transition economy, options to acquire shares may have limited use and be subject to abuses.

Because of the above risks it might be better not to allow the issuance of convertible securities and options to acquire shares in transition economies. An intermediate position, that would permit more flexibility, is to allow issuance of these securities, while requiring that the shareholders approve the number and terms of these securities before they are issued. As a general rule, the same level of protection the company law provides for shareholders during issuance of shares should be required during the issuance of convertible securities and options to acquire shares. Otherwise, the requirements for preemptive rights or those related to the issuance of shares only at market value could be easily evaded by a company issuing convertible securities or options which permit the holder to acquire shares at a price below market value.

Issuance of Bonds

In addition to the need to regulate issuance of securities convertible into shares and options to acquire shares, a question arises as to whether special approval requirements or other procedures should be applied to a company's issuance of ordinary, non convertible bonds.

Some countries leave the issuance of bonds entirely at the discretion of the company's board of directors, based on the assumption that the managers will have an incentive to obtain the best terms available, so shareholder approval is not necessary. A second group of countries, in contrast, look with greater suspicion on issuance of bonds. Some countries prohibit issuance of bonds for a period of time (up to 3 years) after the company's formation and require shareholder approval thereafter. Others limit the nominal value of bonds issued without a guarantee from a third party to the amount of the company's charter capital.

In principle, a requirement for shareholder approval of bond issues would seem to differentiate between various types of borrowing transactions without an apparent reason. This, nevertheless, assumes that proper and enforceable protection against transactions that are based on conflicts of interest exists. If that is not the case, the issuance of bonds can be used by insiders to appropriate part of the income generated by the company. In the transition environment, the law might need to adopt a rather restrictive approach on this point requiring a minimum level of shareholder control over bond issues.

VIII. Transactions Involving a Conflict of Interest

Approval of transactions involving a conflict of interest and remedies. One important issue for company law in every country is the regulation of transactions in which company insiders have a conflict of interest because they have a direct or indirect property interest in the transaction. This problem is especially serious in transition economies, and calls for correspondingly strict regulation.

Three approaches are available. (1) A strict approach, adopted from company laws of the early 20th century prohibits the completion of such transactions. While such an approach can be simple to apply, it may also create serious problems in the day-to-day management of the company, as it may render illegal a number of transactions beneficial to the company entered into by management. (2) A second approach would prohibit most transactions based on a "bright line" prohibition but would also provide some flexibility by permitting approval of specific types of transactions by the non-interested members of the board of directors and by the non interested shareholders. (3) A third option would simply require prior approval of a transaction involving a conflict of interest by the above non-interested parties. In the latter two cases, strict procedural requirements are needed, to reduce the risk that managers will arrange for approval of a transaction by friendly shareholders. In any case, the law should ban two types of transactions for which there is no business justification and a high risk of abuse: payments (kickbacks) by a third person to an insider in connection with a transaction between the company and the third person, and loans by the company to an insider without documentation or without the payment of a reasonable rate of interest.

The law should specify the type of transactions that fall under the scope of its restrictions. It should include those in which insiders, their close family relatives, other persons closely affiliated to them, and members of the management organs of the company's large shareholders, have a direct or indirect property interest. It could also cover cases where the same person is an insider for both parties to a transaction and cases where a close relative of a member of the company's management organs is a member of the management organs of the other party to a transaction. The law should specify the percentage of ownership level at which a large shareholder is considered to be an insider (for example a 20 percent ownership level of a company's common shares), as well as which family members and other affiliated persons are considered insiders.

Remedies for transactions involving a conflict of interest should be specified in the law. The insider who acted while in a conflict of interest situation, should be liable for losses suffered by the company, including lost profits that could have been obtained by contracting on better terms with another party. In cases where it is difficult to prove loss to the company, but possible to show profit to this insider or his family members, or affiliated persons, the insider should be liable up to the amount of profit. The law should, however, limit the circumstances in which a transaction, completed in violation of the conflict of interest procedures, will be invalidated, in order to protect the rights of third parties who conclude a transaction with a company in good faith.

IX. Control and Change in Control

Rules concerning a change in control. Once control of a given company has been acquired by a shareholder, the ability of minority shareholders to sell their shares for a reasonable price often vanishes. This has little to do with the actual performance of the company; it is due to an event which is not connected to their behaviour or the company's potential. In order to respond to this problem, preserve the liquidity of equity markets, and minimize the impact of information asymmetries among shareholders, the law could provide for a system of "takeout" rights: when a shareholder acquires a controlling block of the shares of a widely held company, the shareholder must offer to buy all remaining shares at a fair price. This gives the remaining shareholders an opportunity to decide whether they want to remain as shareholders in the controlled company. The system of takeout rights has been adopted by several countries in Europe and is consistent with the rules envisaged in a draft European Union directive.

Takeout rights should be adopted by transition countries and the company law should provide for their concise definition. It should define a threshold ownership percentage at which a control block of shares is considered to exist (for example 30 percent of the company's common shares). These rights should also be available when control is collectively acquired by a number of affiliated persons. A threshold for the minimum number of shareholders a company must have to be covered by this rule should also be included. Furthermore, it would be desirable that the law defines a minimum offer price, the offer period, and the other terms of the offer to be made by the controlling shareholder to the remaining ones. The offer price could equal the highest price paid by the controlling shareholder and his affiliated persons to acquire the company's shares during a period of time, perhaps 6 months, preceding the date on which the controlling shareholder acquired the control block of shares. Last but not least, the law should prescribe relatively severe sanctions for violation of the requirement to buy all remaining shares, to ensure that this requirement is complied with. The controlling person and his affiliated persons could be deprived of the right to vote their shares, unless the other shareholders vote to restore these voting rights.

In addition to takeout rights, countries with transition economies may want to consider other rules for regulating changes in the control of companies. These rules have two basic elements. The first consists of a minimum notice period prior to the acquisition of a control block of a company's shares: this will give the management of a company time to search for a higher offer for the company's shares from another party or, in the case of a management buy-out, will give outside parties an opportunity to offer a higher price. The second element consists of restrictions on the steps that a company's managers can take to prevent a change of control. If the law provides for a minimum notice period, it is important that management defensive tactics are also restricted during this period. A law that provides a minimum notice period but does not limit defensive tactics may give too much power to a company's managers to act to preserve their own jobs, even when this deprives shareholders of the opportunity to sell their shares at an attractive price.

"Freezeout" transactions

A further issue involving control and acquisition of control involves the right of a controlling shareholder to cause the company to enter into a reorganisation or other transaction. As a result of this transaction, the controlling shareholder will achieve 100 percent ownership of a company's shares or assets and former minority shareholders will have no further opportunity to participate in the company's future profits. This is sometimes called a "freezeout" transaction, because the minority shareholders are frozen out of further participation in the company's profits.

Some countries may choose to restrict freezeout transactions, in order to protect minority rights. For example, general rules on approval of conflict of interest transactions by non-interested shareholders, and the use of appraisal and redemption rights during a reorganisation or major transaction, would help to ensure fair treatment of minority shareholders. These rules would not prevent freezeout transactions, but would help to ensure that the price paid for the shares was fair and that a majority of non interested shareholders agreed to the transaction.

X. Shareholder and Creditor Protection during Payment of Dividends, and A Company's Acquisition and Redemption of its Own Shares

Payments of dividends: In the continental tradition, dividends are understood as a means for companies to distribute some of their accumulated profits to shareholders. In the AngloSaxon common law tradition, dividends can also be used to distribute funds that are no longer needed in the business to the shareholders and to change a company's capital structure. In either case, company laws limit the power of a company to pay dividends or make other distributions to shareholders in order to protect creditors. A company that is insolvent, either in the balance sheet sense (assets are smaller than liabilities) or in the cash flow sense (inability to pay its obligations as they come due) should not be permitted to pay dividends. Companies should also be allowed to pay quarterly or semiannual dividends, as long as the shareholders have approved this practice in their annual meeting.

A system that allows the payment of dividends to shareholders only out of current profits does not encourage equity investment - much needed in the context of transition. It does not allow companies to effectuate long term planning of their own financial structure and reserves, and of their policy towards their shareholders. Shareholders usually prefer a more stable dividend policy than one based exclusively on the distribution of current profits. On the other hand, the unrestricted possibility to distribute capital (in excess of charter capital) to the shareholders might increase creditor risk, especially in an environment of acute information asymmetries that characterises transition economies. Companies could be thus stripped of their most valuable assets without the creditors being informed about it. This is even more likely to happen where the legal framework for secured lending is not yet developed. On the basis of the above considerations, a balanced approach would be to allow only the distribution of past, accumulated as well as current profits as dividends. This should be a default rule; companies should be allowed to further restrict dividend distribution in their charter so that they could become more creditor friendly.

The power to declare dividends is given, in some countries, exclusively to the board of directors. The shareholders in such countries do not have to approve dividends declared by the board and they cannot require the company to declare dividends. In other countries, the shareholders must approve dividends at an annual meeting, though the board of directors may have the power to approve and pay interim dividends, either out of the previous years' profits or as an "advance payment" against the next approved dividend. In transition economies, there may be concern about the motives of the board (or management) in choosing to declare a dividend, or not to do so. In this situation, a rule permitting the shareholders to determine the amount of annual dividends, taking into account the above-mentioned limits on the company's power to pay dividends discussed above, could be appropriate despite the risk that the shareholders will approve larger dividends that the company can afford to pay.

Company's acquisition of its own shares : A company's acquisition of its own shares may raise problems for both creditors and shareholders. From the creditor's perspective, a company's acquisition of its own shares (and also redemption of shares) reduces the property of the company available to pay the creditor's claims. A company's own shares are not an asset of the company in any meaningful sense. If the company's other property is insufficient to pay the claim of creditors, share certificates held in a file drawer in the company's office will have no value. Acquisition of a company's own shares also carries different risks from the shareholders' perspective. A company's acquisition of shares at a price greater than their market value harms shareholders whose shares are not acquired. A company can also take advantage of the shareholders' ignorance of the company's true value to acquire shares for less than their market value, which harms the shareholders whose shares are acquired, and benefits shareholders, especially controlling shareholders, who do not sell their shares.

Some company laws forbid a company's acquisition of its own shares entirely or permit acquisition of shares only in cases specified in the law. Others do not significantly restrict this practice. One solution for transition economies might be to completely ban this type of transaction. This will give maximum protection to the creditors and shareholders. On the other hand, companies might in some cases need the flexibility of acquiring their own shares as a tool of adjusting their financial structure. This might be especially useful in the uncertain transition environment.

An alternative to banning a company's acquisition of its own shares is to allow a company to acquire shares only up to a specific percentage of its charter capital. This then raises the question of how to handle the nominal value of the shares that a company has acquired. In order to provide some protection to creditors, the law could stipulate a period of time, perhaps one year, during which the company must dispose of the shares that it has acquired; it could provide that during this period, the company must either sell the shares, reduce its charter capital by cancelling the acquired shares, or cancel the acquired shares while at the same time increasing the nominal value of its remaining issued shares in an amount sufficient to avoid a reduction in its charter capital. The same restrictions should be applied to the process of appraisal and redemption of shares. A one year period for taking these actions seems to be convenient because it would allow time for a decision, to reduce charter capital or to increase the nominal value of the remaining issued shares, to be taken at the company's next annual shareholder meeting. A shorter period could require the company to convene an extraordinary shareholder meeting, or else to sell shares for a low price, simply to get rid of them. In addition, a company should be permitted to voluntarily acquire its own shares only if, after the acquisition of shares, the company satisfies the same solvency test that applies to dividends.

In order to protect the interests of creditors, a special audit might be required to the effect that a company's acquisition of shares does not impair the company's solvency. In order to reduce the risk of harm to minority shareholders, a company could be required to acquire shares only at their market value. The law could also require shareholder approval of all offers to acquire a company's own shares or, at least, of those offers to acquire shares that are not open to all shareholders in proportion to the number of shares held by each. If the persons whose shares are to be acquired are known, they could be excluded from the vote to approve the acquisition of shares, on the grounds of conflict of interest.

Other Limits on Transactions that Harm Creditors

Any transaction by a company when near or in insolvency can be a vehicle for extracting property from the company, to the detriment of creditors (and, often, shareholders). The challenge is to find a way to block transactions designed to extract property from the company without impeding ordinary business dealings.

Some laws use the concept of "fraudulent conveyance": a transaction is considered to be reversible by a creditor through a petition to court, if the company does not receive equivalent value, and/or the company fails a balance sheet based or liquidity based solvency test after the transaction. The standard of equivalent value is not precise, but it can at least reach egregious cases where a company transfers most of its remaining property to third parties for nominal consideration to evade its creditors. An alternative is for the bankruptcy law to provide a lengthy period prior to the bankruptcy during which suspect transactions can be challenged and reversed in appropriate cases. These rules could be included in the bankruptcy law or in other civil law provisions concerning voidable transactions.

XI. Shareholder Powers

Decisions that require shareholder action: Most company laws require shareholder approval for a limited list of important corporate actions, such as a reorganisation, a liquidation, a large issuance of shares, or amendments to the charter. It is also common for the law to allow a company's charter to assign additional decision-making powers to the shareholders. Company laws typically specify majority voting rules for approval of different actions, but allow a company's charter to specify a higher minimum vote. The only exception to this flexible approach concerns issues relating to election and removal of the company's board of directors, where a higher minimum vote requirement could be used as a device to entrench a company's current managers.

The following issues are required by most legal systems to be decided exclusively by the shareholders and should be considered for adoption as mandatory rules by transition economies:

- Amendments to the company's charter (Paragraphs 38-40). If not all parts of the charter are included, this rule should at least include changes in the company's type, an increase or a decrease in the number of authorised shares of one or more categories (types) of shares, a change in the nominal value of one or more categories of shares, and specification of the number of members of the board of directors;
- Reorganisation of the company (Paragraphs 41-44);
- Conclusion of a major transaction (Paragraphs 47-50);
- Liquidation of the company (Paragraphs 55-56);
- Waiver of the preemptive rights of shareholders to acquire the company's shares (Paragraphs 76-77) or securities convertible into shares (Paragraph 84);
- Approval of issuance of a large amount of shares (Paragraphs 81-82); Issuance of securities convertible into shares and options to acquire shares, if issuance of these securities is permitted by the company law (Paragraphs 83-84);
- Approval of issuance of bonds (Paragraphs 85-87);
- Conclusion of a transaction involving a conflict of interest (Paragraphs 8891);
- Decision on the payment of annual dividends (Paragraphs 97-99); Approval of a company's acquisition of its own shares (Paragraphs 100103); and
- Election of members of the company's board of directors and early termination of their powers.

Where no board exists, election of the managing director and early termination of his/her appointment (Paragraphs 117-119).

Shareholder Power to Act Independently of the Board of Directors

A general question involving shareholder powers concerns the actions shareholders can take on their own, independently of any recommendations from the company's board of directors. In order to protect shareholder authority and the interests of minority shareholders, it may be appropriate for company laws in transition economies to give the shareholders the power to act on their own initiative.

To make the shareholders' right to take decisions without a proposal from the board of directors meaningful, the law should contain procedures for shareholders to include issues on the agenda for a shareholder meeting. These rules could include: (1) a procedure for a shareholder holding a minimum number of shares (perhaps 2 percent of the company's common shares) to submit an issue for consideration at a company's annual shareholder meeting; (2) a procedure for shareholders to obtain a list of other shareholders, in order to solicit support for their proposals; and (3) a procedure for shareholder(s) holding a large number of shares (perhaps 10 percent) to demand that the company's board of directors convenes an extraordinary meeting to discuss specific issues submitted by the shareholder, and to convene the meeting himself if the board of directors refuses to do so.

Procedures for Shareholder Voting

Every company law contains procedures governing the mechanics of shareholder voting. Among the important procedural devices are: a means for shareholders to vote by mail rather than in person, through proxy votes, or written ballots (the use of written ballots should be mandatory for companies that exceed a threshold number of shareholders). In principle, management should be barred from soliciting or voting proxies in transition economies; this prohibition would ensure that shareholders would get a realistic chance to have their motions considered and thus control management which, in these economies is operating under few other constraints. On the other hand, excluding management from proxy representation might result in impasses due to lack of a quorum. That is why proxy voting by management could be envisaged if a credible, enforceable mechanism for solicitation could be insured, that would ensure that other shareholders soliciting proxies are given a fair chance in the process, allowing for an open proxy contest; a mechanism for providing reasonable assuıance that the votes will be counted honestly, such as, for example, the appointment of an independent tabulation commission; a means for shareholders to receive all of the information they need to make an informed decision on the issues that they are asked to vote on; a means for a shareholder to demand a list of the names, addresses and shareholdings of the company's other shareholders, including as much information as is available to the company about beneficial owners of shares who hold their shares indirectly, through nominal holders; and a procedure for shareholders to include proposals and director nominations on the ballot for an annual meeting, and to demand the convening of an extraordinary meeting.

In transition economies characterised by substantial employee share ownership, it may be necessary for the law to include procedures to ensure that the employees can vote and sell their shares freely, without management coercion. For example, the law might forbid a company's managers from receiving a power of attorney from employee-shareholders to vote the employee's share, or from establishing trust management of employee shares which would have the effect of preventing employees from selling or voting shares.

XII. Management and Supervisory Organs Structure and Powers of the Board of Directors

A two-tier board structure is required by some countries, with both a supervisory board and a management board that is appointed by the supervisory board. In transition economies, the company law could allow but not require a two-tier board structure. This flexibility might be achieved by providing for a board of directors, which is elected by the shareholders, and by also allowing the company to have either an individual executive organ (general director or chief executive officer), or a collegial executive organ (a management board). The choice between these two options should be determined either by the company's charter or, if the charter does not specify this structure, by the board of directors.

Some company laws allow companies to specify on their charter that the company will not have a board of directors. In this case, the powers normally exercised by the board of directors are exercised directly by the shareholders. This might be a flexible and cost-effective solution for companies with a very small number of shareholders. Nevertheless, where such options are available, clear alternative sets of rules should be in place; they should include mandatory thresholds (a maximum number of shareholders) under which the possibility to forego the obligation for a board of directors is not possible, and clearly adopt the board of directors as a default solution.

Many company laws give to a board of directors, elected periodically by the shareholders, broad power to oversee the day-to-day management of the company and to select and replace those who carry it out. Some company laws specify the minimum duties of the board of directors, allowing it to undertake additional responsibilities, if such additional powers are specified in the charter or are allowed by a vote of shareholders. Some laws also permit the board of directors to take additional powers away from the management if it believes this is necessary. However, as a practical matter, the ability of the board of directors to act is limited because the members of the board of directors know far less about the company than the day-to-day managers.

The central questions with regard to the power of the board of directors are: (1) which actions by the company must be approved by the shareholders, and therefore cannot be taken solely by decision of the board of directors; (2) which actions can be taken unilaterally by decision of the shareholders, without the approval of the board of directors; (3) what are the minimum tasks assigned to the board of directors; (4) does the board of directors have the power to appoint and remove the officers of the company, especially the chief executive officer; and (5) does the board of directors have the ability to decide what additional tasks it should undertake?

The most important tasks of the board of directors is to select and replace the company's chief executive officer (or collegial executive body). The following is a list of other tasks of the board of directors; this list could be expanded in a company's charter: determining the company's principal business activities; compiling the basic agenda for a shareholder meeting, including proposals submitted by the board of directors and by the shareholders; convening annual and extraordinary shareholder meetings; determining the date for compiling the list of shareholders having the right to vote at a shareholder meeting, and other issues connected to holding a shareholder meeting; approving and submitting for shareholder approval company actions that also require such approval;

- issuing shares within the limits of the number and category (type) of authorised shares, within the limits prescribed by the law and the company's charter;

- issuing bonds and other securities, within the limits of shareholder authorisation, prescribed by the law and the company's charter; borrowing of money in excess of a threshold amount (established by a general shareholder meeting);
- determining the market value of the company's shares or other property, when such a determination is required by the company law; effectuating the company's acquisition and redemption of its own shares, bonds and other securities;
- determining the membership, composition, and competence of the company's executive organ, the compensation of the chief executive officer and other senior officers, and terminating the powers of the chief executive officer and other senior officers;
- approving internal documents that establish the procedure for activities by the company's management organs;
- hiring, and determining the compensation of the company's independent auditor, when the company has one;
- approving the company's annual report and financial statements before their submission to a shareholder meeting; and approving interim payments to the shareholders if the company law permits this decision to be taken by the board of directors.

Election of the Board of Directors

The principal constraint on the board of directors is the right of the shareholders to elect it periodically. In order to protect shareholder control in a transition economy environment, it may be appropriate to provide for a maximum term for the board of directors that is relatively short, perhaps only one year. For the same purpose, the shareholders should have the power to remove, on their own initiative, members of the board at any time and without any stated cause. It may also enhance shareholder power if the law requires that all directors be elected at the same time. Some countries permit the board to be divided into different classes, each of which may serve for 3 or 4 years, with only one class elected each year. The use of such a "staggered" board of directors makes it harder for shareholders to remove a majority of the members of the board of directors, and thus easier for a group of directors to maintain control over company policy.

In transition economies, a legal provision on mandatory cumulative voting for members of the board of directors in companies with a large number of shareholders would be useful. Cumulative voting enables a larger minority shareholder to obtain representation on the board of directors, or a group of small shareholders to put an "outsider" not connected to the majority or the management on the board.

In practice, minority directors elected through cumulative voting will very often be outvoted. Nevertheless, representatives on the board of directors may help minority shareholders to obtain information about the company's business successes and failures, and alert shareholders to a particular problem under discussion or consideration. Also, some decisions by the board will be taken not by the entire board, but by the independent or non-interested members of the board (for example, approving a transaction in which a member of the board or a company's officer has a direct or indirect property interest). For these decisions, the directors elected by the minority shareholders through cumulative voting might sometimes control the outcome. Moreover, there will be other decisions, such as decisions involving determination of the market value of a company's shares, in which a dissenting vote by one director may substantially increase the risk that the assenting board members may face personal liability for a breach of their duty to the company. This may lead the majority directors to adopt more careful or fairer decisions that improve outcomes for minority shareholders.

Obligations and Liability of Members of a Company's Management Organs

The company law should specify standards of conduct for members of the board of directors and the members of a company's other management organs. Some countries allow for liability of members of a company's management organs (including its board of directors) if they do not act reasonably. Other countries require serious fault before these persons can be found liable. However, even in countries where mere negligence can in principle form the basis for liability, cases where the courts have actually found liability are rare.

In general, the minimum standards of conduct imposed by the company law on the members of a company's management organs should be anchored on the concepts of good faith and the interest of the company. These are general principles covering all transactions. They should be applied together with more specific rules on conflicts of interest to ensure that managers fulfill their duties as regards the company. There is good reason to limit the circumstances in which members of a company's management organs are liable for actions taken in good faith and without a conflict of interest. Business decisions necessarily involve risk, and must often be taken based on limited information. Some risky decisions will prove highly profitable, while others will look foolish with the benefit of hindsight. If managers can be found liable for decisions that look foolish in hindsight, they will be reluctant to take risks. Moreover, judges are not very well placed for assessing whether a business decision that has turned out badly was reasonable at the time it was taken.

The company law should give members of a company's board of directors and also a company's shareholders the right to bring an action in court against the members of a company's management organs, in which the board members and /or the shareholder(s) seeks damages on behalf of the corporation for violation of these persons' obligations to the corporation. It is appropriate to require that a shareholder hold some minimum percentage of shares in order to sue. This can help to avoid "nuisance" suits, brought to force directors to settle the suit for a sum of money which is significant, but less than the expense of defending themselves in court. A member of the board of directors or a shareholder who brings such a suit and is successful in recovering damages on behalf of the company should have the right to receive compensation for his/her expenses, including legal fees, as long as these expenses are reasonable in relation to the amount of the damages.

XIII. Disclosure of Information about a Company Independent Audit and Other Reviews of a Company's Financial Statements

A requirement that a company's financial statements be reviewed by an auditor can be an important protection against fraud by the company's officers. At the same time, for a company with a small turnover or a small number of shareholders, an annual audit may be a substantial and largely unnecessary expense. Thus, the company law should as a rule require an annual audit; it should allow companies with a small annual turnover or with a small number of shareholders to adopt charter provisions which waive the audit requirement; alternatively, it could allow the latter to be audited at less frequent intervals or only at the request of shareholders. In any event, these charter provisions should be considered non-applicable when the company exceeds the turnover or share thresholds provided for in the law.

Disclosure to Shareholders

All company laws require a company to provide basic information to shareholders periodically. The law should require a company to provide to shareholders, at least once a year, a balance sheet, statement of profits and losses, and a written report on the company's activities. As discussed earlier, a shareholder should also have the right to obtain a list of the company's other shareholders, their addresses, and shareholdings. This information can be used by the shareholder to solicit support at a shareholder meeting for his/her nominees for the board of directors or other proposals. The law could impose a threshold requirement for such requests to avoid nuisance requests.

A more difficult question involves shareholder rights to obtain additional financial information about the company. Access rights may need to be limited, both to avoid expense to the company and to prevent disclosure of sensitive business information that competitors might want to know. The law could provide for access rights to be subject to a threshold percentage, such as 5 or 10 percent of a company's shares, and/or subject to a pledge of confidentiality by the shareholder. It could also disallow access to information the dissemination of which could seriously damage the company's business. This exception would have to be defined carefully, however, as it could be used by managers to restrict shareholder access to any important information. In any event, all members of a company's board of directors (including minority directors elected through cumulative voting) should have the right to inspect a company's accounts and other relevant information. The general duty to act in good faith and in the company's interests provides here adequate protection against this information being used in an abusive manner.

Public Disclosure

A company's charter should be available for inspection at the state registration office for a reasonable fee.

Information about the founders could also be made available to the public, as well as financial statements of large companies, exceeding a threshold number of shareholders, for example 50. However, a company with a small number of shareholders should not be required to publicly disclose its financial statements. This is important in countries in which criminal activities, such as extortion, have not yet been effectively contained.

9

Potential for Increased Institutional Monitoring and Financing

Introduction

A brief mention should be made about industry-wide monitoring. It would appear that, in the light of the focus given to board structure and composition by the Cadbury Committee in the UK and the Bosch Committee and the AIMA in Australia, there is only limited scope for further industry-wide action by institutions and their trade associations in that area. On the other hand, in areas such as disclosure of executive remuneration, and disclosure generally, there is considerable room for more industry-wide monitoring.

Direct Firm-Level Monitoring

This section deals with the disincentives to, and incentives for, the performance of *detailed* firm-level monitoring by fund managers. Several of the disincentives and incentives relate specifically to institutional interventions to change management, but some relate to detailed monitoring in a broader sense: encompassing vigorous, continual examination of the performance of the management of all portfolio companies.

Structural Disincentives to Detailed Monitoring

The disincentives discussed under this subsection are characterized as 'structural' disincentives. The reason for this is that they all flow from either the structure of the system of corporate ownership and governance, the structure and workings of the fund-management industry, or the structure of the institutions themselves. Most of the 11 disincentives discussed below fall within one of the following three broad groupings. First, the 'outsider' system of corporate ownership and governance in the UK quoted sector (a) entails the real option of sale rather than costly monitoring, and thus perpetuates the collective-action problem (associated with monitoring) even where the largest few shareholders hold a significant proportion of the equity; and (b) means that fund managers have very limited personnel available to perform the monitoring function. Secondly, there are divergences between the interests of the various parties composing an institutional shareholder (for example the fund manager, trustees, and members of a pension fund), which means that the optimal amount of monitoring from the point of view of the ultimate beneficiaries is normally greater than the amount of monitoring that is actually performed. Thirdly, the highly competitive nature of the fund-management business, and of the insurance, unit-trust, and investment-trust sectors, means that co-operation between different institutions is not easy.

i. The Structure of Corporate Ownership and Governance: Institutions as Arm's-Length Investors

It was demonstrated in the previous chapter that there is a fundamental difference between the type of shareholder or shareholders which have ultimate control over quoted

German and Japanese companies, and the type of shareholders which ultimately control most quoted UK companies (and about half of all quoted Australian companies). The ultimate controllers of German and Japanese firms are 'committed' shareholders, whilst the ultimate controllers of UK companies and widely held Australian companies are 'arm's-length' shareholders. This has a major ramification: when there are serious problems with the management of a UK company or a widely held Australian company, the first instinct of many institutional shareholders is to try to extricate themselves from the situation by selling the shares. The dominant shareholders of German and Japanese companies, on the other hand, have a default strategy of staying put whilst a restructuring is conducted. In Japan, this often involves the main bank'. In Germany, it occasionally involves the 'house bank' (but not as often as in Japan), sometimes involves the supervisory board, and sometimes involves no external intervention at all. It is of some significance that the main/ house bank typically has an equity holding in the company as well as a lender-borrower relationship with it. In Coffee's terminology, the German and Japanese banks, and other committed shareholders, have traded liquidity for control.

One caveat to the above concerns the monitoring of the management of Japanese and German firms whilst performance is satisfactory, or at least not clearly inadequate. Some commentators believe that Japanese main banks, and German banks and supervisory boards, play an active role in routinely monitoring the management of firms. Kallfass, for example, states:

Through the exercise of voting rights the big banks greatly influence hirings and firings in West German corporations' [non-]executive bodies, the supervisory boards; as well as on managing boards. They have a voice in all fundamental business decisions. This is evident not only from the high proportion of bank representatives on supervisory boards, but also from the frequent namings of bank managers as chairs of corporate supervisory boards.

However, the latest evidence supports strongly the view that, in normal states, the managers of Japanese and German firms have substantial discretion and leeway.

In the normal course of events the Japanese main bank exercises explicit control neither in the selection of management nor in corporate policy making. Well-run companies that incur little or no debt from banks appear to be virtually free from banks' intervention, and their managements enjoy the highest degree of autonomy Banks remain as silent business partners in good profit states. Their power becomes visible only in bad states.

It must be emphasized that, despite the problems associated with selling a large stake (resulting from the depressing effect upon the share price if it is not done with great caution), the UK and Australian interview studies revealed that sale is still very much a major option for most institutions when serious problems emerge at a portfolio company. One fund manager from a large UK insurer explained how a sale in these circumstances would not necessarily involve a large discount:

Poor managerial performance occasionally surfaces like a crevasse, down which one falls. More often, however, one has what I would perhaps describe as a 'creeping effect' of poor managerial performance, which is a long sliding slope. And depending on quite where you are on that slope when you realise that it is poor management, and the dimensions of the slope, can influence the judgment that you take in that situation. In this situation it is generally speaking more appropriate to sell your shares to somebody who sees the hill going up rather than down.

The nature of the outsider system of corporate ownership and governance means that, although the benefits from exit decrease as concentration of shareholding increases, exit will always be a reasonably attractive option. The outsider system seems, therefore, to have perpetuated the collective action problem (associated with monitoring) during the period when increased institutional share ownership was increasing substantially the concentration of shareholding in the UK and Australia.

Another effect of the outsider system, where institutions have the option of sale in the market or to a hostile bidder, is that even large institutions have only a fairly small number of fund managers and analysts available to perform detailed monitoring, and those persons each have only a short time that they can spend on any one company.

ii. Collective-Action and Free-Rider Problems

Once a company has more than one shareholder, the 'collective-action' problem surfaces. The monitoring of management is a collective good: any positive effects from monitoring are enjoyed by all shareholders regardless of whether or not they have participated in, or contributed to, the monitoring. For this reason, a shareholder behaving in an economically rational way will undertake monitoring only in limited circumstances. At the most basic level, it seems that a shareholder will provide the collective good of monitoring if the costs to that shareholder are outweighed by the benefits it receives from the monitoring. However, as Rock points out, in the context of companies, the basic theory of collective action needs to be adjusted for the possibility of alternative courses of action: simply holding the shares (and free-riding on the monitoring efforts, if any, of others); selling the shares; or acquiring the company in a takeover or (of more relevance in the present context) engineering a takeover bid for the company. The crucial condition for the provision of monitoring is, as it happens, that the shareholder in question must stand to gain more from monitoring than from any alternative course of action. If this condition is satisfied then, in contrast to the basic theory of collective action, it is rational for a shareholder to perform monitoring even if the gains derived by that shareholder are exceeded by the cost of the monitoring. Also, and importantly, if a shareholder stands to gain more from an alternative course of action than from monitoring, then it is not in the shareholder's economic interests to perform any monitoring even if the shareholder would enjoy a net gain from monitoring. The latter scenario can lead to a classic prisoners' dilemma, where (a) shareholders would gain collectively if each contributed to monitoring, but (b) it is in the interests of each shareholder not to contribute, so (c) no monitoring occurs and all shareholders are worse off than if they had all contributed.

Of importance for present purposes is the fact that greater concentration of shareholding makes monitoring more rational for large shareholders for two reasons. First, it increases the benefits which flow from, and lowers the costs of, monitoring. Secondly, it decreases the benefits from alternative courses of action: free-riding becomes less likely, and selling out becomes comparatively less attractive compared to monitoring. The increase in institutional share ownership in the UK and Australia from the 1960s until the 1990s led to greater concentration in shareholding. Why, then, are most large fund managers still more likely to sell than intervene when serious managerial problems arise? It was suggested in the previous subsection that the nature of the outsider system of corporate ownership and governance means that, although the benefits from exit decrease as concentration of shareholding increases, exit will always be a reasonably attractive option. There are, however, other explanatory factors.

The discussion to this point has been based on the assumption that the ultimate beneficial owners (for example the beneficiaries of pension and superannuation schemes, and the unit-holders in unit trusts) of the institutions' equity holdings are the persons who decide whether or not to partake in monitoring. In practice, of course, this decision is taken in most cases by the fund manager (external or in-house), and in some cases by the trustees (in the case of a pension or superannuation scheme) or the board (in the case of an insurance company or investment-trust company).

Just as the divergence between the interests of shareholders and managers of a company gives rise to agency costs, agency costs also arise from divergences between the interests of (a) an external fund manager and its clients (for example the trustees of pension and superannuation schemes, and charities; investment-trust companies; private clients); (b) the manager and unit-holders of a unit trust; and (c) *some* of the trustees (namely the sponsor's representatives) and the body of members of a pension or superannuation scheme. The agency problem in (c) is being diminished by the recent moves towards compulsory member-trustees in UK and Australian pension and superannuation schemes. Problems (a) and (b) are, however, much more difficult to reduce to any great extent. The significance of the divergences detailed in (a) and (b) has been described as follows: 'Because of this divergence between the interests of [fund] managers and the interests of their principals, one cannot assume that because improving corporate governance may increase the value of the managed portfolios, improving corporate governance will be in the interests of the [fund] managers.'

As demonstrated in the next subsection, monitoring that increases the value of a company is a collective good for external fund managers. On the other hand, the next four subsections show that only rarely will it be in the interests of individual fund managers to provide that collective good. The divergence between the interests of external fund managers and their clients means that the factors influencing whether it would be rational for a particular fund manager to engage in monitoring are different from those which would determine the rationality of monitoring if that decision were in the hands of that fund manager's clients. As a result, less monitoring is performed by external fund managers than is optimal from the point of view of their clients.

iii. Fund-Manager Performance Measurement

In the UK, the US, and Australia, the performance of a fund-management firm is measured relatively rather than absolutely. The performance of external managers of pension funds, and the performance of unit trusts, is assessed mostly in comparison to that of other pension-fund managers and other (equivalent) unit trusts, respectively, and less frequently in comparison to stock indices. Therefore, in the (not so extreme) case where the holdings of each external fund manager with a stake in company X are index-weight, or near index-weight, Rock says that monitoring 'that benefits all will benefit none'. This is correct in regard to benefit in the form of winning new clients through better relative performance. However, it disregards another benefit that a fund manager derives from an increase in the value of a portfolio company: the great majority of UK, US, and Australian fund managers charge their clients an *ad valorem* fee-a (decreasing) percentage of the value of funds managed. Therefore, any monitoring which increases the value of the funds under management also leads to an increase in the fund manager's fee. This is discussed further in the next subsection. For the moment it is enough to say that, where every external fund manager has an index-weight or near index-weight holding, even though it may be irrational for any one fund manager to provide the collective good (monitoring), the fund managers as a group would be better off if the good were provided. It is at this point that the writer's analysis departs from that of Rock, who suspects that not monitoring is normally the collective good as far as external fund managers are concerned. This is because Rock does not take into consideration the increase in fee that flows from an increase in the value of a portfolio company.

Once one relaxes the assumption that all external fund managers have an index-weight holding in company X, it becomes clear that some fund managers (namely, those with an overweight holding) have a greater incentive than others (namely, those with either an index-weight or an underweight holding) to engage in monitoring. Even though monitoring conducted by an over weighted fund manager would also benefit the performance of index-weighted and underweighted competitors, it would benefit the performance of the overweighted fund manager to a greater degree. By the same token, an underweighted fund manager would probably never have an incentive to expend resources on monitoring. Any increase in its fee would be overridden by the cost in terms of having improved the performance of those competitors which had index-weight or overweight holdings even more than it improved its own performance-and possibly for no cost to those competitors! That UK-based fund managers do not participate in interventions when they have underweight holdings has been confirmed in (separate) interviews conducted by Coffee and the present author. The way in which the performance of external fund managers is measured is thus part of the reason why less monitoring is performed by fund managers than is optimal from the point of view of their clients.

In-house pension-fund managers should not be affected by this consideration, because they are not competing for clients. However, the performance of most in-house investment managers used by UK pension funds is measured using league tables. An in-house management team that consistently under-performs the industry's average manager may well be replaced by one or more external fund manager(s). An in-house manager with an underweight holding or even an index-weight holding may not, therefore, wish to take part in an intervention which, if successful, would improve the performance of other fund managers proportionally more than the performance of its own fund. This raises the question of whether other fund managers which have solely or predominantly internal funds under management particularly the fund-management arms of insurance companies are influenced by whether they are overweighted, underweighted, or market-weighted, when it comes to deciding whether or not to participate in an intervention. Certainly, from the point of view of the policyholders, an insurance company's fund managers should not take this matter into consideration. But the executives of the insurance company want to win new policyholders, and there are many insurance companies in competition for potential new policyholders. If an underweighted insurer (with, say, a 1% holding) plays a major part in a successful intervention, which improves the performance of its life fund for its existing policyholders, it might also be making a rod for its own back when the performance tables for with-profits funds are next published. A rival insurer with an overweight holding (say 6%) would, whether or not it also took part in the intervention, have achieved a gross return relatively greater (500% greater, in this example) than that of the underweighted insurer. Nevertheless, it may be significant that, of the four UK fund managers interviewed by the author who were engaged full-time (or almost full time) on matters of corporate governance and problem companies, two were senior executives of fund-management arms of large insurers, and one was a senior officer of an in-house pension-fund manager.

iv. Financial Constraints

Any form of monitoring involves costs for the fund manager(s) concerned. An intervention obviously entails greater costs than less vigorous actions. Before discussing the actual outlays involved in an intervention, it is important to note that there are other substantial costs involved. Some which are termed 'private costs' are discussed in Subsection B.1. (6), below. Another one is the opportunity cost of the time spent by senior fund managers in organizing and conducting the intervention. As mentioned in Chapter 9, it is only senior fund managers who are involved in detailed monitoring actions. When tied up in an intervention at one portfolio company, a senior fund manager loses the chance to market the firm to potential clients, and to consolidate relationships with existing clients. A fund manager interviewed by the author said that, in one major intervention, he had spent a total of 48 hours in meetings, not including travelling time.

There are numerous outlays involved in an intervention. Legal fees are commonly a major expense, as it is usual for the advice of solicitors to be obtained. It is also common for a merchant bank to be engaged to find a new management team. Sometimes the members of a potential new management team will require that they be indemnified by the intervening institutions as a condition of accepting their positions. (This is especially the case where the company is in very poor financial shape, as is often the case here.) If the matter gets to the stage of an extraordinary general meeting, there is the expense of an explanatory circular to all shareholders a right which the intervening institutions would invariably wish to utilize. If the intervening institutions send out their circular themselves, they must bear the cost of that. They are entitled to have the company circulate it for them. In the latter case, the intervening institutions would have to pay (up front) the company's expenses, but these can be reimbursed if the general meeting so resolves (which it probably would do if the institutions had the numbers to implement successfully their other resolutions at the meeting).

In one UK intervention, the solicitors' bill came to £60,000, and another intervention described by an interviewee had expenses of £20,000. In each case, two institutions were forced to share those expenses it is difficult for the proactive member(s) of an institutional coalition to persuade the supporting institutions (who are business competitors) to contribute to the outlays. Most external fund managers do not even bother to ask their pension-fund trustee clients for a contribution towards such expenses, due to the highly competitive nature of the pension-fund management business. But, as Black and Coffee point out, if an external 'pension fund manager does not seek reimbursement from its clients for expenses, then the expected benefit [from the intervention] must be huge to justify the manager incurring any expense'

Black and Coffee give the example of an external fund manager with a 1% stake in a company capitalized at £1,000 million. As this stake is worth £10 million, a proposed intervention thought likely to increase the company's share price by 10% would yield the fund manager's clients a £1 million gain. It would clearly be in the interests of the fund manager's clients for the fund manager to contribute £30,000 towards the cost of an intervention (assuming total costs of £60,000 and only two institutions footing the bill). It was mentioned earlier that UK fund managers charge their clients an *ad valorem* fee. For standard discretionary balanced management for pension funds, the average fees in 1994 were 49.6 basis points (i.e. 0.496 of 1%) for the first £10-50 million of funds under management; 30.7 basis points for funds between £50-100 million; 23 basis points for funds between £100-200 million; and 19.8 basis points for funds above £200 million. Even taking the fee for the smallest portfolios (49.6 basis points) the expected £1 million increase in the value of the shareholding in the above example would yield the fund manager an increase in remuneration of only £4,960. Clearly, the expected increase in share price from an intervention in a small or medium-sized quoted company (which is where most interventions have occurred) must be very large to vindicate an *external* fund manager becoming an expense-sharing member of an institutional coalition. And, of course, it would be rational for an external fund manager to perform some monitoring only if (a) the expected increase in its fee exceeded the total costs (direct and indirect) incurred by it in the monitoring, *and* (b) the expected net gain from monitoring exceeded the expected gain from alternative courses of action.

Coffee proposes incentive compensation for external fund managers as a partial cure of the agency problem just described. He was, however, told in his interviews with UK fund managers that the introduction of worthwhile incentive compensation is commercially infeasible in the UK due to client distrust of high fees and the highly competitive market for fund management. Indeed, as at early 1993, the investment-management contracts of only 6% of UK pension funds made provision for performance related compensation.

Managers of internal funds, such as fund-management arms of insurance companies and in-house pension-fund managers, do not have the disincentive just described. For them, the relevant consideration for present purposes is whether the sums add up from the point of view of their fund(s). On the other hand, they do not seem to be entirely free from the agency problem set out in the previous subsection.

v. Increased Level of Indexed Investing

The gradual trend towards passive fund-management techniques, whereby index-weight stakes are held in a wide spread of companies, can be expected to exacerbate the problems referred to in the previous two subsections. In the first instance, an indexer will not, by definition, have any significantly overweight holdings, and thus (especially if an external manager) will always face the disincentive of improving the relative performance of overweighted rivals if it considers intervening at a portfolio company. Secondly, the fees charged for managing funds passively are, naturally, much lower than for discretionary management. The average fees charged in 1994 for managing a segregated fund, tracking the FT-A All Share index, were just 12 basis points (for a £10 million fund), 10 basis points (for a £75 million fund), and 5.5 basis points (for a £200 million fund). These fees are so low that a fund manager would virtually never recoup the expense of organizing and implementing an intervention.

Consistent with these predictions, two Australian fund managers interviewed by the author, whose firms used indexing and quantitative management techniques, said that their institutions did not even have the usual meetings with the senior management of portfolio companies, on the ground that they would hold the stock regardless of what the management had to say. It would be a waste of money for them to expend resources on monitoring of any sort, let alone an intervention. In contrast, two UK interviewees said that their institutions did engage in monitoring despite the fact that they indexed most of their holdings. As *in-house* pension-fund managers, they did not have the same interest in cost minimizing as *external* indexers; their interest was in the benefit to their funds that would flow from any increase in the value of portfolio companies, resulting from their monitoring.

vi. Structural Conflicts of Interest

Several US works have analysed in detail the conflicts of interest which serve to dissuade various types of institution from becoming involved actively in corporate governance. The evidence indicates that many UK and Australian institutions face similar conflicts, although, overall, conflicts of interest would seem not to have been as large a deterrent to activism as in the US. This is possibly explicable by the fact that most institutional interventions, and other detailed monitoring actions, occur 'behind closed doors' in the UK and Australia, whereas institutional activism in the US has mostly been very public. Since some conflicts of interest are 'reputational', there is less at stake in monitoring in private compared to monitoring in the public arena.

Most large UK and Australian fund-management firms are affiliated with firms that provide services (besides fund management) to quoted companies. These firms may incur 'private costs' from being involved in an intervention or other form of detailed monitoring action, especially if the detailed monitoring takes place at a company with which other relationships exist. If a fund manager intervenes at company X, company X might take business away from another arm of the fund manager's firm (for example commercial banking, corporate advisory, stock broking, or commercial insurance), or it may take business away from the fund manager itself where the fund manager manages assets for company X's pension/superannuation scheme. However, business may also be lost by both a fund-management firm and its affiliates even where they have no relationship (other than the fund manager's shareholding) with the company subject to the intervention. Such a loss of business could occur as a result of the fund manager gaining a 'bad' reputation amongst corporate managements that is, the reputation of being an 'interventionist'. Corporate managements may switch business to more 'loyal' financial firms. The fund manager may also find that the managements of other portfolio companies start to 'clam up'. Thus, one insider has said that UK fund managers that are affiliated with merchant banks 'like to keep their profile [on corporate-governance matters] below the level of the floor'.

Despite these possibilities, it is clear that the fund-management subsidiaries of merchant-banking companies ('financial conglomerates') have been involved in many interventions in the UK. When an illiquid stake of, say, 12% or 18% is held, the possible private costs (and other costs) of intervening may be outweighed by the potential benefits from installing a new management. In addition, there has been at least one well-publicized case where the fund-management arm of a financial conglomerate, holding a 13.5% stake in a company to which the fund manager's affiliate merchant bank was the key adviser, sold out to a hostile bidder despite the obvious resultant loss of business for its affiliate.

The AIMA has directly addressed this issue. The *AIMA Corporate Governance Guidelines* recommend that AIMA members should have a written policy on the exercising of voting rights. The *Guidelines* continue:

> *Each investment manager's proxy voting policy and procedures should include a statement recognising that the investment manager must only vote in the client's interest, and that it is the investment manager's duty to put any other client relationship or interest to one side when deciding how to vote on behalf of clients. It is recommended that the investment manager have in place a*

> *procedure for dealing with conflicts of interest. It is recommended that wherever a client delegates responsibility for exercising proxy votes, the investment manager should report back to the client when votes are cast (including abstentions) on investments owned by the client. The report should include a positive statement that the investment manager has complied with its obligation to exercise voting rights in the client's interests only. If an investment manager is unable to make this statement without qualification, the report should include an explanation.*

Company executives in the US, acting in their capacity as pension-scheme trustees, have applied pressure to the external fund managers of their companies' pension funds to take a pro-management approach to the voting of shares. It is unclear whether the (management-appointed) trustees of UK and Australian pension funds have taken such action. In any case, the recent move towards compulsory member-trustees is a positive step towards removing this potential conflict of interest.

vii. Qualification Constraints

The disincentives discussed to this point, which relate to the problems of collective action and agency, represent a fairly formidable set of obstacles to serious intervention by managers of external funds, and a sizeable set of obstacles for managers of internal funds. Even assuming that those barriers do not suppress the desire to monitor of all of a company's major institutional shareholders, there are other barriers that serve to discourage the performance of, and diminish the probability of success of, any detailed monitoring either contemplated or initiated by the otherwise-undeterred institution(s).

One such disincentive is that, whilst fund managers are probably adequately qualified to monitor the performance of company managers, many may lack the skills necessary to run a campaign to replace an underperforming management team. In the words of one fund manager with experience in this area, 'fund managers are listeners, not persuaders'.

viii. Informational Constraints

Following on from the previous factor, there is the problem that, even if the intervenor (or prospective intervenor) has 'a flair for presentation' (to assist in winning over other uncommitted institutions), it would be 'difficult to match the management's arguments because [the intervenor would be] working only on the basis of the information' provided by the management. As conceded by one of the participants in the UK interview study, institutions 'operate from a position, really, of very limited knowledge'. The reason why this factor appears under the head of 'structural disincentives' is because part of the reason for its existence lies in the fact that UK and Australian institutions typically have information solely from their equity holdings. They do not benefit (as do German and Japanese banks) from other relationships besides that of an equity holder. Even where a fund-management firm is affiliated with a commercial bank which lends to the company in question, or with an investment bank which provides financial-advisory or broking services to the company, any useful information possessed by the other divisions or subsidiaries would be (or should be) inaccessible due to Chinese Walls.

ix. Lack of Homogeneity amongst Institutional Viewpoints

A UK fund manager interviewed by the author said that he believed that institutional interventions happened too late in the day. He continued: 'We pick up things very early. In a number of cases we've picked up things very early that are going wrong, but profits are going up; dividends are going up; everybody loves them; the shares are sky high. It's very difficult to influence, or go and see, other shareholders when everything appears fine but you've picked things up.' Another UK fund manager said: 'The problem you've got is that institutions consist of people with widely differing views on an interpretation of markets and events.

In the case of institutional interventions to change under-performing managements, this lack of homogeneity in views can play a destabilizing role at two stages. First, as implied by the first of the quotations above, it can delay or prevent the formation of an institutional coalition. Secondly, where a coalition is up and running, it can either (a) defeat altogether the goals of the coalition this has occurred where non-coalition institutions have sided with the impugned management; or (b) lead to a more moderate outcome than that sought initially. Looking at the first case in more detail, UK fund managers interviewed by the author commented that the ideal coalition would have two or three members, that four is the maximum for a workable group, and that these institutions should, ideally, represent at least 20-30% of the equity.

Differing institutional views affect not only attempted ousting of underperforming managements. The UK practice of pre-marketing of large transactions, rights issues, etc. It was noted that most pre-marketed proposals elicit a diversity of views some favourable, some unfavourable (to varying degrees), and some indifferent and that some proposals are, therefore, carried into effect in spite of the strong opposition of a major shareholder.

In conclusion, it is only when something is blatantly wrong that there will be sufficient like-minded institutions for a successful intervention to be possible. However, it seems likely that, from a comparative perspective, this is not a weakness in the UK and Australian systems. Interventions in Germany and Japan rarely occur until a late stage of under-performance.

x. Logistical and Practical Constraints

The UK interview study revealed that there are logistical problems which add to the expected cost of a planned intervention. In combination with other factors, they could deter some possible actions from taking place. They certainly hinder those interventions which do occur. Getting a group of just three or four institutions together for meetings at a mutually convenient time, at short notice, is difficult. This is the case even in the City of London, which is tailor-made for interventions because most of the large English institutions are based there. This is one of the reasons why coalitions larger than four members become unwieldy. It is difficult for the Scottish institutions to play an active role in a coalition because of the distance factor. This is also a problem in Australia, where it would not be uncommon to find that half of the potential members of an institutional coalition are located in Sydney and the other half are located in Melbourne. Another practical difficulty for a minority of institutions is a requirement to obtain the prior blessing of all or many clients before voting or taking other action in relation to controversial matters.

xi. Presence of a Non-Institutional Controlling Shareholder

Thus, the disincentive to institutional intervention which this entails flows from the structure of the corporate sector. Where a non-institutional shareholder has a stake of such a size that a successful institutional intervention is not possible, the institutional shareholders in the company would be aware of this and would adopt an even more arm's-length approach to the investment than in the case of their investments in widely held firms. If there is a 30% + (non-institutional) shareholder, and it is prepared to suffer bad management, then disaffected institutions will in most cases be better off by taking an alternative course of action to monitoring.

Other Factors which Inhibit Detailed Monitoring

The following are some further factors which serve as disincentives to detailed monitoring. These factors are not related to the structure of the system of corporate ownership and governance, the structure and workings of the fund-management industry, or the structure of the institutions themselves.

i. Non-Structural Conflicts of Interest

Conflicts of interest which arise out of the organizational structure of the institutions are not the only conflicts which deter monitoring. There are also non-structural conflicts, which deter certain institutions from conducting monitoring in certain areas. For instance, one UK fund-management firm would be unlikely to join other institutions in pushing for the enfranchisement of non-voting shares at portfolio companies because its listed parent company has non-voting shares. A second example is that some listed UK merchant-banking companies, which have large fund management subsidiaries, have a tradition of scanty disclosure in their accounts in an age when institutions are increasingly urging their portfolio companies to disclose more information. A third example is that a listed UK insurance company, which did not comply with the *Cadbury Code* in four respects in 1994, reportedly failed to provide in its 1994 annual report a 'material reason for non-compliance' as required by paragraph 12.43(j) of the *Listing Rules*. In a fourth instance, one listed UK fund manager recently implemented an executive share-option scheme which did not comply with the ABI and NAPF guidelines on performance criteria. Finally, the executive directors of several listed UK insurers had three-year rolling service contracts as at 1993-4, which explained the reluctance of the ABI Investment Committee to join the call for rolling contracts to be shortened or changed to fixed-term contracts.

ii. Fear of Political Repercussions

There is no doubt that, during the 1960s and 1970s, the UK institutions (in particular, the large insurers) were extremely wary about the extent of their potential power over corporate managements being seized upon as an excuse for nationalization or other major regulatory intervention. There were still some concerns in the early

1980s, but the 1992 interview study of Coffee suggested that fear of political retaliation was not then a significant deterrent to intervention. It is possible that a change of government could alter the perception of fund managers on this matter.

As regards Australia, there has been an instance of political retaliation against institutional power. A provision was introduced into the companies legislation in 1961 which required that unit-trust deeds contain a covenant barring the manager and the trustee from voting on the election of directors in portfolio companies, without the consent of a majority of unit holders. The Minister for Justice, speaking on the Bill, said: 'The restrictions imposed by the Bill arise out of the necessity to impose some curb on the enormous power capable of being exercised, not by the interest holders themselves but by the managers of the [unit trust] who actually may have little financial interest in a particular trust.' None of the participants in the author's Australian interview study mentioned fear of political repercussions as a disincentive to detailed monitoring. It should be noted that a Parliamentary inquiry into the role of institutional shareholders in Australia was conducted during 1993-5. The inquiry was, however, concerned more about a lack of, rather than too much, institutional involvement in corporate governance.

iii. Legal Constraints

UK institutional shareholders are subject to significantly less legal constraints than their US counterparts. None of the interviewees in the UK interview project cited legal constraints as a major deterrent to their intervening at a problem company. The situation for Australian institutions falls somewhere between the restrictive US situation and the UK situation. Several of the Australia-based fund managers interviewed by the author said that legal constraints served as a significant deterrent to their engaging in collective action at a portfolio company. The main provisions affecting UK and Australian institutions are detailed below.

Both countries have insider-trading legislation. It does not matter if an institution comes into possession of insider information during the course of monitoring, so long as it does not trade on it, encourage or procure another party to trade in the shares, or communicate the information to others. But does the insider-trading legislation cause institutions to conduct significantly less monitoring than they would conduct in its absence? First, the legislation is not a barrier to routine meetings with company managements. Secondly, it is difficult to see how the legislation could stymie interventions, because institutions only initiate or join coalitions when they have decided that they do not want to sell their shares at the prevailing price. Thirdly, in relation to pre-marketing of proposed large transactions, although most of the UK institutions covered in the interview project were happy to be made insiders for a few days, it might be argued that without the prohibition on insider trading they would be able to become involved at an earlier stage. However, it is likely that, even in the absence of the legislation, a company's management would divulge undisclosed price-sensitive information to an institutional shareholder only if the institution first gave an undertaking not to trade in the shares until the information became public. The desire for freedom to trade would ensure the same relatively short period during which the institution would be happy to be an insider. Finally, inability to trade the shares is cited commonly as a reason why institutions do not want 'institutional' non-executive directors. A Chinese Wall could, however, be utilized to enable the institution to trade the shares of a company at which one of its fund managers or a nominee was a non-executive director. In addition, there are several other reasons usually given by institutions when explaining their antipathy to the concept of institutional non-executives. These other factors would remain as strong disincentives to institutional non-executives even if there were no insider-trading legislation.

It is possible in each country for an institution to be held liable for wrongful or insolvent trading at a portfolio company, if the institution is a party in accordance with whose directions or instructions the directors of the company are accustomed to act (i.e. a 'shadow director'). In addition, in Australia, if it is a shadow director, an institution is subject to all of the provisions of the Corporations Law to which any director is subject. Importantly, there are numerous directors' duties codified in the Australian legislation, and these would be applicable. Despite the fact that this is a rather harsh eventuality, most of the UK fund managers interviewed by Coffee denied that this possibility entered their thinking when intervening at, or otherwise monitoring the management of, a portfolio company. Whether an institution is a party in accordance with whose instructions the board is accustomed to act must be determined from the point of view of the board. However, probably the last thing that a board, which was the subject of an institutional intervention, would do would be to act in accordance with the instructions of the institutions (if any were given, which is most unlikely). It is not surprising then that, as Coffee's interviews indicated, this potential legal problem is not considered to be of practical importance by UK institutions.

Australia has a statutory system for regulating takeovers and, as Hill points out, the provisions 'are more than capable of catching conduct not strictly associated with a takeover bid at all'. Section 615 of the Corporations Law prohibits an acquisition of shares in a company if it would result in (a) any person presently 'entitled' to less than 20% of the voting shares in the company becoming entitled to more than 20% of the voting shares; or (b) any person already entitled to between 20-90% of the voting shares becoming entitled to a greater percentage of the voting shares. Part 6.7 of the Corporations Law contains a regime under which any person who becomes a 'substantial shareholder', or whose substantial shareholding changes by a certain amount, or who ceases to be a substantial shareholder, must notify the company and the ASX of certain prescribed particulars. A person has a substantial shareholding for the purposes of Part 6.7 if the person is 'entitled' to 5% or more of the voting shares. The crucial concept in section 615 and Part 6.7 is, therefore, 'entitlement' to shares. The shares to which a person is entitled include not only shares in which that person has a 'relevant interest', but also shares in which an 'associate' has a relevant interest. An associate includes a person in concert with whom the primary person is acting or proposes to act; and a person with whom the primary person has, or proposes to enter into, an agreement, arrangement, or understanding (formal or informal, written or oral, legally enforceable or otherwise) for the purpose of controlling or influencing the composition of the company's board or the conduct of the company's affairs.

A handful of institutions which form a loose coalition in order to replace an under-performing management team or board would almost certainly be 'associates'. Even co-operation between a group of institutions in relation to a non-control issue (for example a proposed, excessively generous, executive share-option scheme) may constitute the institutions associates of each other. A breach of Part 6.7 and possibly also section 615 could result. Section 615 is, for two reasons, less likely to be breached than Part 6.7. First, the threshold for Part 6.7 is 5% of the voting shares whereas the threshold for section 615 is 20% of the voting shares. Secondly, section 615 has the extra requirement that there must be an 'acquisition' of shares. Nevertheless, in the case of most large Australia-based institutions, the total shareholding in a particular company consists of many-possibly dozens of separate holdings for particular funds and/ or clients. The acquisition element of section 615 could therefore be satisfied almost unintentionally. For example, by an 'index' purchase of shares for a unit trust which tracks an ASX index of which the particular company is a constituent.

It might be argued that the foregoing is largely academic, and that in practice there is little likelihood of institutions ever suffering any consequences as a result of a 'technical' breach of section 615 or Part 6.7. Any such argument would, for two reasons, be misconceived. First, several interviewees in the Australian interview project said that the potential application of these provisions served as a significant deterrent to their engaging in collective action at a portfolio company. Secondly, the overseas experience suggests that there is cause for concern. In the US, where there are provisions similar to those in Part 6.7 of the Corporations Law, lawyers who advise corporate managements provided the following advice in a public forum: 'If several institutional investors communicate with each other with respect to an election of registrant directors or an alternative slate of nominees, registrants should consider asserting the application of Schedule 13D [i.e. the equivalent of Corporations Law, Part 6.7].' It is reasonable to expect that equivalent advice would be given by advisers to an Australian corporate management which was subject to an institutional intervention. A significant weapon in this context could be section 1324 of the Corporations Law. Under this provision, the Australian Securities Commission or any person whose interests have been, are, or would be affected by a contravention of the Corporations Law has standing to apply to the court for an injunction or damages. The impugned directors could bring an application under section 1324 in the name of the company, alleging a breach of Part 6.7 and/or section 615. There is also the prospect of criminal prosecution. Any person who breaches the prohibition in section 615 or one of the notification provisions in Part 6.7 is guilty of a criminal offence, and is subject to a fine of up to A$2,500 (or A$12,500 if the person is a body corporate), or imprisonment for 6 months, or both.

The potential for collective action by institutions to contravene section 615 and/or Part 6.7 of the Corporations Law does not sit comfortably with a model of corporate governance in which monitoring by institutional shareholders plays an important role. Therefore, in the final chapter a recommendation is made for legislative reform in this area.

There are several other legal and regulatory restrictions which may affect institutional investors. First, the Reserve Bank of Australia discourages banks from holding equity in non-financial companies. Secondly, an Australian investment company (a closed-end fund) is barred from holding more than 5% of the issued ordinary shares of any company. Thirdly, the London Stock Exchange requires that investment trusts, investment companies, and unit trusts wishing to list on the Exchange must be passive investors, and must not control or seek to control, or be actively involved in the management of, their portfolio companies. Fourthly, the minimum notice period for extraordinary general meetings is just 14 days.

Factors which Precipitate Detailed Monitoring

The UK interview study revealed four main factors which serve to increase an institution's propensity to intervene to change an under-performing management: (a) unattractiveness of alternative strategies; (b) an overweight holding in the company; (c) fundamental soundness of the underlying business; and (d) deliberate misrepresentations by the management. Observation of the reported interventions suggests a further factor: (e) entrepreneurs.

In relation to (a), it is fairly obvious why an institution, when it considers itself 'locked in' (essentially, unable to dispose of its shareholding at a sensible price), and can see no prospect of or cannot engineer-a takeover, should be more inclined to intervene than at other times. Factor (b) is discussed in Section B.1.(3), above. Three of the four UK interviewees who mentioned factor (c) worked for firms which managed predominantly external funds. This indicates that the fund manager believes that, with better management, the company's share price would improve to such an extent that the costs of the intervention would be more than offset by the anticipated increase in the fund manager's fees (which are based on the value of funds under management). Regarding (d), three of the UK interviewees mentioned that they had initiated, or taken part in, an institutional intervention where they believed that they had been 'lied to' by the impugned management. In one case, the institution had been buying more and more shares in the company right up until it issued a profits warning because of the very positive sentiments being expressed at its meetings with the management. Obviously, as in other areas of life, considerations other than purely financial ones may carry weight in this sort of situation.

As regards (e), there is no evidence of US-style political entrepreneurs operating on a significant scale in either the UK or Australia. There is, on the other hand, evidence that an entrepreneur of another type contributed to some institutional interventions in the UK. Fidelity Investments International, the UK arm of the large US-based mutual-fund manager, Fidelity Investments, appears to have taken a deliberately high profile approach to corporate governance in the early 1990s. Despite its relatively small size (it was not amongst the largest 50 managers of quoted UK equities at the end of 1991), it employed a full-time Corporate Finance Director to deal with 'problem companies' in its portfolio. This seems to be an example of an external fund manager believing that it can derive 'private benefits [for example an increase in investors into its unit trusts] from being perceived as an active shareholder advocate'. Ironically, however, Fidelity parted company with this fellow in 1992 because 'his actions had received too much adverse publicity'.

Summary

There are numerous disincentives to institutional activism in both the UK and Australia, which affect particularly the managers of external funds. It would be only in rare circumstances that an external fund manager would stand to gain more from an intervention than from an alternative course of action. In the absence of positive regulatory changes, it is probable that here will be no significant increase on the current level of detailed firm level monitoring in the UK, and only a small increase on the current level in Australia.

10

Reducing the Cost of Capital by Managing Risk

Introduction

Violations of certain M&M assumptions resulting in imperfections in the capital market, unequal access of participants to the capital market, and asymmetric information across market participants can all motivate firms to manage risk in a manner that is consistent with value maximizing behavior of the firm's security holders. But the implications of these motivations on the actual strategy and tactics of the risk management program cannot be fully appreciated if the justifications for risk management are used to force the firm into a Johnson-Stein trader hedging model.

The sections that follow and the other chapters survey the rationales for value-added risk management in the theory of corporate finance. As subsequent chapters will explain, however, some of the rationales have implications that are completely unrealistic. Others have realistic implications but are inconsistent with the actual evidence on how firms manage risk. And still other theories make sense theoretically and practically and are consistent with observed actions by firms.

The theories of value-added risk management explored in this and the next three chapters are separated into four categories, all of which can be associated back to Jensen and Meckling's conception of a firm as a nexus of contracting relationships. The four types of opportunities for risk management to add value to the firm are as follows:

1. Pure frictions in the capital market.
2. Conflicts between managers and stakeholders (i.e., shareholders and/or creditors).
3. Conflicts among stakeholders (i.e., equity and debt holders).
4. Asymmetries in information.

These categories are not unrelated to one another. The second and third categories, for example, both illustrate problems in principal-agent relationships when a principal such as a shareholder engages an agent such as a manager to implement his wishes. Agency problems arise in large part due to frictions in the capital market, such as the cost to principals of monitoring and verifying the actions of their agents. Nevertheless, presenting the various justifications for corporate risk management using the four categories above will make the discussion clearer than trying to define *mutually exclusive* categories of risk management theories.

Also note that there is no clear correspondence between these four categories of risk management models and the M&M assumptions violated to justify risk management. In the category where risk management by firms is justified on the basis of manager-shareholder conflicts, for example, any or all of the M&M assumptions of perfect capital markets, equal access, or symmetric information may be violated depending on the specific nature of the manager-stakeholder conflict. As we will see later, however, the M&M assumption being violated is not the key factor in appreciating how the strategy and tactics of risk management trace back to the rationale for risk management. Again, these four categories will serve us better than others for the purpose of tying the strategy and tactics of risk management to the reason risk management makes sense in the first place.

Value-Added Risk Management

One of the M&M assumptions is that investment decisions made by the firm are taken as given. But because the firm is a complex set of contractual relations between different types of participants, who makes the investment decision is important. Who makes the financing and risk management decisions of the firm is equally important.

The basic variable underlying all the analysis here is the value of the firm. When the parties comprising the nexus of contracts that is the firm do not take actions that maximize the firm's value, under the M&M assumptions the firm will be taken over and replaced by decision makers who will maximize the value of the firm.

We know that the investment rule that maximizes the value of a firm is one that maximizes total security holder welfare, or the left-hand side of Equation 10.1:

$$[E_{t-1}(t) + \delta(t)] + [D_{t-1}(t) + \rho(t)] = V(t) + X(t) - I(t) \qquad (10.1)$$

Maximizing security holder welfare is commensurate with maximizing the value of the firm. When this does not happen, the firm becomes a takeover target.

Suppose the managers, shareholders, and creditors of a firm all agree on policies that result in a value of $V^{\circ}(t)$ for their firm at time *t*. Suppose this value results from the collective decision by all parties to buy a lot of unnecessary corporate jets and wander around the U.S. sightseeing in them at the company's expense. Under the M&M assumption of symmetric information, everyone in the market agrees that the assets of the firm could be deployed without these frivolous expenditures to achieve a true value of $V^*(t) > V^\circ(t)$. With equal access and perfect capital markets, other investors will either buy out the existing firm's security holders (and sack the management) for $V^*(t)$ - $V^\circ(t)$ or will open a new firm worth $V^*(t)$ that will operate more efficiently and drive the demand for the original firm's securities to zero.

So, the name of the game is maximizing the value of the firm in a M&M world, and the way to win the game is by maximizing the value of combined security holder welfare. Risk management, to the extent that it can be value enhancing for a firm, thus must somehow help the firm in playing this game. Sources of opportunity for value-added risk management can best be seen by remembering that $V(t)$ in Equation 10.1 can be rewritten as follows:

$$V(t) = \sum_{j=1}^{\infty} \frac{E_t[X(t+j) - I(t+j)}{1 + \lambda_{t,t+j}}$$

where the firm's cost of capital is λ. Risk management can add value when either it reduces the firm's cost of capital or increases its expected future net cash flows. As we will see later, risk management can, in certain circumstances, be a way to do both.

On a more dynamic basis, risk management can also be a source of value added by improving the process by which the firm's different participants work together and sometimes work against one another in order to maximize $V(t)$ and to maximize combined security holder welfare. To the extent that risk management is a low-cost way to reduce conflicts over policies that affect this value maximization criterion, risk management can be a source of value added, as well.

We assume that the M&M assumptions regarding symmetric information, equal access, and given investment strategies hold. We focus solely on violations of the assumption that capital markets are perfect. More specifically, we confine our attention here to sources of capital market imperfections that affect a corporation's managers, creditors, and shareholders in essentially the same way. In other words, all of the stakeholders in the company consider these imperfections bad, and all would support a means of reducing the costs associated with these imperfections in order to increase the value of the firm (via the increase in expected cash flows accompanying a decline in expected costs).

Reducing Expected Taxes

Suppose we consider an open corporation whose shareholders are capable of fully diversifying away idiosyncratic risks. In this situation, risk management cannot affect the firm's cost of capital. The only way that risk management can add value to the firm for a given risk level or, equivalently, preserve value while reducing risk is by increasing the expected cash flows to the firm.

As long as that remains true, it is impossible, as shown when we examined hedging as a capital budgeting problem, for hedging tactics alone to add value to the firm. Hedging is itself, after all, a zero NPV project.

Much of the literature on corporate finance has attempted to explain risk management by value-maximizing corporations by trying to force corporations into a Johnson-Stein-Ederington-style model. In other words, if we can somehow treat the corporation as if it is a risk-averse investor with a concave utility function, then the same mean-variance portfolio framework will lead companies to undertake optimal mean-variance.

Merton Miller has referred to this as the process of "concavifying" the firm's value function. Figure 10.1 shows the value of the firm as a function of assets and liabilities in a M&M world. As you can see, the function is *linear.* Over

20 years of corporate finance research has focused on how to introduce a concavity into this curve that makes it more similar to Figure 10.3.

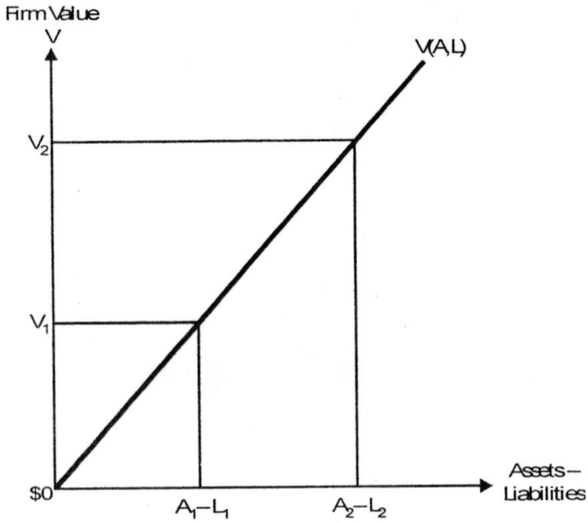

Fig. 10.1. The value of the firm in a Modigliani-Miller world

One of the strong assumptions underlying M&M is perfect capital markets and the absence of institutional frictions, including corporate taxes. If the individual stakeholders that comprise a corporation face positive taxes, their own portfolio optimization decisions will incorporate these taxes. In other words, *personal* taxation is not enough to affect the *firm's* risk management decision. But *corporate* taxes specifically, a *convex* corporate tax schedule will concavify the firm's value function and can lead to benefits from managing risk.

A convex tax schedule is one in which a firm's average tax rate rises as pre-tax income rises. Shown in Figure 10.2 as compared to a linear tax schedule, the following factors can contribute to the convexity of a firm's tax schedule:

- Progressivity in the tax rate.
- The alternative minimum tax (AMT).
- Tax carry-forwards and tax credits.

- Other tax shields that defer taxation.

Figure 10.3 shows graphically how the value of the firm *after taxes* can be higher if risk management programs are used to hedge fluctuations in the value of the firm. Suppose V_1 and V_2 denote two possible pre-tax values of the firm. At those levels of pre-tax income or earnings, the firm faces tax liabilities T_1 and T_2, respectively, as shown in the top panel of the figure. If we assume for simplicity that these pairs of pre-tax income levels, firm values, and tax liabilities will occur with equal probability—making a different assumption adds complexity but does not change the results then the expected pre-tax value of the firm is indicated on the lower panel of the figure as $E(V)$, where

$$E(V) = \tfrac{1}{2}V_1 + \tfrac{1}{2}V_2$$

If the firm does not hedge, the firm's expected tax liability is the probability weighted tax liability corresponding to the two possible firm values and tax liabilities, or

$$E(T) = \tfrac{1}{2}T_1 + \tfrac{1}{2}T_2$$

which implies an expected *post*-tax value of the firm of $E(V) - E(T)$.

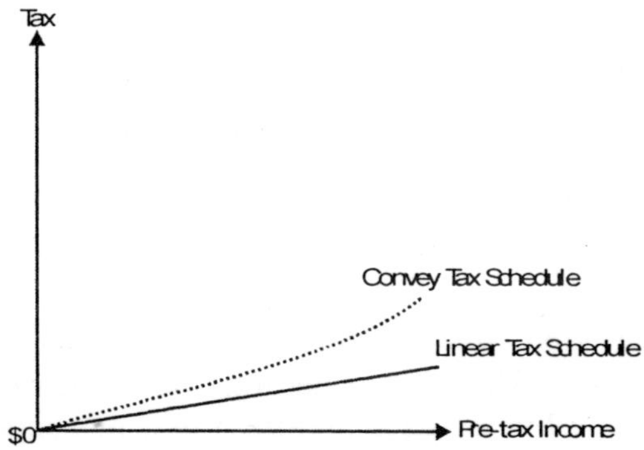

Fig.10.2. Corporate tax as a function of pre-tax income.

Now suppose the firm constructs a *perfect hedge* of its value, so that the value of the firm is locked in at $V_H = E(V)$.

At this value of the firm, the tax liability is *known* and indicated on the upper panel of Figure 10.3 as T_H. The post-tax value of the firm is then also known and locked in as $V_H - T_H$.

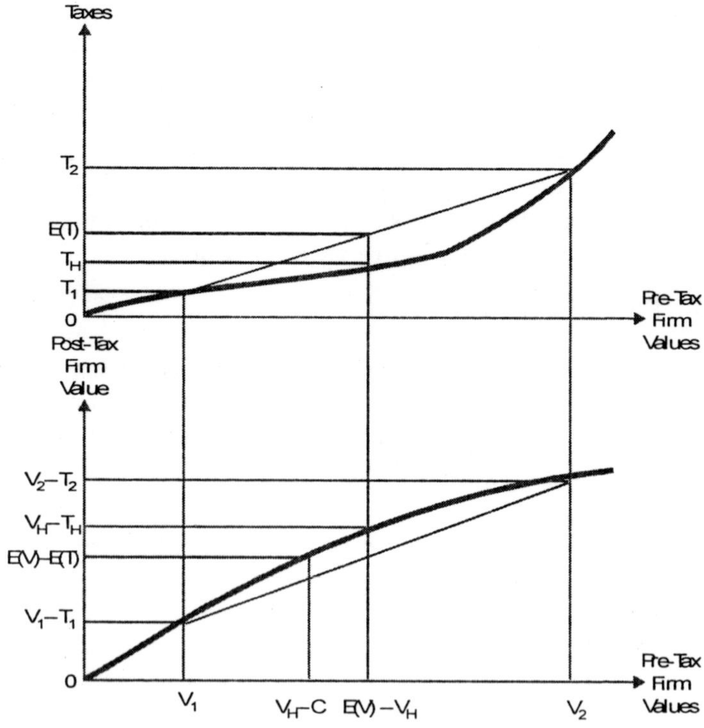

Fig. 10.3. The value of the firm with progressive corporate taxation

The post-tax known value of the firm is higher than the post-tax expected value of the firm. Notice that this would not be true if the firm's tax schedule was linear rather than convex. With a linear tax schedule, the firm's expected tax liability *E (T)* would equal the known tax liability T_H that the firm could lock in with a perfect hedge of firm value. In this case, the expected post-tax value of the firm without hedging would equal the known value of the firm with hedging.

Because the tax schedule facing the firm is convex, however, the expected tax liability without hedging is higher than the known tax liability with hedging. The probability of the firm's value being high results in a more than proportional increase in taxes than the liability associated with the value of the firm in its low albeit equally likely state.

The lower panel also indicates what the firm is willing to pay for this hedge. Without the hedge, the value of the firm is expected to be $E(V) - E(T)$, whereas the known value of the hedged firm is $V_H - T_H$, or $E(V) - T_H$ because $V_H = E(V)$. The firm's expected *savings* thus *is* $T_H - 1/2(T_1 + T_2) = C$. The lower panel indicates graphically that any cost of hedging up to *C*, the actual value of the firm is no less than the expected post-tax value while remaining unhedged.

This analysis demonstrates plainly that a firm whose objective is maximizing post-tax firm value can benefit from risk management. The M&M assumption of frictionless capital markets was the only such assumption we needed to violate in order to explain why a company might manage risk.

But how should a company manage risk in this situation? Here, theory fails us. Compare Figure 10.3 again to Figure 10.1. The introduction of a convex tax schedule was enough to *concavify* an otherwise linear value function. With a convex tax schedule, the firm now knows that it will pay up to *C* for a perfect hedge when two values of the firm are equally likely, V_1 and V_2. But what about situations when a whole distribution of outcomes of V is possible?

Assuming that changes in the value of the firm are normally distributed, the *optimal* hedge is the hedge that minimizes the variance of changes in the value of the firm in order to minimize the expected tax liability. True, the rationale for risk management does not immediate imply the need to assume a normal distribution or a variance minimizing hedge. As long as some criterion is developed to link the distribution of changes in the value of the firm to the expected tax liability minimization, the distribution need not be normal. Nevertheless, in practice, the rationale for hedging presented in Figure 10.3 usually leads straight to a retreat back to the Johnson-Stein variance minimization model.

Also worth noting is that this rationale for hedging has a very specific connection to *accounting earnings,* which determine the tax liability of the firm.

Reducing Expected Exogenous Bankruptcy Costs

Perhaps the most intuitive reason for firms to manage risk is to avoid financial explosions that result in bankruptcy or financial distress. In a M&M world, however, this would not matter. With no transaction costs, bankruptcy merely results in the prorated redistribution of assets to the firm's liability holders.

We assume that bankruptcy costs are *exogenous.* In other words, the costs of financial distress may be constant or may vary with the size of the financial disaster we will explore both cases but these costs are *not* determined directly or indirectly by any of the financing decisions of the firm. If it helps to have an example, suppose in this chapter that we are limiting our discussion of bankruptcy to those situations arising only from natural risk exposures that the firm inherited by virtue of its normal business operations. Assume specifically that we are not considering financial distress costs that might somehow be tied to investment decisions in future projects.

Figure 10.4 shows the value of a firm with no liabilities except outstanding debt of face value FV on the date that the firm is presumed to both pay off its debt holders *and* to liquidate its assets and pay equity holders a liquidating dividend. If the firm has assets of A_2, the surplus assets over the face value of the debt A_2 - FV—is the total value of equity, and debt holders receive FV. If instead the value of the firm's assets is below FV—say, A_1 — then equity receives nothing. Debt holders each receive a prorated share of the residual assets A_1, and thus lose FV - A_1.

With costless bankruptcy, the remaining assets of the firm are distributed to debt holders such that they receive exactly what they are entitled to. Even when the value of the firm's assets declines to zero, the relation between the value of the firm and the value of its assets remains a perfectly linear one. No concavities here, and no need for risk management per se.

But when the costs of bankruptcy are positive and borne by the firm (i.e., taken from the proceeds from the liquidation of its remaining assets), the situation changes. We explore two such situations—constant bankruptcy costs, and costs of financial distress that are proportional to the shortfall of assets below liabilities.

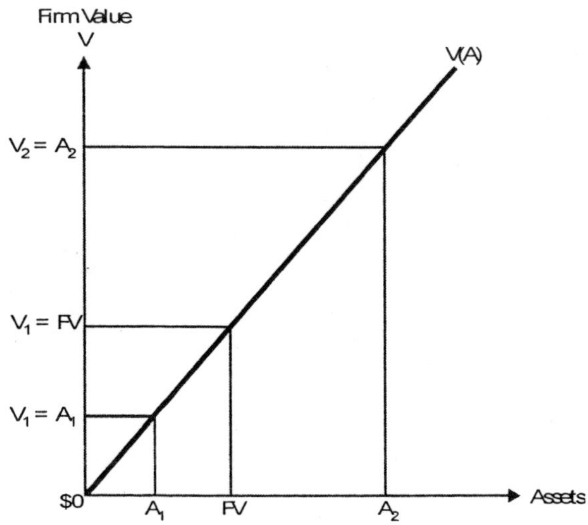

Fig. 10.4. The value of a firm with debt and no bankruptcy costs

Constant Bankruptcy Costs

First consider a situation where bankruptcy results in a fixed cost that is borne by the firm. This cost might include lawyers and court fees, costs of distributing the remaining assets to debt holders, and the like. Importantly, the fixed cost denoted *B* does not vary based on how bad the situation is. In other words, any situation in which the firm's assets are below the face value of its debt results in bankruptcy, the cost of which does not depend on the amount of the asset shortfall.

For any asset value below FV, the fixed costs of bankruptcy incurred by the firm represent a shift down in the curve that denotes the value of the firm as a function of assets. In Figure 10.4 where bankruptcy was costless, assets of value $A_1 < FV$ resulted in a value of the firm of V_1. Denoted V^*_1 on Figure 10.5, that amount is now above the value of the firm when assets are worth A_1. With bankruptcy costs *B*, the value of the firm is now $V_1 = A_1 B < V^*_1$.

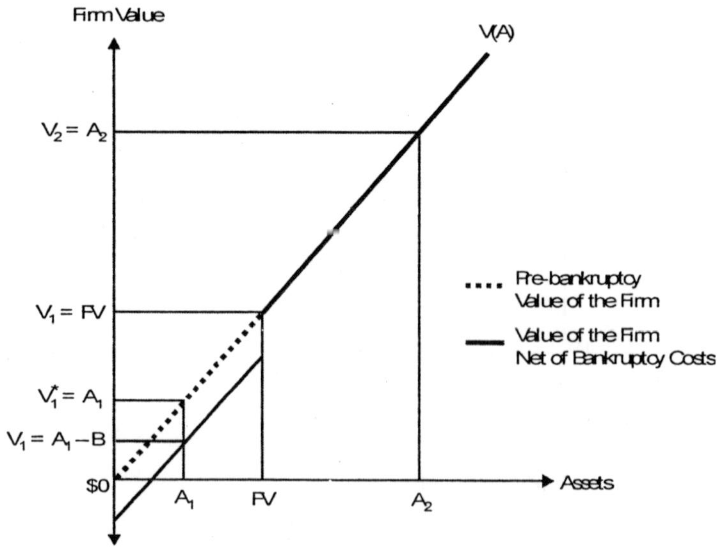

Fig. 10.5. The value of a firm with debt and no bankruptcy costs

Risk management can help reduce the expected costs of bankruptcy in this situation. To see how, consider Figure 10.6, which shows the value of the firm as a function of its assets and fixed bankruptcy costs *B* on the *y*-axis just as in

Figure 10.5. But in Figure 10.6, the second *y*-axis now indicates the probability of various asset values on the assumed liquidation date of the firm.

The solid line is the probability distribution for values of the assets underlying the firm given that the firm does not hedge. In this case, the expected value of the firm is the asset value less expected bankruptcy costs:

$$E(V) = E(A) - \Lambda B$$

where Λ is the probability that assets are below FV, equal to the area under the solid unhedged distribution of asset values of 0 up to FV.

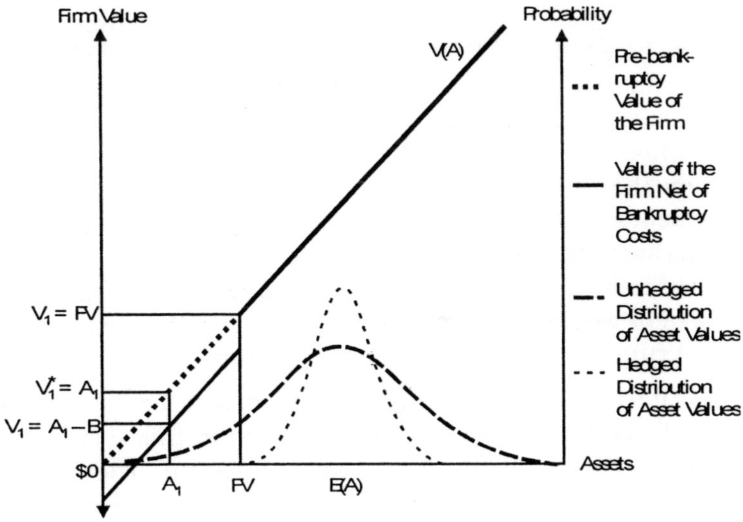

Fig. 10.6. Hedging with debt and constant bankruptcy costs.

Now suppose the firm hedges in a manner that reduces the probability of bankruptcy to zero. This requires a new probability distribution where asset values below FV never occur. Such a distribution is shown on Figure 10.6 as a dotted curve. If the hedge is costless, the expected value of the assets does not change because, as we have seen, hedging is a zero NPV project. But the support of the probability distribution the values on the *x*-axis with positive probability associated with them is now tighter than before. In other words, the upside has shrunk proportionately to the downside. In our earlier terminology, the hedge has left the expected value of assets the same but has decreased the variance of asset value changes.

What is the expected value of the firm in this situation? Now that bankruptcy costs have been reduced to zero, the expected value of the firm is now E (A), which is higher than $E(A) - \Lambda B$.

Even though the expected value of the firm's assets has not changed, equity holders benefit from an increase in the expected value of the firm when expected bankruptcy costs are reduced to zero. But debt holders do not necessarily enjoy the same windfall. In fact, whether or not debt holders enjoy any gains from the elimination of bankruptcy costs depends on whether or not they knew the firm was going to hedge when they bought the debt. At original issue, the price of the debt and the interest paid by the firm would have reflected some assumption on the part of debt holders about the firm's credit risk. If debt holders knew the firm would hedge, then the debt would have been priced at issue with zero expected bankruptcy costs and no states of default.

The result of introducing bankruptcy costs even as simple as those constant costs explored in this section has been to concavify the firm's value function. The optimal hedge in this case, however, is not necessarily a variance-minimizing hedge because of the nature of the concavity we have introduced. In this example, the value function is concave exclusively because of a discontinuity we introduced at the point the firm reaches bankruptcy. The risk management objective function here is just the reduction of expected bankruptcy costs that occur after that threshold is reached. With no costs of hedging, the optimal hedge is the hedge that reduces bankruptcy costs to zero by eliminating the possibility entirely. This may or may not also be the hedge that reduces variance the most.

Proportionate Bankruptcy Costs

Now consider a slightly different situation in which a corporation incurs costs of bankruptcy that are proportional to the shortfall of assets below liabilities. Denote bankruptcy costs in this case as B (A), and suppose that bankruptcy costs rise at an increasing rate as the market value of assets fall. Mathematically,

$$B(A) > 0 \quad \text{where } A < FV$$
$$B_A(A) < 0 \quad \text{where } A < FV$$
$$B_{AA}(A) > 0 \quad \text{where } A < FV$$

Figure 10.7 shows the assumed bankruptcy cost function in the top panel, and the resulting value of the firm in the lower panel. In the lower panel, the solid line represents the value of the firm as a function of its assets and bankruptcy costs.

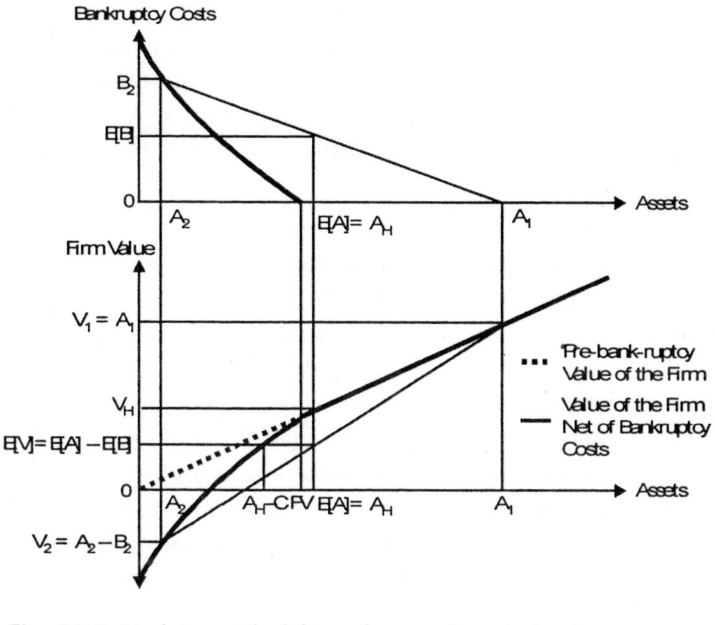

Fig. 10.7. Hedging with debt and proportionate bankruptcy costs

The heavy dashed line represents the value of the firm in the absence of bankruptcy costs—a 45° line. The heavy solid line in the lower panel is essentially the bankruptcy cost function subtracted from the 45° line. When assets are worth A_2, for example, debt holders would still have some small positive prorated distribution to enjoy in the absence of bankruptcy costs. But at asset value A_2, bankruptcy costs are B_2 and the value of the firm is thus $V_2 = A_2 - B_2$. Similarly, when assets are worth A_1, the firm is solvent and its value is $V_1 = A_1$.

Specifically, suppose any two asset values— A_1 and A_2 —are equally likely to occur. The expected value of assets is the midpoint of A_1 and A_2. If the firm does not hedge, its expected value is just the expected value of its assets, *E (A)*, less expected bankruptcy costs, *E (B)*. Graphically, *E (B)* is the *y*-axis value in the top panel that corresponds to the midpoint of the line drawn between where A_1 and A_2 intersect the bankruptcy cost function—0 and B_2, respectively. Similarly, the expected value of the firm in the lower panel is the *y*-axis value corresponding to the midpoint of the line drawn between where A_1 and A_2 intersect the firm's post-bankruptcy value function—V_1 and V_2, respectively.

Now consider a situation where the firm hedges its assets and locks in an asset value of A_H, which is equal to the expected value of assets. At this known asset level, bankruptcy costs are now zero, and the value of the firm is now $V_H = A_H = E(A)$. This is a higher value of the firm than its expected unhedged value of *E (V)*—higher by exactly the expected cost of bankruptcy. The firm thus would be willing to spend up to *C* to hedge its assets and lock in value V_H even though it means eliminating the potential for realizing the higher value V_1. *At this level of expenditure on the hedge, the firm is worth the same in known terms that it expected to be worth facing a possibility of bankruptcy, but without that risk of bankruptcy.*

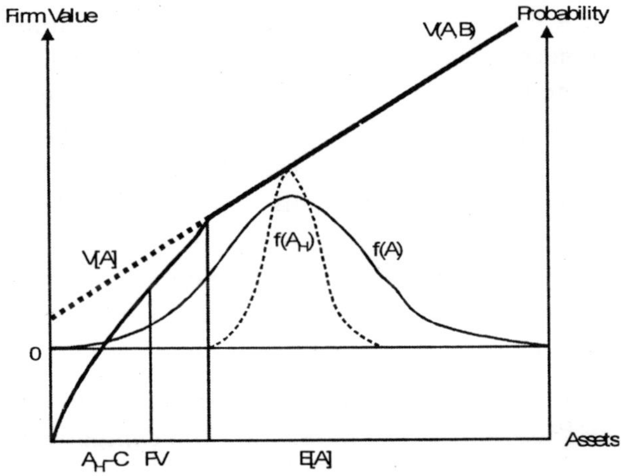

Fig. 10.8. Hedging with debt and proportionate bankruptcy costs, Part II.

The problem with this particular hedge, however, is that $A_H - C$ is less than FV, which means that the firm would go bankrupt from the cost of the hedge! Figure 10.8 makes this point more dramatically. As in Figure 10.6, this figure has two *y* axes one indicating firm value as a function of bankruptcy costs and asset value, and the second one showing the probability distribution for assets. The distribution $f(A)$ is the unhedged distribution, and $f(A_H)$ is the hedged distribution. The hedged distribution is clearly lower in variance and associates a zero probability with all situations that would make it impossible for the firm to repay its debt. But as shown, that particular hedge is simply too expensive.

We have successfully concavified the corporate value function in a manner that allows us to treat *corporate* hedging as indistinct from trader hedging. And in fact, many theorists would simply put their pens down here and argue that if we assume normally distributed returns, we could proceed straight to the Johnson-Stein optimal hedge ratio to determine how the firm should manage its risks.

In fact, as in the prior section, the theory itself does not prescribe a variance-minimizing hedge in this situation at least not necessarily. A properly formatted problem would be to choose the hedge ratio that equates the marginal cost of hedging to the marginal reduction in expected bankruptcy costs subject to the constraint that the hedging cost cannot bankrupt the firm. Indeed, this would be one way for a company to hedge when facing these types of costs. Unfortunately, most theoreticians and practitioners alike stop once the concavity has been identified and simply solve the problem incorrectlya la Johnson, Stein, and Ederington.

Note, by the way, that the firm need not begin incurring costs like those discussed here when the company actually goes bust. In fact, this is not very realistic. Instead, one can imagine that a firm begins to incur financial distress costs before the exact point at which the current value of assets net of liabilities falls below the face value of outstanding debt. For the moment, we do not include in this category the costs of financing continuing operations by issuing new, distressed debt. But even setting aside distressed debt, other costs of financial distress might include, for example, a premium you would need to pay to employees to stop them from leaving, lawyers fees, fees paid to consultants you engage to try to keep you out of bankruptcy, and so on.

On Figure 10.7 and 10.8, the point where bankruptcy costs become positive, now labeled FV to correspond to the face value of debt, is simply shifted somewhere to the right of FV. Alternatively, you could imagine that FV no longer stands for face value and merely indicates the level of assets at which the firm begins encountering distress costs. Whether or not the firm is or is not bankrupt is a legal question. The point at which the firm begins incurring bankruptcy or financial distress *costs* is what drives the analysis, and this may or may not coincide with the firm's level of outstanding liabilities.

Reducing the Cost of Capital

We know we can rewrite the firm's cost of capital as

$$\lambda_{t,t+j} = E\left(R_{t+j}^{j}\right) = R_{t+j}^{f} + \beta_{j,m}\Phi_m$$

where

$$\beta_{j,m} = \frac{\operatorname{cov}\left(R_{t+j}^{j}, m_{t+j}\right)}{\operatorname{var}(m_{t+j})} \qquad \Phi_m = \frac{-\operatorname{var}(m_{t+j})}{E_t(m_{t+j})}$$

See Cochrane for an explanation of the correspondence in the two expressions, which is not actually as obvious as would seem from simple substitution.

For risk management to reduce the cost of capital, one of two things would have to be true. First, the risk management program would have to somehow change the way that returns on the firm covary with the stochastic discount factor. This is highly unlikely, as this part of the FVE is based on systematic risk, not diversifiable firm-specific risks. All but one dimension of market risk and all the other risks discussed liquidity, credit, operational, and legal risks are diversifiable by open corporations. Accordingly, risk management cannot affect the value of the firm through the cost of capital, which remains unaffected by financial policies, including risk management and hedging.

A second case in which hedging can reduce the cost of capital is when the organization is a closed corporation whose owners are not well-diversified. Indeed, these shareholders must be incapable of holding diversified portfolios because so much of their wealth is tied up in their own firm in order for hedging to reduce the cost of capital. In this case, the idiosyncratic risk of the firm will affect its cost of capital:

$$\lambda_{t,t+j} = E\left(R_{t+j}^{j}\right) = R_{t+j}^{f} + \beta_{j,m}\Phi_m + \varepsilon$$

where ε is the idiosyncratic risk of the firm that is no longer fully diversified away. If $E(\varepsilon) > 0$, then the idiosyncratic risk of the firm raises the average cost of capital. To the extent that hedging or risk management can reduce $E(\varepsilon)$, the firm's cost of capital will decline and the value of the firm will rise as a result of the risk management program.

Unlike reducing expected taxes and bankruptcy costs, the particular nature of the capital market imperfection that allows firms' risk management initiatives to reduce their cost of capital also requires that the M&M assumption of equal access be violated. Otherwise, badly diversified managers of a closed corporation could create securities to reverse out the portion of their portfolios that is disproportionately weighted toward their own closed firm. In fact, existing restrictions on insider purchases and sales of stocks and on the disposition of stock-based compensation lends some plausibility to the assumption that not all small firm managers have the ability to issue securities based on the performance of their own firms cost lessly. Without such equal access, risk management may be the only viable solution.

11

Controlling and Managing Finance by Managing Risk

Introduction

The specifics of how risk management can add value when people have different information, a moment should be spent on what we do and do not mean by the term asymmetric information. The M&M assumption itself essentially requires that all market participants shareholders, creditors, managers, other investors, etc. have access to the same information and accurately perceive the true impact of that information on security prices. The assumption is typically extended to mean that everyone also has the same information about things like investment opportunities for example, managers and shareholders both accurately perceive whether or not a project is positive NPV.

More generally, the true state of nature is sometimes accessible to all, but only at a positive cost of verifying what that state of nature is. Assuming everyone can have access to the same information but that it is costly is not quite the same as asymmetric information, where some parties are basically just structurally less-informed than others that is to say that the costs of obtaining and verifying that information are effectively limitless. A typical principal-agent problem illustrates this important distinction. Suppose first that shareholders, willing to tolerate some mistakes by managers and others that occur for totally exogenous reasons, are primarily interested in the effort their manager agents expend. In a world of symmetric information, it may be costly for shareholders to verify that effort, but it is possible. More formally, contracts can be written such as compensation agreements that depend on a manager's effort, which, if the shareholders are willing to spend the number, is a knowable fact.

Now consider the analogous situation when information is asymmetric. In that case, shareholders simply cannot ever determine how much effort the manager put in at any reasonable cost. In that case, shareholders and managers can only write contracts based on other variables that may be noisy proxies for effort, such as sales or growth.

We saw that some believe managers might be inclined to grow their divisions to suboptimal levels. We did not assume that shareholders were incapable of recognizing that. All that was required to motivate monitoring, the issuance of debt, or the adoption of risk management is that it is expensive for shareholders to know when managers are pursuing excessive growth. In this sense, the agency cost of equity and free cash flow models are not models that rely on asymmetric information.

We review the potential for firms to increase their value by reducing the costs of or exploiting the benefits of information that is really and truly asymmetric known by one party and both unknown and unobservable to some other party. In the free cash flow model, the notion that something must be done to stop managers from spending excess cash on negative NPV projects becomes even more compelling if we assume that shareholders can never know the true NPV of the investments managers are accepting, and so on.

To avoid repetition, we do not repeat the agency models discussed in prior chapters here, but we do note that the agency costs of these models not only persist when information is asymmetric, but the costs grow. Risk management thus can add even more value when information is asymmetric between either security holders and managers or amongst security holders. Although we do not simply repeat the models explored earlier to evaluate the impact of asymmetric information, we do note in some specific instances how the models are relevant and in several cases present new models that are quite similar to some of the ones we have already explored.

Reducing Noise from "Signals"

In a world where information is not equivalent across all market participants, firms can sometimes have trouble signaling the true value of their investment opportunities. Consider, for example, a pharmaceutical company whose scientists have a unique perception of the potential value they could create 10 years down the road with a new drug. In the meantime, the investment expenditures on the drug can be quite high, which can lead to problems if not everyone has the same information about the expected value of the new drug.

Aggravated Agency Costs of Reducing Conflicts

When bondholders, for example, cannot ascertain whether or not the NPV of the projects shareholders are accepting is positive, they cannot tell whether they are being expropriated and whether or not shareholders have deviated from optimal investment policies. At the same time, shareholders may be equally in the dark, to the extent the inside information about the new drug is possessed by managers and not shareholders. In turn, shareholders could become concerned that managers are taking actions inconsistent with optimal investment policies, which could also further exacerbate bondholders concerns with stockholders and vice versa. All in all, when information is asymmetric across stakeholders of the firm shareholders, creditors, and managers about investment opportunities, the desire to incur significantly greater costs monitoring those investments becomes significant. In the absence of such monitoring, the securities issued by the firm could trade at a discount, thereby raising the cost of capital for the firm and decreasing the value of the firm.

Risk management can serve as a substitute for monitoring. As will be discussed later, for example, firms may embed derivatives positions into their debt and equity securities in order to signal their confidence in or information about future investment opportunities. To use the pharmaceutical example, the company might choose to issue debt whose coupons are payable in the foreign currency of a country where it expects significant drug sales to occur. By embedding a forward foreign exchange transaction into the debt, the firm is either taking a blind exposure to currency fluctuations or pre committing itself to a sufficient volume of sales in that currency to offset the new liability incurred through the bond issue.

Bondholders will be indifferent to this currency risk, of course, because they themselves can simply turn around and hedge it. We have not relaxed the equal access or perfect capital market assumptions of M&M, after all, and the informational asymmetry in question has nothing to do with the exchange rate. Nevertheless, hedging the exchange rate risk can signal to bondholders the managers' or shareholders' expectations about future drug sales, thus potentially reducing the expropriation premium bondholders might demand as discussed in the previous section. And similarly for equity holders, whose dividends could be paid in foreign currency to achieve the same results.

Analysts and Asset Valuation

In a world of imperfect information, there can be little doubt that investors rightly or wrongly pay serious attention to analysts. One of the supposed tasks of analysts is to try and evaluate the quality of the investment decisions made by the firms they follow. When analysts receive poor information, they can easily undervalue a project, especially when the project is intangible like a patentable process or a new drug.

In the same way that hedging and risk management can help better informed stakeholders signal less-informed stakeholders that investment projects are sensible, a properly designed risk management program can also help send a similar signal to analysts.

DeMarzo and Duffie and others have explored the use of risk management and hedging to increase the ratio of signal to noise in the informational content of financial variables. Returning to our pharmaceutical firm, suppose the firm is subject to significant risk from foreign exchange fluctuations on the sales of its existing drugs, as well as the new one being developed whose value is largely unknown outside the firm. In an M&M world, the firm should be indifferent to hedging its exchange rate risk. But suppose 90% of the firm's earnings volatility comes from exchange rate exposure. The firm might choose to hedge its exchange rate risk and reduce its earnings volatility so that less-informed parties do not assume the volatility is due to perceived problems with the drug development.

In this example, the earnings volatility associated with the actual investments of the firm could be considered the true state of the world that only the firm knows. The total earnings volatility is all that analysts and others can observe, and if exchange rate fluctuations go unhedged, the noise in the signal sent by earnings will be high relative to the true volatility associated with the firm's actual investments. Hedging to increase this signal-tonoise ratio can help reduce the information asymmetry that might lead to undervaluation of the firm's investment projects, which, in turn, will depress equity and debt prices and increase the firm's cost of capital.

Consider an even more basic but plausible example of a firm whose balance sheet is denominated in U.S. dollars that is building a factory in Malaysia. Under FAS 133, the firm may be able to get hedge accounting treatment if its assets and liabilities are matched (i.e., if the firm funds the Malaysian factory in ringgit, thereby creating a ringgit liability to fund a ringgit asset). Importantly, the firm is still exposed to the risk of exchange rate fluctuations between the ringgit and the dollar on both the asset and liability. But suppose the exchange rate vis-à-vis the dollar is reasonably stable except for periodic major devaluations. The firm may actually prefer to run the risk of a major devaluation periodically in exchange for reducing the noise in its earnings that would be created if the ringgit asset were funded with, say, a dollar liability. In other words, the firm may be willing to assume a larger risk that it can explain than tolerate a smaller one that shows up as unattributable earnings volatility.

Managerial Risk Aversion

We explained that a risk-averse manager might be tempted to take actions that do not maximize security holder welfare when monitoring is costly. We saw that the degree to which the manager would either fully hedge the firm or simply walk away from risky projects was in large part based on whether or not the expected utility of manager wealth is a convex function of the value of the firm.

Now consider a related situation in which information is asymmetric. Specifically, suppose that a firm is owned by a collection of risk-neutral shareholders that appoint a risk-averse manager to make the financial and investment decisions on behalf of security holders. Managers can tell the difference between idiosyncratic risk and systematic risk, but shareholders cannot. In other words, shareholders can only observe the total volatility of the firm's value, not its various component risks.

In this situation, Diamond and Verrechia have argued that it makes sense for managers to pursue a risk management policy. Specifically, if given the opportunity to hedge, managers will engage in the management of those risks that are under their control and within the purview of their own information. Those risks about which the managers are as ill-informed as shareholders will be left alone. But by reducing risks that are under the manager's control, the temptation for them to walk away from risky projects is reduced. At the same time, the signal sent to equity holders is similar to that explored earlier in the analysts' case. By reducing the noise of the signal, managers can better signal to shareholders that they are taking actions consistent with the NPV criterion.

Reducing the Costs of External Debt Financing for New Investments

New investments made by equity holders may be so heavily weighted to paying off debt holders that equity receives few of the benefits despite bearing most of the costs if the project goes bad. So, firms sometimes reject positive NPV projects because of the cost of external finance.

The basic underinvestment model is driven primarily by the value of investment projects, and how the value of those projects comes to bear on the value of debt and the value of equity. An alternative formulation has been offered by Froot, Scharfstein, and Stein henceforth, FSS in which the underinvestment problem is recast in terms of cash flows.

The FSS Cash Flow Hedging Model

The intuition behind the FSS underinvestment model is that it is costly for firms to finance their projects by issuing new debt. Debt is costly in the FSS model for several reasons. The first is that financial distress is presumed to be costly a violation of the M&M perfect capital markets assumption.

The closer a firm gets to financial distress in the FSS model, the more firms are penalized with higher borrowing costs. This does not require the firm to be near bankruptcy, but can also occur because the firm is experiencing liquidity problems.

A second reason that debt can be costly in a FSS world is also a result of capital market imperfections. Namely, as we have seen in several cases already, it can be costly for principals to monitor their agents.

Finally, debt can be costly when external creditors have less information than internal managers and stakeholders about the quality of the firm's investment projects and growth opportunities a violation of the symmetric information assumption in M&M. The more intangible a firm's assets, the more trouble outsiders have determining the true value of its assets. And the more trouble the firm has raising money to fund those opportunities.

A sufficient but not necessary condition for underinvestment problems to arise in a cash flow sense is that prospective creditors have less information than managers about investment opportunities and thus may charge higher interest rates than if the quality of all investments was observable. But the only necessary and sufficient condition for underinvestment problems to occur in a cash flow sense is that the marginal cost of issuing new debt is positive and increasing in the amount of external financing required.

We could thus easily get to a cash flow-based version of Myers' underinvestment problem without assuming any differences in information by focusing on one of the two other costs of debt. But the fact is that the FSS theory tends to be much more interesting and relevant when information asymmetries exaggerate the costs of external finance.

To see why underinvestment occurs purely because of the costs of external finance, consider the simple model set up by FSS in which a firm's NPV is

$$F(I) = f(I) - I.$$

where I is the investment expenditure and $f\ (I)$ the subsequent level of production output, such that $f_I > 0$ and $f_{II} < 0$. In the normal case where investment and financing decisions are independent of one another, optimal investment occurs where $f_I = 1$—the marginal product of the investment equals its marginal cost. This optimal investment expenditure can be denoted I^*.

To motivate underinvestment, FSS assume that investment expenditures can be financed from internal funds, denoted w, and external funds, denoted e:

$$I = w + e.$$

External financing is assumed to be costly for reasons noted. If C denotes these costs, bonds issued by the firm earn C/e over the risk less rate. Internal financing is not presumed to give rise to such "deadweight costs."

The firm now chooses I to maximize $F\ (I) - C\ (e)$, where costs depend on the total amount of external financing $e = I - w$. The first-order condition for the firm now says that investment expenditures are optimal when

$$F_1 - C_e = f_1 - 1 - C_e = 0$$

or when $f_I - C_e = 1$. Because $f_I(I) > 0$ and $C_e(e) = C_e(I - w) > 0$, the optimal investment expenditure I is below the I^* that satisfies the normal first-order condition

$f_I = 1$. Thus, the firm invests too little because debt is costly to issue.

Even from this simple model, the direction taken by FSS is a pretty easy one to anticipate. Namely, the more a firm can finance investment from its internal funds w, the less it needs to rely on external funds. The less external funding, the lower C_e and the closer investment comes to its optimal level. In the limiting case where $e = 0$, $f_I - C_e = f_I$ *and the original, optimal level of investment* I^* occurs.

The intuition behind the FSS cash flow hedging model is best seen from the example offered by FSS in a shortened version of their major article that appeared in the *Harvard Business Review*. Their example is based on a hypothetical pharmaceutical company called "Omega Pharmaceutical" whose revenues are at risk from sales in Japan and Germany specifically, from fluctuations in the mark/dollar and yen/dollar exchange rates. Omega is dollar-based and expects its net cash flows to be worth about $200 million per annum. Exchange rate swings, however, could change the dollar value of these revenues to either $100 million or $300 million per annum with equal likelihood.

As a pharmaceutical firm, the company's investment expenditures are heavily weighted toward R&D. As part of its normal capital budgeting exercises, Omega has forecast cash flows associated with different investment levels in new drugs. These investment expenditures, cost-of-capital discounted cash flows, and NPVs are shown in Table 11.1 from FSS. The firm's R&D budget was $180 million last year and will be $200 million next year. FSS (1994) argue that the choice of $200 million is based on the higher NPV at that level of spending as seen from the capital budget shown in Table 11.1. However, that corporate finance theory does not tell firms to accept the highest NPV project of several, but rather to take all of them. In truth, the choice of a $200 million investment decision for Omega thus is driven primarily by intuition.

Table 11.1. Omega Pharmaceutical's Capital Budget (Million of U.S. Dollars)

R&D Expenditure	Discounted Cash Flows	NPV
100	160	60
200	290	90
300	360	60

FSS then suppose that Omega does not have the ability to borrow funds to finance its R&D program and is unwilling to issue equity to do so. Internal cash funding thus is the only option for Omega. In this situation, Omega is quite vulnerable to exchange rate changes that can impact its net cash flows. If the dollar appreciates and Omega's net revenues decline in value to $100 million, only $100 million can be spent on new investment and R&D. By contrast, a dollar depreciation would leave Omega with an extra $100 million above its planned $200 million spending level.

If Omega were to perfectly hedge its cash flows against exchange rate risk, the net revenue from its drug sales would be locked in at $200 million per annum. If the dollar appreciates and the dollar value of foreign sales declines from $200 million to $100 million, this means that the hedge will generate a cash inflow of $100 million. Conversely, a depreciation of the dollar that increases the dollar value of foreign sales by $100 million is offset with a $100 million loss on the hedge.

Table 11.2. The Impact of Hedging on Omega Pharmaceutical's Investments (Million of U.S. Dollars)

Dollar	Internal Funds	R&D without Hedging	Cash Flows on Hedge	Additional R&D with Hedging	Value from Hedging
Appreciates	100	100	+100	100	+130
Stable	200	200	0	0	0
Depreciates	300	200	–100	0	–100

Ignoring the cost of the hedge, Table 11.2 shows the impact of the hedge on the available funds for R&D as compared to the no hedging alternative. For a depreciating dollar, the hedge does not change anything because the cash outflow on the hedge just offsets the cash inflow on the foreign currency denominated sales. But with an appreciating dollar, the cash inflow on the hedge that offsets the $100 million decline in foreign currency-denominated sales is just enough to finance the additional $100 million in investment that the firm decided to make. Consulting Table 11.2, the increased investment expenditure from $100 million to $200 million increases future expected cash flows by \$130 million. Because the \$130 million gain exceeds the \$100 million loss in a NPV sense, Omega Pharmaceutical can increase the value of the firm from hedging.

The FSS story thus is all about using risk management to match the *demand* for internal funds with the *supply* of external funds in order to avoid the presumed costs of issuing new debt to finance future investment projects. The demand/supply calculus is illustrated in Figure 11.1. The demand for R&D spending is shown at \$200 million, the presumed target level. The supply of internal funds is represented by a 45° line that changes in value dollar-for-dollar with appreciations or depreciations in the dollar price of yen and Deutsche marks. The two are equalized at the point where the hedge perfectly locks in the current dollar value of foreign sales. The gain from hedging, in general, is indicated as anything that tilts the supply of internal funds curve close to the demand for those funds.

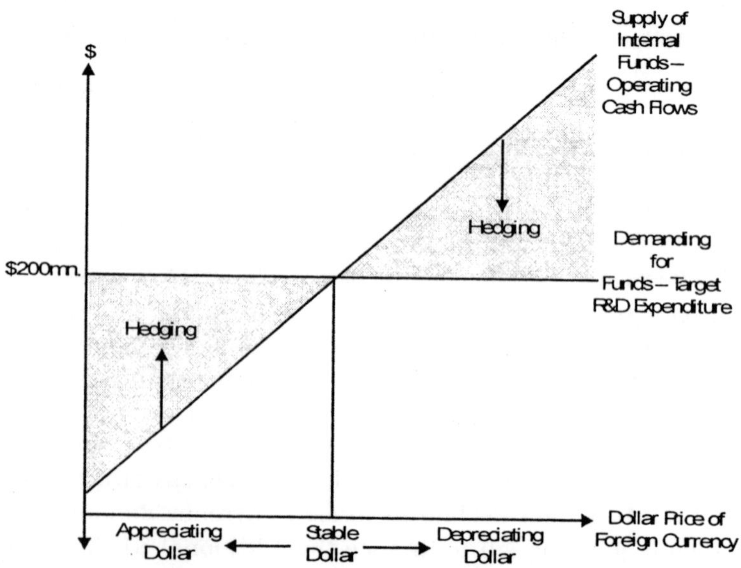

Figure 11.1. Using hedging to match the demand for and supply of internal funds at Omega Pharmaceutical.

In this example, the demand for internal funds is presumed to be perfectly elastic with respect to exchange rate changes. In other words, the exchange rate may ultimately affect how the investment expenditure is financed, but the exchange rate does not affect the demand for the investment.

FSS offer another example to illustrate what happens when the investment itself depends on the value of a diversifiable risk, such as exchange rates. They describe a new company called Omega Oil whose supply of internal funds is clearly affected by oil prices. When prices rise, revenues rise and conversely. But FSS then assume the demand for investments is also related to the price of oil. When prices are low, they posit that the demand for exploration and new reserves declines and conversely. Unlike revenues which clearly depend on the price of oil in a one-for-one manner, however, investments are a bit less sensitive to oil price changes. Prices could, after all, recover before oil is pumped from the ground. Although the demand for and supply of internal funds both are affected by oil prices, they are not exactly matched as Figure 11.2 illustrates.

Comparing Figure 11.1 and Figure 11.2 shows that the gains from hedging are higher for Omega Pharmaceutical than for Omega Oil. In the latter case, the natural exposure of the firm to oil prices exists both in its investments and its sales, thereby providing a bit of a natural hedge. Nevertheless, as Figure 11.2 shows, there is still some room for the firm to protect its investment opportunities by hedging to ensure that cash flows are always adequate to fund new investment opportunities.

So, the FSS model tells us that whenever the marginal cost of *external* finance is increasing in the amount of funds required and the marginal cost of *internal* finance is not, it makes sense for firms to reduce the volatility of their cash flows. Note that this is not the same as saying that firms should hedge their cash flows when external finance is more expensive than internal finance. If the rate a firm pays to bond holders is always 50 bps higher than its shadow price of internal funds, then the FSS model collapses. The firm can in that case always issue debt to finance investments, albeit at a cost of 50 bps. Whether or not external finance makes sense depends on the comparative cost of hedging and the cost of maintaining free cash flows (as we will discuss now).

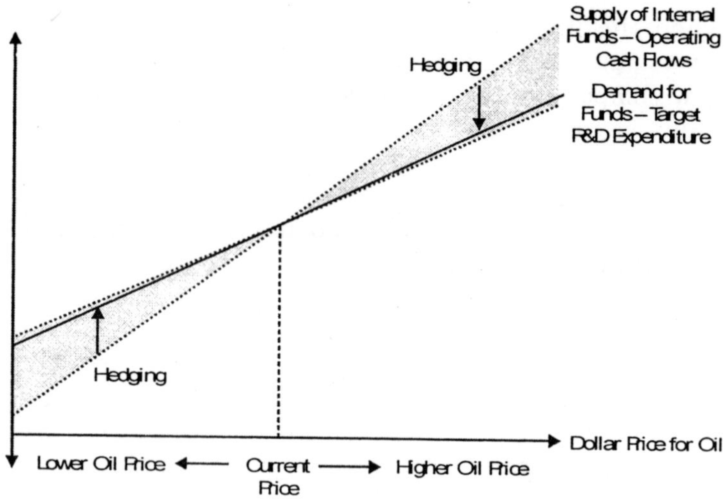

Figure 11.2. Using hedging to match the demand for and supply of internal funds at Omega Oil.

The FSS justification for risk management adding to firm value really kicks in when the marginal cost of external finance is not a constant but the marginal cost of internal finance is. In this case, more funds required mean proportionally increasing costs of external funding vis-a - vis internal funding. As noted earlier, asymmetric information is not strictly required to motivate the FSS model, but it helps a lot. Aside from firms that near bankruptcy that encounter distressed debt problems as they lever up, it is hard to imagine how external marginal financing costs can increase with the level of debt unless it is because the capital market simply cannot perceive the quality of the firm's investment opportunities. They instead simply observe the increase in leverage and mistake this for a distressed debt situation.

Carrying Charge Hedging

We saw that the variance-minimizing hedge ratio is not necessarily the *optimal* hedge ratio. The optimal hedge ratio was, rather, the tangency point between the trader's mean-variance indifference curve and the frontier of possibilities that a combination of hedged and unhedged positions in the market creates in mean-variance space. Is there an analogous *partial hedging* concept for corporations that can be consistent with the maximization of security holder welfare? In a world where information is asymmetric, the answer can be yes.

Types of "Hedging" in the World of Holbrook Working

Any discussion of the important role that asymmetric information can play in theories of corporate risk management must begin with some background on the work of Holbrook Working, an agricultural economist writing from the Food Research Institute at Stanford University in the mid-twentieth century. Working did much to increase our knowledge of the functioning of futures markets, including why people speculate and why people hedge. His work was both theoretically and empirically sound.

Because Working published his work in the agricultural economics journals really the only place to publish research on futures in the 1940s and 1950s the corporate finance literature has largely ignored his contributions. Nevertheless, they remain solid contributions to the theory and practice of risk management even today.

The Convenience Yield, the Basis, and the Supply of Storage, the fair quoted price of a futures contract can be expressed using the cost of carry formulation as follows:

$$F(t,T) = S(t) + b(t,T) \tag{11.1}$$

where $b(t, T)$ is the basis comprised of the capital and physical costs of storing a commodity from time t to time T less the *convenience yield* or implicit dividend earned by the marginal storer of the commodity. We can express the basis as

$$b(t,T) = R(t,T), W(t,T) - D(t,T) \tag{11.2}$$

where $R_{t,} T$ is the all-in interest cost prevailing from t to T, $W_{t,} T$ is the lump sum cost of physical storage from t to T, and $D_{t,} T$ is the dividend earned on the physical asset from t to T.

It is easy to reformulate this expression in any number of ways if you are unhappy with either the presumption of compounding implicit in the above or with the expression of W and D as lump-sum amounts. For example, if $w(t, T)$ and $d(t, T)$ denote the physical storage cost and convenience yield as a function of the spot price and $r(t, T)$ is the interest rate, then Equation 11.2 becomes and Equation 11.1 becomes

$$b(t,T) = r(t,T) + w(t,T) - d(t,T) \tag{11.3}$$

and Equation 11.1 becomes

$$F(t,T) = S(t)[1 + b(t,T)] \tag{11.4}$$

Or if you like continuous compounding becomes

$$F(t,T) = S(t)\exp[b(t,T)] \tag{11.5}$$

with $b(t, T)$ defined as in Equation 11.3 using continuous rates.

For financial futures and forwards, the cost of carry relation given in Equations 11.1, 11.4, or 11.5 is basic and intuitive. The formula is based on the construction of a transaction in the physical market that replicates the forward position and thus, in the absence of arbitrage, allows us to write the quoted forward purchase price as a function of carrying costs. A Treasury security, for example, can be carried over time at its financing rate, the repurchase (repo) rate you get for loaning a Treasury security out. For financial instruments, physical costs are zero. So, you have enough to know the futures price—$S(t)[1 + R(t, T) - d(t, T)]$ where $R(t, T)$ is the rate you earn on the Treasury and $d(t, T)$ is the rate you pay to borrow the Treasury. Foreign currency futures can be priced similarly— $S(t)[1 + R(t, T) - d(t, T)]$ where $R(t, T)$ is the rate you earn on domestic currency and $d(t, T)$ is the rate you are giving up by not holding the foreign currency, and so on.

Things get much more interesting when the underlying of the forward contract is a physical commodity. In that case, the physical storage cost $w(t, T)$ has some meaning, but $d(t, T)$ the so-called convenience yield is a lot more complicated.

Let us take a step backward and ask the reverse of the question we are considering when we ask why firms hedge: Why might firms want to hold on to a physical product rather than a substitute derivatives transaction? The answer lies in the convenience yield.

Working argued that there are four reasons why people store physical commodities. First, the transactional demand for storage leads some firms to store products to avoid the transaction costs of getting rid of them. People store pennies for this reason the benefit of getting rid of five pennies for a nickel is surely smaller than waiting until you have 100 or even 1,000 pennies saved up.

Second, firms sometimes have a "pure storage" motive for storage, as Working calls it. This simply means that storage is required for a purely physical reason usually having to do with some production process. Some auto manufacturers let every car leave their assembly lines, for example, with at least some gas in the tank. In order for this to be possible, they must store some gas near the assembly lines.

A third motivation for storage is speculative people store an asset in anticipation of an increase in its value. This is the classical rationale for hiding money under a mattress or, better still, for buying gold bullion. Gold has virtually no appreciable use in any major production process, but people hold on to it as a store of value and in the hope that its value will rise.

Finally and most importantly, Working characterizes the "precautionary demand" for storage. Firms sometimes have a precautionary demand for storage not because of current production needs that is, the "pure storage" rationale for inventory but because of unanticipated shocks to future production needs. These shocks can come either on the demand side or the supply side. The important thing to motivate the precautionary demand for storage is the cost associated with an inventory stock out. How many customers would Bally Switzerland on the Bahnhofstrasse in Zurich lose if it had to announce one day that it was out of shoes? How expensive would it be if an oil refinery had to cease all gasoline and heating oil production because it ran out of crude? How many shareholders of DeBeers would complain if they heard the company telling all of its resellers: "Sorry, but all our diamonds are still in the mines for the next few months."

The distinctions between these four motivations for physical inventory holdings are not always clear. Bally needs some shoes on hand to keep its store open. But the company might choose to inventory more than it needs for, say, a week's sales to avoid turning customers away a week later because of a problem with its shipping agent. The shoes it needs to open the store and sell this week is a pure storage motive for inventory, whereas keeping enough shoes to last another week is precautionary.

Or consider a jewelry manufacturer that caters primarily to the Japanese market, where the non industrial demand for platinum is extremely high. The jeweler might hold extra stocks of platinum to avoid a cessation in production in the event of a platinum shortage. But the jeweler might fine-tune those inventory holdings based on his beliefs about platinum prices, holding more than needed to satisfy precautionary demand in order to try and make a speculative profit on the actual metal.

The different motives for storage have a close linkage to the forward and futures market, as Keynes and his peer Pierro Sraffa observed in the 1930s. Specifically, the demand for holding physical inventory or, equivalently, the demand for immediacy is directly related to the premium placed on selling inventory in the future relative to selling into the spot market today. In other words, futures and forward markets act as intertemporal lending markets to move inventory from the present to the future or vice versa based on relative scarcity.

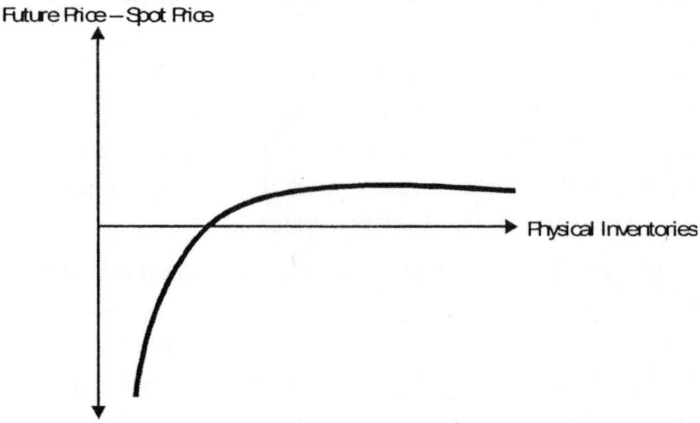

Figure 11.3. The demand for immediacy

Figure 11.3 illustrates this demand for immediacy. When inventories are high, the relative premium that a commodity commands in the future relative to the present is reasonably small. Plenty of the commodity is on hand to assure producers and intermediaries that a future stock out will not occur given reasonable demand and supply conditions. On the other hand, as inventories start to decline, the spot price rises relative to the futures price in order to give producers an incentive to take physical product out of inventory and give it to the current spot market. A high spot price alone would not do that. But a high spot price relative to the price for the sale of the same commodity in the future is signaling the market that inventories are tight today relative to the future.

The demand for immediacy is sometimes viewed from the opposite perspective and called the supply of storage, as shown in Figure 11.4. The basic relations between relative futures/spot prices and inventories is the same as in Figure 11.3, but now the y-axis is reversed and is expressed in terms of the spot price premium over the price at some point in the future for subsequent delivery of the commodity. Note in both Figure 11.3 and Figure 11.4 that the sensitivity of the price relation between current and future sale prices for the commodity varies based on the actual amount of the goods in storage. When inventories are high, the price relationship between current and future prices does not change much. But as inventories get tighter and tighter, the spot price becomes more and more responsive to that scarcity relative to the futures price.

Consulting the cost of carry characterization of futures prices is instructive and allows us to assign a good deal more economic interpretation to Figure 11.3 and Figure 11.4 than without it. Rearranging Equation 11.1 tells us the maximum the futures price can ever be relative to the spot price, or

$$F(t,T) - S(t) = R(t,T) + W(t,T) - D(t,T) \qquad 11.6$$

Clearly, the differential between the futures and spot price achieves its maximum when the convenience yield is at its minimum, or zero. Given what we know about the convenience yield, this means that firms essentially place no value on having physical inventories on hand during this time period. Accordingly, the futures price is left to drift above the spot price to reflect only the pure physical and capital costs of moving a unit of commodity over time. When the convenience yield is zero and futures prices exceed spot prices by exactly the capital and physical cost of storage, a market is said to be in full carry.

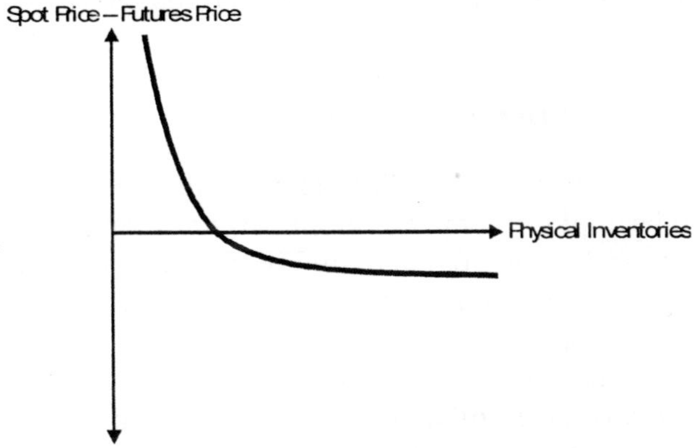

Figure 11.4. The supply of storage.

In most developed countries, physical and capital costs of storage do not fluctuate much and remain below a certain level. Some developing countries can experience hyperinflations that put tremendous upward pressure on rates, but even that does not radically affect the cost of physical storage. Consequently, the quantity $R(t, T) + W(t, T)$ does not fluctuate much and does not usually rise above some upper reflecting barrier or boundary. We can denote this *de facto* maximum as $R^{\circ}(t, T) + W^{\circ}(t, T)$, the level at which the market is in full carry. Figure 11.5 shows this point graphically. No matter how large inventories grow, at some point they grow large enough to drive the convenience yield to zero, at which point the premium of the futures price over the spot price never really gets any larger than $R^{\circ}(t, T) + W^{\circ}(t, T)$.

The convenience yield is overlaid on Figure 11.5 as a dotted line. As inventories shrink, however, the convenience yield becomes positive. And as inventories get lower and lower, the convenience yield rises at an increasing rate. The less there is available in inventory, the less there is for firms to meet *current* production demands and the more the firms *need* physical inventory, which is the implicit dividend to physical product that the convenience yield is intended to reflect.

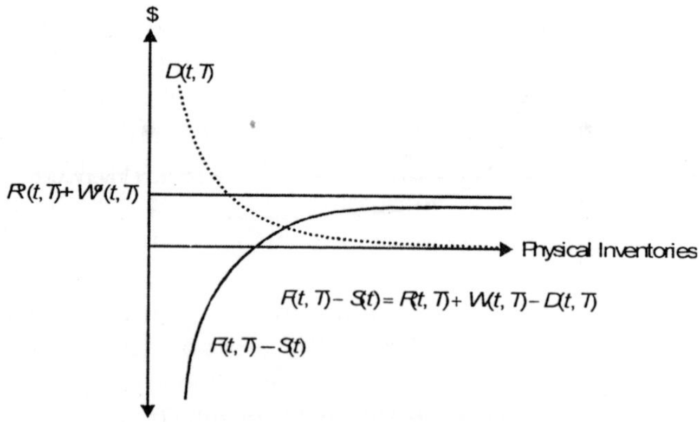

Figure 11.5. The demand for immediacy and cost of carry futures pricing.

Many people become confused when first encountering the convenience yield because of confusions over demand and supply shocks. From Equation 11.1, we know that the futures price is a function of the spot price. In an efficient capital market with rational expectations, we have already seen that the futures price is an unbiased predictor of the future spot price. Consequently, demand and supply shocks should be reflected in the spot price. If demand in one year is known with certainty to be above average, the price will rise today in anticipation of this. And the futures price will also rise because it is a function of the spot price.

French has carefully studied relations between spot and futures prices and has shown that the impact of supply and demand shocks on spot prices and the spot-futures price relation depends primarily on the level of inventories when the shock occurs. If inventories are high, demand and supply shocks tend to impact the spot price and the futures price in much the same way. In other words, because the shock hits the spot price it also hits the futures price proportionately. But the convenience yield does not change much, and so the relation between the futures and spot price the basis, as we have called it remains nearly constant. But as inventories shrink, a shock to supply or demand impacts the spot price much more significantly than the futures price. This is the convenience yield responding to the level of inventories and acting as an adjustment mechanism for moving inventory across time.

The Term Structure of Futures Prices Our discussion thus far has included nothing about the relationship between prices for the delivery of a commodity at multiple points in time. Yet, all of our discussion thus far generalizes for any value of T we may consider. As it is, we could simply redraw Figure 11.3 through Figure 11.5 using two different futures prices. When we refer to the spot-futures basis, we are referring to what is sometimes known as the calendar basis, or the relation between the prices of two identical commodities to be delivered at different calendar times. Just as the spot-futures basis is the difference between the spot price and the futures price observed at the same time, we can define any pair wise basis accordingly. The one-to-three month calendar basis is the difference between the current price of a contract for delivery one month hence and the current price of a contract for delivery three months hence.

The relation between several futures or forward prices and the spot price defines the term structure of futures prices. Some examples of futures price term structures all based on futures settlement prices observed on September 6, 2000 are shown in Figure 11.6 to Figure 11.8. Figure 11.6 shows the relation between the price of lumber per thousand board feet and the month in which the lumber will be delivered. The futures price rises steadily each month. The slope of the term structure of futures prices is positive. This tells us that lumber inventories are probably reasonably high and expected to remain high relative to demand through September of 2001. Why? As noted earlier, when inventories are high the difference between any given futures price and the spot price is roughly equal to the cost of storing the commodity over time; the convenience yield is negligible because supply is aplenty. We expect some increase in prices over time, of course, because the cost of storage rises that is, it costs more to store a thousand board feet of lumber for one year than for one month.

The lumber market shown in Figure 11.6 is said to be in contango because the slope of the term structure of futures prices is positive throughout. Figure 11.7, by contrast, shows that the world sugar market is in a state of what is called backwardation in which futures prices decline with successively more distant delivery dates. Sugar is selling for about 10.45 cents per pound today in the spot market, but the exact same quantity and quality and type of sugar to be delivered in the same place (s) in July 2002 is selling for only 8.90 cents per pound today.

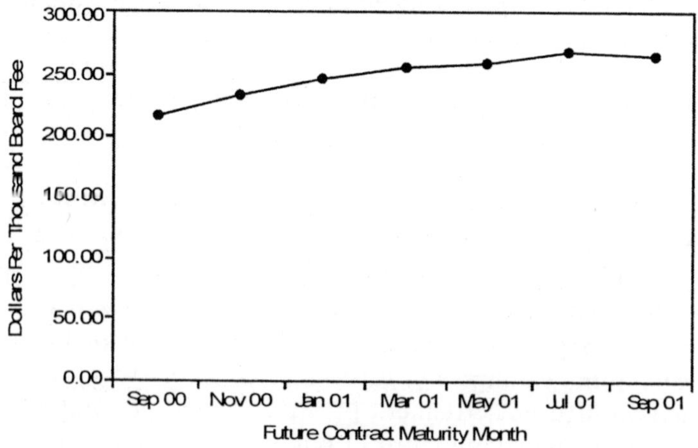

Figure 11.6. Term structure of futures prices as of 9/6/00 for lumber (CME).

A market in backwardation has a calendar basis futures price minus the spot price that is negative. Returning to Figure 11.5, $F(t, T) - S(t)$ becomes negative only when inventories are getting tight and, consequently, the convenience yield associated with physical storage is starting to rise. In fact, we know from Equations 11.1 and 11.2 that the only way the spot price can exceed the futures price is if

$$D(t,T) > R(t,T) + W(t,T) \qquad 11.7$$

so that the convenience yield earned from holding physical product exceeds the capital and physical cost of storing the product. We thus can make a fairly well-educated guess from Figure 11.7 that world sugar inventories are not at their highest levels right now and that demand is high relative to supply in the short run.

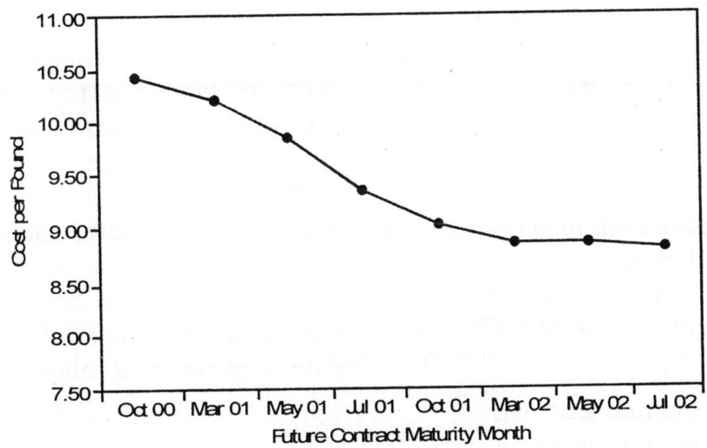

Figure 11.7. Term structure of futures prices as of 9/6/00 for sugar (NYBOT).

The third example, Figure 11.8, shows the term structure of copper futures prices as quoted on the New York Mercantile Exchange on September 6, 2000 at about 90.90 cents per pound. Copper is currently selling in the spot market for about 90.10 cents per pound.

Figure 11.8 is instructive because it illustrates that a market can exhibit both backwardation and contango at the same time. The price of copper to be delivered from now through March 2001 is rising steadily. This contango market reflects a low convenience yield relative to physical storage costs. But in March 2001, the market turns and prices start to decline.

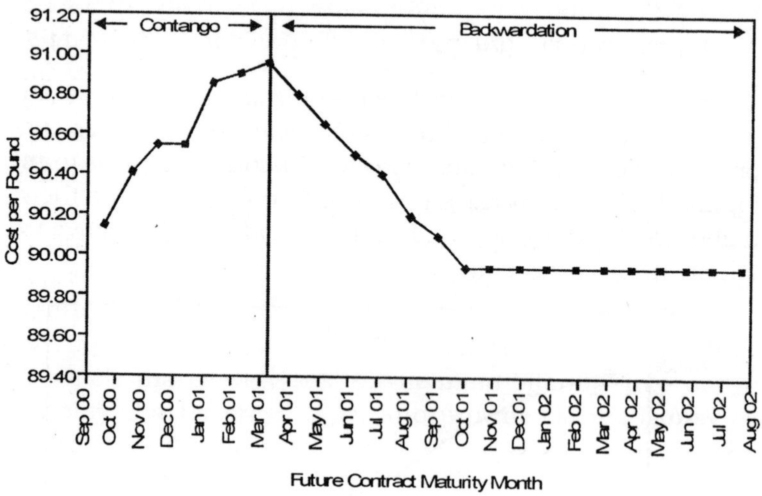

Figure 11.8. Term structure of futures prices as of 9/6/00 for copper (NYMEX).

A variety of factors can cause a market to shift from backwardation to contango at some future delivery date. In the case of the copper market, it might be the case that current inventories are enough to meet demand, but a mine could, for example, be going temporarily out of production in March. That would lead to a contraction in supply that would affect future inventories, even though inventories are presently reasonably high.

It is important to keep in mind, moreover, that the term structure of futures prices much like the term structure of interest rates, or yield curve represents a snapshot of the market at a single point in time. The behavior of a market over time can be quite different. As new supply and demand shocks occur, the convenience yield can be quite volatile, sending a market from backwardation into contango one week and then back to a negatively sloped term structure the next week.

Petroleum markets tend to exhibit particular volatility in the convenience yield, in large part because OPEC pursues cartel pricing whose stability depends at any given moment on the credibility of its production quotas for member nations. Figure 11.9 shows the impact this can have on the slope of the term structure of futures prices, depicted specifically for the 24 month calendar basis the price of the futures contract with 24 months to maturity less the spot price. As you can see from Figure 11.9, the market for light, sweet, West Texas Intermediate (WTI) crude was in backwardation for most of the period shown with the notable exception of most of 1998, when the market went as far as $6 per barrel into contango.

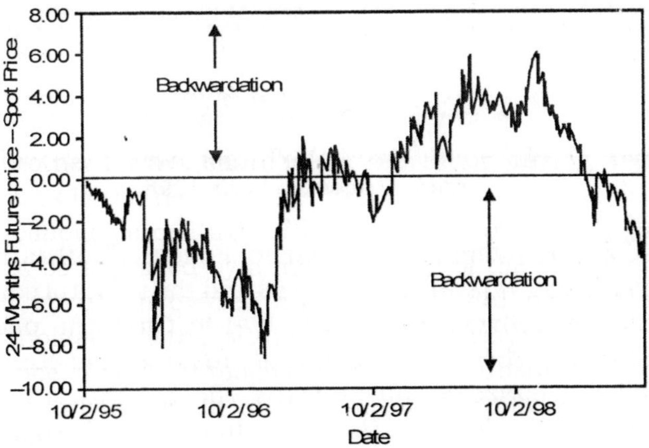

Figure 11.9. Slope of term structure of futures prices for light, sweet, west Texas intermediate crude oil (NYMEX), 10/95–8/99.

To add a different perspective, Figure 11.10 shows the slopes of some specific oil price term structures on October 2 for the years 1995 to 1998. The information conveyed by these term structures is quite different from the information we can deduce from the time series graphs in Figure 11.9, which tells us only whether the market was in backwardation or contango and by how much. In Figure 11.10, we can see that the driving force appears to be shifts in the spot price and the prices of near-term futures. The long end of the term structures stays relatively stable around $18 to $22 per barrel, whereas the spot price fluctuates from around $15 to almost $25 per barrel.

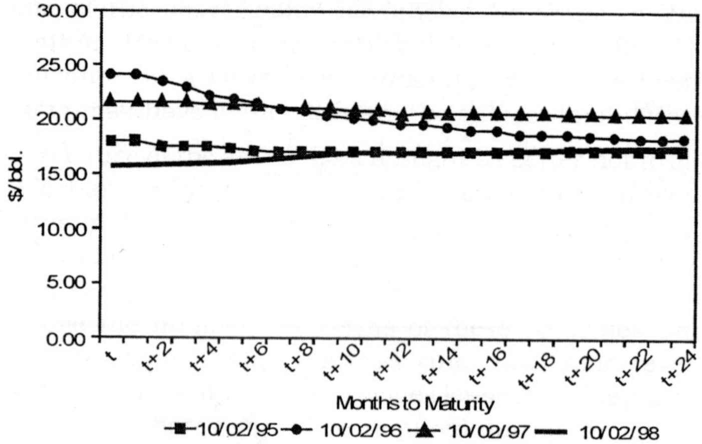

Figure 11.10. Term structures of WTI light, sweet crude oil futures prices October 2, 1995–1998

The phenomenon depicted in Figure 11.10 is not an unusual one. Typically, spot prices and the prices of contracts nearer to delivery are more volatile than the prices of contracts for delivery further in the futures. Sometimes this is called a *horizontal diving board* effect, because the term structures in Figure 11.10 appear to trace the movement of a diving board bouncing a lot at one end and not much at the other.

This horizontal diving board should not come as a shock, given what we saw in Figure 11.5. As inventories decline further and further, the convenience yield gets higher and higher. And at the same time, the spot price becomes quite sensitive to small changes in anticipated supply and demand. Consequently, it does not take much to move short-term prices in a market like oil, despite the relative stability of the prices of oil to be delivered two years and beyond in the future.

The dividend portion of the cost of carry futures pricing formula is not as interesting for financial assets as it is for commodities. For financial assets like foreign currency, equity indices, and Treasuries, the dividend foregone by holding the futures contract is *an explicit dividend* or cash flow. The current time t price of a futures contract on the S&P 500 that matures at time T is just

$$F(t,T) = I(t) + R(t,T) - D(t,T)$$

where $I(t)$ is the current index level, $R(t, T)$ is the all-in cost of borrowing the index value today and financing it through date T, and $D(t, T)$ are the cumulative dividends paid on all the stocks in the index over the time period. By holding a long futures position, you guarantee the purchase of the stocks in the index (or their cash equivalent) at time T, but you forego the dividends. As a benefit, you pay nothing to enter the position today. Buying the stocks now and holding them, by contrast, allows you to earn the dividends, but you must borrow the money to buy the stocks and finance the loan in turn. Any way you cut it, buying and holding the stocks is equivalent to going long the futures.

For commodities, it is not always true that going long the futures is exactly equivalent to buying and storing the physical good. Whereas the dividends paid on the S&P 500 are either known or fairly predictable and do not depend on who holds the stocks, any given firm may have a different physical storage cost and convenience yield than the basis reflected in the current futures price. Inventories may be high enough in aggregate that the convenience yield reflected in futures price is negligible, but any particular firm may be in an inventory squeeze.

The cost of carry formula for futures and forwards based on financial assets thus is an *arbitrage* relationship. If the price of S&P 500 futures is above its fair value by more than transaction costs, any firm can short the futures and buy the stocks for a risk less profit. At any given time, by contrast, the basis priced into a commodity futures contract is the marginal cost of storage less the marginal convenience yield for the marginal entrant into physical storage. The convenience yield thus is unobservable, different across firms, and not explicitly associated with a cash flow. It serves to establish equilibrium between futures and spot prices in order to move inventory across time, but consequently, it cannot be arbitraged easily.

At the same time, the fact that the convenience yield is an unobservable, equilibrium relation rather than an observable quantity means that, as Holbrook Working recognized, it is precisely the place to look for the impact of asymmetric information on trading and risk management activities.

Working describes a type of hedging he calls "carrying-charge hedging" in which the basic intent is to exploit a perceived informational advantage. When a firm believes that one market is mis-priced relative to another, the firm can essentially engage in a basis trade to exploit that perceived mispricing until, of course, its own actions reveal its information and drive away the profit opportunity. Why would such a firm not simply sell the overpriced asset outright? The answer, for Working, was that firms could not acquire enough information about a financial asset being mis-priced without having a natural exposure in the underlying market. By definition, then, any trading decisions would be basis trading decisions. That explanation is not entirely satisfactory, however, because the firm would want to keep trading even after its natural exposure had long since been offset with trades attempting to exploit its information about the basis. But, as we shall see in the next two subsections, the minor addition of positive expected bankruptcy costs takes care of this problem.

A Simple Model of Carrying-Charge Hedging

One obvious way that a firm can make money or advantageously avoid losing money in a financial market is if this edict of finance is violated and securities are mis-priced. Can such mis-pricings of securities occur? Indeed, in a world of asymmetric information, they can under one very strong assumption (in addition to the assumption of information asymmetries). Trading is itself informative, so security mis-pricings can persist only when information is asymmetric and the actions taken by a firm or a trader to exploit the mispricing do not drive the mis-pricing away.

With Holbrook Working's "theory of supply of storage" in hand, we can illustrate the relation between risk management and information asymmetry using a simple model. Our example involves three periods, $t = (0, 1, 2)$. Suppose at time 0 a marketing firm contracts to deliver one barrel of oil at time 1 and time 2 to retail customers for fixed price K (henceforth the *customer swap*). Assume for simplicity there is no demand for the marketer to offer swaps in which it receives oil. In addition, the marketing firm is a price taker in all derivatives; its actions cannot influence quoted futures prices or swap rates, and it cannot offer swaps with rates different from dealer-offered fair swap rates.

Assume that the per-period interest rate r is constant but that the net cost of oil storage is not. The net cost of storage from time 0 to 1, denoted $z(0, 1)$, is the difference between the marginal cost of physical storage $w(0, 1)$ and the marginal convenience yield $d(0, 1)$ between time 0 and time 1 expressed as a proportion of the spot price. The net convenience yield from time 0 to time 1 is a random variable realized at time 0.

The expected future spot price one period hence is presumed equal to the current spot price adjusted for the observable basis (i.e., capital and physical storage costs less convenience yield) plus a zero expected value error term:

$$E_0[S(1)] = S(0)(1 + r)[1 + w(0,1)]$$
$$E_1[S(2)] = S(1)(1 + r)[1 + w(0,2)]$$

where E_0 and E_1 are expected value operators conditional on information available at times 0 and 1, respectively.

The marketing firm perceives itself as having superior information to all external market participants customers, futures traders, swap dealers, and so on. We do not assume the information asymmetry exists vis-à-vis external or internal financing sources, although we must assume the marketing firm's actions do not affect market prices.

To capture the asymmetry of information, we adopt some simple notation. For any random variable X, denote an expected value conditional on time 0 public information as $E_0[X]^2$ and an expectation conditional on the marketing firm's information as $E_0{}^*[X]$.

$$E_0^*[S(1)] = E_0[S(1)] + \theta$$
$$E_1^*[S(2)] = E_1[S(2)] + \theta$$

where $\theta > 0$. Futures and other derivatives are opriced as unbiased predictors of expected future spot prices from the public perspective. The uoted price of a contract maturing one period hence thus is,

$$F(0,1) = E_0[S(1)] = S(0)(1+r)[1+w(0,1)]$$
$$F(1,2) = E_1[S(2)] = S(1)(1+r)[1+w(1,2)]$$

At maturity, the futures price must equal the *realized* spot price for example, $F(2) = S(2)$. In other words, the expected profit on all futures trades conditional on public information.

To express the price of a two-period futures contract quoted at time 0 and maturing at time 2, we assume that futures are marked to market each period. Rational futures pricing then requires that

$$\frac{E_0[F(1,2)] - F(0,2)}{1+r} = 0 \qquad 11.7$$

Purely for simplicity, we assume throughout that the spot price is independent of the contemporaneous net storage cost—$E_0[S(1)w(1,2)] = E_0[S(1)]E_0[w(1,2)]$ and $E_0^*[S(1)w(1,2)] = E_0^*[S(1)]E_0^*[w(1,2)]$. Using this assumption together with the law of iterated expectations, we can solve Equation 11.7 for $F(0,2)$:

$$\begin{aligned} F(0,2) &= E_0[E_1S(2)] = E_0\{S(1)(1+r)[1+w(1,2)]\} \\ &= S(0)(1+r)^2[1+w(0,1)][1+E_1w(1,2)] \end{aligned} \qquad 11.8$$

The arbitrage-free swap rate on a dealer-offered commodity swaps is just the rate equates the conditional expected NPV of the commodity swap to zero at its inception, or the K that solves:

$$\frac{K}{1+r} + \frac{K}{(1+r)^2} = \frac{E_0[S(t)]}{1+r} + \frac{E_1[S(2)]}{(1+r)^2}$$

which is

$$K = \frac{\dfrac{E_0[S(1)]}{1+r} + \dfrac{E_1[S(2)]}{(1+r)^2}}{\dfrac{1}{1+r} + \dfrac{1}{(1+r)^2}} \qquad 11.9$$

$$= \frac{S(0)[1+w(0,1)] + S(0)[1+w(0,1)][1+E_0w(1,2)]}{\dfrac{1}{1+r} + \dfrac{1}{(1+r)^2}} \qquad 11.10$$

Because the marketer is a price taker in both futures and swaps, the equilibrium quoted futures and swap prices above are unaffected by the firm's private information. In addition, the arbitrage-free swap rate K shown in Equation 11.9 is not only the rate that the marketer would be quoted by a dealer on a hedge, but also the rate that the marketing firm must charge its customers on the customer swaps. Note, however, that from the perspective of the marketing firm, derivatives are no longer unbiased predictors of subsequent spot rates. From the firm's perspective, the information asymmetry results in a mis-pricing of futures and swaps that creates a profit opportunity.

The Unhedged Program Private information about the basis implies private information about either spot or derivatives prices. If all M&M assumptions are retained except for symmetric information, the marketer has an expected profit function that is linear in firm value. Consequently, there is no reason at this stage to assume the firm would need to hedge.

By assumption, the marketing firm may only enter into swaps in which it receives fixed and delivers oil. If the company does not hedge the customer swap, the time 1 and time 2 cash flows on the unhedged position are as follows:

$$E_0^*(\pi_2) = K - E_0^*[S(2)] = K - E_0[S(2)] - \theta \qquad 11.11$$

Discounting the expected cash flows in Equations 11.10 and 11.11 and substituting the fair swap rate from Equation 7.9 into the resulting NPV expression yields the following time 0 conditional expected NPV of the program for the marketer:

$$NPV = \frac{-\theta}{1+r} + \frac{-\theta}{(1+r)^2} \qquad 11.12$$

Because of the nature of the assumed information asymmetry, the marketer will reject the unhedged program as a negative NPV project. In this stylized example, the private information thus leads the marketing firm not to offer the customer contracts at all.

An Outright Futures Position The marketer's linear profit function enables it to accept positive NPV profits in an essentially limitless manner. Because the customer swap has a negative NPV and the firm cannot by assumption offer the opposite swap deal, the firm will exploit its private information through futures trading. We consider two such strategies, both of which are intended to function as *synthetic storage* programs synthetic purchase of oil in each of periods 1 and 2 to mimic the swap or some physical storage program. For now, assume an exogenous one-for-one hedge ratio in both strategies.

The first trading strategy the multimaturity trade involves a long one-period contract held from time 0 to 1 and another long contract held from time 0 to time 2. The realized cash flows on the multimaturity strategy are as follows:

$$\begin{aligned}\pi_1 &= [F(1,1) - F(0,1)] + [F(1,2) - F(0,2)] \\ &= S(1) - F(0,1) + F(1,2) - F(0,2) \\ \pi_2 &= [F(2,2) - F(1,2)] = S(2) - F(1,2)\end{aligned}$$

The time 0 conditional expected cash flows then can be written using the marketing firm's specific private information:

$$E_0^*(\pi_1) = E_0^*[S(1)] + E_0[S(2)] - E_0[S(2)] = \theta \qquad 11.13$$

$$E_0^*(\pi_2) = E_0^*[S(2)] - E_0[S(2)] = \theta \qquad 11.14$$

The NPV of the strategy is clearly then

$$NPV = \frac{\theta}{1+r} + \frac{\theta}{(1+r)^2} \qquad 11.15$$

which is positive. The firm accepts the project.

The second strategy is called a *stack-and-roll* trade in which the marketer goes long two one-period contracts from 0 to 1 and a single one-period contract from 1 to 2. Now consider the cash flows on the stack-and-roll trade:

$$\begin{aligned}\pi_1 &= 2[F(1,1) - F(0,1)] = 2[S(1) - F(0,1)] \\ \pi_2 &= 2[F(2,2) - F(1,2)] = S(1) - F(1,2)\end{aligned}$$

which implies time 0 conditional expected cash flows of

$$E_0^*(\pi_1) = 2E_0^*[S(1)] - 2E_0[S(1)] = \theta$$
$$E_0^*(\pi_2) = E_0^*[S(2)] - E_0^*\{E_1[S(2)]\} = E_0^*[S(2)] - E_0[S(2)] = \theta$$

The NVP of the stack-and-roll is

$$NPV = \frac{2\theta}{1+r} + \frac{\theta}{(1+r)^2} \qquad 11.16$$

which is positive. The firm again accepts the project.

Several important points emerge from the NPVs shown in Equations 11.15 and 11.16. First, the NPV criterion literally states that firms should accept all positive NPV projects. With no assumptions about capital constraints and a linear expected profit function, theory tells us that the firm will accept both of these projects. In the limit, the firm actually will load up on an essentially unlimited number of long futures contracts. Or if not unlimited, the positions the firm will take at least will be enough to make tenuous our assumption that the marketer's trades never reveal its private information.

The other important point to note from Equations 11.15 and 11.16 is that the NPV of the stack-and-roll trade has expected profits that are strictly increasing in the size of the stack. Consequently, if the firm was, say, capital constrained (e.g., by funding requirements), the preferability of the stack-and-roll program over the multi maturity program in terms of expected profit alone would be clear.

The reason that the futures trades allow the firm to exploit its perceived informational advantage arises from the mis-pricing of the futures relative to the expected future spot price. When the futures contract matures, its value to the firm is equal to the then-prevailing spot price. At time 0, this is the firm's expectation of the future spot price. When the futures contracts are either initially quoted or marked to market, their values are based on the public's expectation of future spot prices. Consequently, the firm can appropriate the gain only when a contract actually reaches maturity.

Marking a contract to public information repeatedly yields a gain for the firm only when the contract matures. Rolling over from one maturing contract into a new one, however, enables the firm to earn a private information premium upon each rollover.

Information Acquisition and the Hedged Customer Swap Because the NPV of the customer contracts is negative and the NPV of a futures trade is positive, the firm would never engage in the former without some additional reason for doing so. But in a world of asymmetric information, the customer contracts themselves may be the key mechanisms by which the firm acquires its perceived superior information. By learning its customers' demand functions, some firms can better anticipate calendar and geographical basis shifts. Viewed in this way, the θ paid each period in the swap can be viewed as the marginal cost of information acquisition that enables the firm to profit by combining the futures with the swap.

First suppose the marketing firm offers the customer swap hedged with multi maturity futures. In this case, the realized cash flows each period are

$$\begin{aligned} \pi_1 &= K - S(1) + F(1,1) - F(0,1) + F(1,2) - F(0,2) \\ &= [K - F(0,1)] + [F(1,2) - F(0,2)] \\ \pi_2 &= K - S(2) + F(2,2) - F(1,2) - K - F(1,2) \end{aligned}$$

The time 0 conditional expected cash flows of the firm are:

$$\begin{aligned} E_0^*(\pi_1) &= K - E_0[S(1)] \\ E_0^*(\pi_2) &= K - E_0[S(2)] \end{aligned}$$

When we substitute in the competitive swap rate from Equation 11.9, we see that the NPV of the program is zero. More specifically, the θ earned each period on the hedge is exactly offset by the θ paid each period on the customer marketing contracts. The cost of information acquisition thus is equal to its benefit at the margin, and the firm cannot take advantage of its proprietary information at all.

Now consider the stack-and-roll as a hedge of the marketing contract. The time 1 and 2 realized cash flows are

$$\pi_1 = K - S(1) + 2[F(1,1) - F(0,1)] = K - F(0,1) + S(1) - F(0,1)$$
$$\pi_2 = K - S(2) + F(2,2) - F(1,2) = K - F(1,2)$$

which yields conditional expected cash flows of

$$E_0^*(\pi_1) = K - E_0[S(1)] + E_0^*[S(1)] - E_0[S(1)] = K - E_0[S(1)] + \theta$$
$$E_0^*(\pi_2) = K - E_0[S(2)]$$

When the competitive swap rate is substituted into these expected cash flows, the time 0 conditional expected net present value of the customer contract hedged with the stack-and-roll is

$$NPV = \frac{\theta}{1+r}.$$

which is strictly positive. This is not surprising given what we saw earlier in Equation 11.16. Namely, the rollover of two contracts at time 1 nets the firm 2θ at that time. Because only θ is paid in the customer contract for information acquisition costs in that period, the firm earns the residual θ as pure expected profit.

In this example, the asymmetry of information between the marketing firm, its customers, and the general futures market allows the firm to make money on the information it has. This profit is limited, however, by the cost of acquiring its special information, which is the cost of the swap program itself. Nevertheless, in this model the firm makes money and increases its value from exploiting its perceived information advantage in the manner set forth.

Importance of Financial Distress

The model in the prior section is hardly a justification by itself for "risk management." Even assuming the customer swaps are required to give the firm its private information, which it exploits by hedging those swaps, the particular assumptions we made about the nature of the informational symmetry drive the result. In general terms, if a firm has private information about the relation between a spot and futures price, it must have private information either about the spot price itself or the futures price itself. And if it does, then "hedging" is a stylized excuse for outright position taking. The firm should simply short unlimited quantities of the overpriced security and buy unlimited quantities of the under priced security.

A more palatable justification for risk management in the world of private information is when we combine our present assumption about asymmetric information with our earlier assumption about exogenous bankruptcy costs to generate a theory of selective hedging a la Working. In this case, a firm with private information could not simply buy or sell unlimited quantities of a mis-priced security not without greatly increasing its expected bankruptcy costs. Risk management thus enables firms with private information to exploit that information without increasing the risk of bankruptcy.

Recall that we have argued risk management is essentially a substitute for equity capital. Accordingly, the types of firms we might most expect to engage in the sort of selective risk management that Working describes as carrying-charge hedging will have capital structures that predispose them to some form of financial distress possibility. To illustrate the link between capital structure and risk management when a firm has the opportunity to exploit a comparative information advantage. In Figure 11.11, the value of the firm is depicted in the presence of bankruptcy costs that increase linearly with the shortfall of net assets below the face value of debt outstanding, FV. When assets are equal to A_2, for example, the value of the firm is $V_2 = A_2 - C$, where C is the cost of financial distress that gets larger the lower that assets fall.

Four probability distributions are shown for four different types of firms. The distribution denoted $f_3(A)$ is clearly a well-capitalized, highly rated firm. The probability that its assets will fall below the face value of debt is virtually zero. The opportunities for value-added risk management may not be very pronounced at a firm like this. The firm would likely not encounter distressed debt costs in the cash flow sense of FSS any more than it would run into traditional underinvestment problems. Risk management might well best be undertaken by the shareholders of a firm like this, just as M&M predicts.

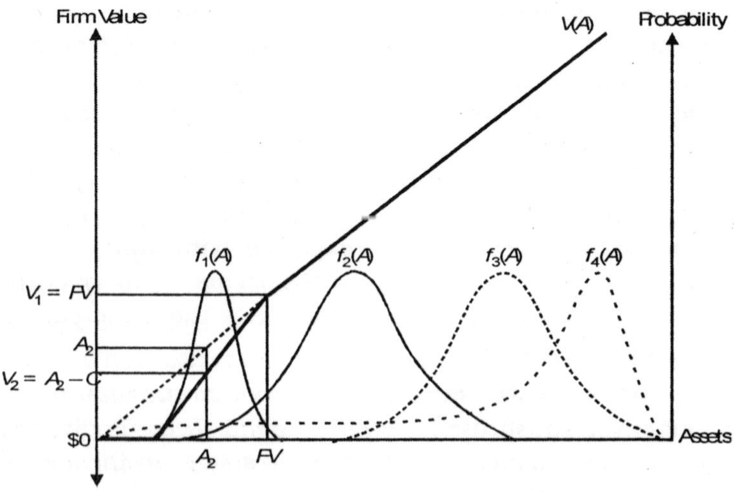

Figure 11.11. Capital Structure and Hedging

As shown, opportunities to exploit asymmetric information also would not necessarily lead to hedging behavior for the firm whose assets have a distribution that looks like $f_3(A)$. Especially if that distribution already reflects the trading activities in which it might engage to exploit an information advantage, the firm simply has no threat of incurring bankruptcy costs. If anything, this is the kind of firm you might well expect to take outright speculative positions in the market.

You might also expect the firm whose asset values are drawn from the distribution $f_1(A)$ to undertake speculative trading activities if it has an informational advantage, but for entirely different reasons. Clearly, the firm whose asset values are shown in distribution f_1 is in trouble. Debt holders will receive their full face value in almost no scenario, which means the equity of this firm is virtually worthless. You could expect the asset substitution problem at a firm like this to be quite severe. About the only way that equity will extract any value from its shares is to pursue extremely high variance projects. If the firm believes itself better informed about a market or basis relation and covenants or other restrictions are not in place to prevent asset substitution, the firm well might try to exploit its informational advantage through outright position-taking as the proverbial "last punt."

Now consider the firm whose assets are drawn from the distribution $f_2(A)$. Here the firm could appreciably reduce its expected costs of financial distress through hedging. But does that mean the firm should not take a position in the market to exploit its comparative information advantages?

Not necessarily. A firm like this one would have to be careful just how it constructs its hedge, but a well-constructed basis trade could actually involve a net reduction in expected bankruptcy costs while at the same time allowing the firm to trade the basis and try to exploit a comparative informational advantage.

Consider our earlier simple model of the oil marketing firm. If the firm offers unhedged customer contracts, its NPV is negative. And if the firm offers those contracts with a maturity matched hedge, it breaks even in a NPV sense and does not appreciably increase the probability it will run into financial distress. But if the firm tries to exploit its private information with the stack-and-roll hedge, there is almost no way it can generate a positive expected NPV strategy without also increasing its expected costs of financial distress. A firm with the distribution f_2 (A) is probably not the firm that would adopt this strategy.

Now consider a different example say, an oil company that owns its own fields and tank farms. Suppose this firm considers its information about the convenience yield better than the rest of the market and believes futures are overpriced. In this case, the firm could short the futures against the oil field, simultaneously exploiting its perception that the futures are overpriced and reducing its expected bankruptcy costs. A firm with an asset distribution like f_3 might be tempted to overhedge. If its trading does not reveal its private information, after all, it will keep selling futures until the market corrects the mis-pricing. Because the firm with asset distribution f_3 has a long way to go before it ever encounters bankruptcy costs, there is no reason for the firm to stop hedging when the size of the hedge reaches the size of the oil field.

If the oil firm has a distribution f_2, however, the firm would stop at a 1:1 hedge, where every barrel of the oil field is hedged with a short futures position. The hedge, of course, is really an attempt to exploit its information that futures are mis-priced. The natural long exposure created by the oil field, however, is what makes it possible for the firm to exploit its information advantage through this hedge without increasing its expected bankruptcy costs.

What kind of distribution would our firm need to have to adopt the strategy we discussed earlier for the marketing firm that makes money only on the volatile stack-and-roll hedge? An example of such a firm might be the distribution denoted f_4 (A) in Figure 11.11. This distribution has a very high expected value, suggesting a high level of equity capital like the firm in f_3. But unlike the f_3 firm, this firm does face a positive probability, albeit small, of incurring financial distress costs. On the one hand, the high level of equity capital in this firm might lead it to try and exploit its comparative informational advantage through an outright position in the market.

Bibliography

Aaron Richard I. (1980) "The Bankruptcy Reform Act of 1978: The FullEmployment-for-Lawyers Bill: Overview and Legislative History", *Corporate Practice Commentator*, 22 (2): 201.

Abbott Andrew (1981) "Status and Status Strain in the Professions", *American Journal of Sociology*. 86: 819-35.

Abowd John M. (1990) "Does Performance-Based Managerial Compensation Affect Corporate Performance?" *Industrial and Labor Relations Review* 43: 52S-73S.

Adler Barry E. (1993) "Financial and Political Theories of American Corporate Bankruptcy", *Stanford Law Review* 45: 311-46.

Aghion Philippe, Oliver Hart and John Moore (1994) "Improving Bankruptcy Procedure", *Washington University Law Quarterly* 72: 849-72.

Bacon Richard L. and James L. Billinger (1979) "Analyzing the Operation and Tax Effects of the New Bankruptcy Act", *Journal of Taxation* 50(2): 76-80.

Baird Douglas G. and Thomas H. Jackson (1990) *Cases, Problems, and Materials on Bankruptcy*, (2nd edn.) Boston: Little, Brown.

Baron James, F. Dobbin and P. D. Jennings (1986) "War and Peace: The Evolution of Modern Personnel Administration in U.S. Industry", *American Journal of Sociology* 92: 350-83.

Barzel Yoram (1989) *Economic Analysis of Property Rights*, Cambridge: Cambridge University Press.

Campbell John L. and Leon N. Lindberg (1990) "Property Rights and the Organization of Economic Activity by the State", *American Sociological Review*, 55: 634-47.

Campbell Steve (1994) "Brother, Can You Spare a Ruble? The Development of Bankruptcy Legislation in the New Russia", *Bankruptcy Developments Journal*, 10: 343-95.

Carruthers Bruce and Wendy Espeland (1991) "Accounting for Rationality: Double-Entry Bookkeeping and the Rhetoric of Economic Rationality", *American Journal of Sociology*, 97: 31-69.

Derthick, Martha and Paul J. Quirk (1985) *The Politics of Deregulation*, Washington DC: Brookings Institution.

DiMaggio Paul and Walter W. Power (1983) "The Iron Cage Revisited: Institutional Isomorphism and Collective Rationality in Organizational Fields", *American Sociological Review*, 48: 147-60.

Dobbin Frank, Lauren Edelman, John W. Meyer and W. Richard Scott (1988) "The Expansion of Due Process in Organizations", in*Institutional Patterns in Organizations*, Lynn G. Zucker (ed.) Cambridge: Ballinger.

Edelman Lauren (1990) "Legal Environments and Organizational Governance: The Expansion of Due Process in the American Workplace",*American Journal of Sociology*, 95: 1401-40.

Flaschen Evan D. and Timothy B. DeSieno (1992) "The Development of Insolvency Law as Part of the Transition from a Centrally Planned to a Market Economy", *The International Lawyer*, 26: 671.

Fletcher Ian F. (1981) "Bankruptcy Law Reform: the Interim Report of the Cork Committee, and the Department of Trade Green Paper",*Modern Law Review*, 44: 77-87.

Galanter Marc and Thomas Palay (1991) *Tournament of Lawyers: The Growth and Transformation of the Large Law Firms*, Chicago: University of Chicago Press.

Gamble Andrew (1988) "Privatization, Thatcherism, and the British State", *Journal of Law and Society*, 16: 1-20.

Grimmig Robert J. (1986) "Handling Problem Loans", in *The Loan Officer's Handbook*, William J. Korsvik and Charles O. Meiburg (eds.) Homewood, Ill.: Dow Jones-Irwin.

Hall Peter A. (1992) "The Movement from Keynesianism to Monetarism: Institutional Analysis and British Economic Policy in the 1970s", in *Structuring Politics*, Sven Steinmo, Kathleen Thelen, and Frank Longstreth (eds.) Cambridge: Cambridge University Press.

Halliday Terence C. (1982) "The Idiom of Legalism in Bar Politics: Lawyers, McCarthyism, and the Civil Rights Era", *American Bar Foundation Research Journal*, 982 (Fall): 911-89.

Joskow Paul L. and Roger G. Noll (1994) "Economic Regulation", in *American Economic Policy in the 1980s*, Martin Feldstein (ed.) Chicago: University of Chicago Press.

Justman Harold Anthony (1976) "Comments on the Bank's Right of Setoff under the Proposed Bankruptcy Act of 1973", *The Business Lawyer*, 31: 1607-18.

Kahn-Freund Otto (1954) "Legal Framework", in *The System of Industrial Relations in Great Britain*, Allan Flanders and H. A. Clegg (eds.) Oxford: Blackwell.

Lake William H. (1982) "Representing Secured Creditors under the Bankruptcy Code", *Business Lawyer*, 37: 1153-83.

Large Peter (1992) "From swanimote to disafforestation: Feckenham Forest in the early seventeenth century", in *The Estates of the English Crown 1558-1640*, R. W. Hoyle (ed.) Cambridge: Cambridge University Press.

Larr Peter (1994) "Two Sides of Collateral: Security and Danger", *Journal of Commercial Lending*, 76: 8-17.

Lee Judge Joe (1975) "A Critical Comparison of the Commission Bill and the Judges' Bill for the

Amendment of the Bankruptcy Act",*American Bankruptcy Law Journal*, 49: 1-48.

Lester V. Markham (1995) *Victorian Insolvency: Bankruptcy, Imprisonment for Debt, and Company Winding-up in Nineteenth Century England*, Oxford: Oxford University Press.

Macpherson C. B. (1978) "The Meaning of Property", in *Property: Mainstream and Critical Positions*, C. B. Macpherson (ed.) Toronto: University of Toronto Press.

McEvoy Arthur F. (1986) *The Fisherman's Problem: Ecology and Law in the California Fisheries 1850-1980*, Cambridge: Cambridge University Press.

Miller Harvey R. (1984) "The Rejection of Collective Bargaining Agreements under the Bankruptcy Code—An Abuse or Proper Exercise of the Congressional Bankruptcy Power?" *Proceedings of the New York University 7th Annual National Conference on Labor*: 5.1-5.21.

Miller Peter and Michael Power (1993) "Calculating Corporate Failure," *Professional Competition and the Social Construction of Markets: Lawyers, Accountants, and the Emergence of the Transnational State*, Y. D. Dezalay and D. Sugarman (eds.) London: Routledge.

Napier B. W. (1991) "The Protection of Workers' Interests in Insolvency in the United Kingdom," in *The Protection of Workers' Claims in the Event of the Employer's Insolvency*, Edward Yemin and Arturo S. Bronstein (eds.) Geneva: International Labour Office.

Nelson Michael A. (1986) "An Empirical Analysis of State and Local Tax Structure in the Context of the Leviathan Model of Government,"*Public Choice*, 49: 283-94.

O'Shaughnessy Terry (1994) "Economic Policy," in *A Conservative Revolution? The Thatcher-Reagan Decade in Perspective*, Andrew Adonis and Tim Hanes (eds.) Manchester: Manchester University Press.

Palmer Donald, Roger Friedland and Jitendra V. Singh (1986) "The Ties That Bind: Organizational and Class Bases of Stability in aCorporate Interlock Network," *American Sociological Review*, 51: 781-96.

Powell Walter W. (1991) "Introduction", in *The New Institutionalism in Organizational Analysis*, W. W. Powell and P. J. DiMaggio (eds.) Chicago: University of Chicago Press.

Przeworski Adam (1991) *Democracy and the Market*, Cambridge: Cambridge University Press.

Riddell Peter (1994) "Ideology in Practice", in *A Conservative Revolution? The Thatcher-Reagan Decade in Perspective, Andrew Adonis and Tim Hanes* (eds.) Manchester: Manchester University Press.

Riker William H. and Itai Sened (1991) "A Political Theory of the Origin of Property Rights: Airport Slots", *American Journal of Political Science*, 35: 951-69.

Robert Morris Associates (1976) "RMA State on the Proposed New Bankruptcy Act", *Journal of Commercial Bank Lending*, 58: 2-17.

Rostow Eugene V. and Lloyd N. Cutler (1939) "Competing Systems of Corporate Reorganization: Chapters X and XI of the Bankruptcy Act", *Yale Law Journal*, 48: 1334-76.

Rowthorn Bob and Andrew Glyn (1990) "The Diversity of Unemployment Experience since 1973", in *The Golden Age of Capitalism: Reinterpreting the Postwar Experience*, Stephen Marglin and Juliet Schor (eds.) Oxford: Clarendon Press.

Scott W. Richard (1994) "Institutions and Organizations: Toward a Theoretical Synthesis", in *Institutional Environments and Organizations: Structural Complexity and Individualism*, W. Richard Scott, John W. Meyer and Associates (eds.) Thousand Oaks: Sage Publications, 55-80.

Scott W. Richard and J. Meyer (1991) "The Organization of Societal Sectors: Propositions and Early Evidence", in *The New Institutionalism in Organizational Analysis,* P. J. DiMaggio and W. W. Powell (eds.) Chicago: University of Chicago, 108-40.

Sullivan Teresa E., Elizabeth Warren and W. J. Westbrook (1989) *As We Forgive Our Debtors: Consumer Bankruptcy in America*, Oxford: Oxford University Press.

Sutton John R. and Frank Dobbin (1996) "The Two Faces of Governance: Responses to Legal Uncertainty in US Firms, 1955-1985",*American Sociological Review*, 61: 794-811.

Thompson F. Corine and Richard L. Norgaard (1967) *Sinking Funds: Their Use and Value*, New York: Financial Executives Research Foundation.

Treister George (1973) "The New Bankruptcy Rules", *California State Bar Journal*, 48 (Sept/Oct): 522-604.

Useem Michael (1993) "Executive Defense: Shareholder Power and Corporate Reorganization", Cambridge: Harvard University Press.

Utgoff Kathleen P. (1993) "The PBGC: A Costly Lesson in the Economics of Federal Insurance", in *Government Risk-Bearing*, Mark S. Sniderman (ed.) Boston: Kluwer.

Weintraub Benjamin and Alan N. Resnick (1983) "Freezing the Debtor's Account: A Banker's Dilemma Under the Bankruptcy Code", *BankingLaw Journal*, 100: 316-24.

Weisman Morris (ed.) (1976) *A History of the Commercial Law League of America*, Chicago: Morris Weisman Educational Foundation, Inc.

Zander Michael (1994) *The Law-Making Process*, (4th edn.) London: Butterworths.

Zinbarg Edward D. (1975) "The Private Placement Loan Agreement", *Financial Analysts Journal*, 31: 33-5.

Index

U

V